DREAM
ESP

CARL LLEWELLYN WESCHCKE is Chairman of Llewellyn Worldwide, Ltd., one of the oldest and largest publishers of New Age, Metaphysical, Self-Help, and Spirituality books in the world. He has a Bachelor of Science degree in Business Administration (Babson), studied Law (LaSalle Extension University), advanced academic work toward a doctorate in Philosophy (University of Minnesota), has a certificate in clinical hypnosis, and honorary recognitions in divinity and magical philosophy.

In addition to book publishing he has worked in the pharmaceutical industry, furniture manufacture, and real estate management. With Llewellyn, he has worked in all aspects of the business: advertising, editing, production, writing, astrological calculation, design and layout, typesetting, cover design, direct selling, bookstore management, trade sales, designing systems and procedures, printing and purchasing, warehouse and shipping, and mopping floors.

He is a life-long student of a broad range of Metaphysical, Spiritual and Psychological subjects, and variously studied with the Rosicrucian Order and the Society of the Inner Light. After corresponding with Gerald Gardner and several of his associates in the late 1950s and early 1960s, he became known for holding the "Weschcke Documents" including a carbon copy of Gardner's own Book of Shadows.

He is a former Wiccan High Priest and played a leading role in the rise of Wicca and Neo-Paganism during the 1960s and 1970s. Authors Scott Cunningham and Donald Michael Kraig together referred to him as "the Father of the New Age" because of his early and aggressive public sponsorship of a new understanding of old occult subjects. In the fall of 1973 Weschcke helped organize the Council of American Witches and became its chairperson. Weschcke rightfully prides himself on having drafted "The Thirteen Principles of Belief" Statement, a cornerstone of modern Wicca. This document was incorporated into the U.S. Army's handbook for chaplains.

While no longer active in the Craft, he retains ties to the Wiccan and Neo-Pagan communities through Llewellyn. He is 7th Past Grandmaster of Aurum Solis, an international magical order founded in Great Britain in 1897. He withdrew from the order in 1991, and is not actively affiliated with any group at the present time.

Still actively associated with Llewellyn, he is devoting more time to studies and practical research in Parapsychology, Quantum Theory, Kabbalah, Self-Hypnosis, Psychology, Tantra, Taoism, Tarot, Astrology, Shamanism, Wicca, Magick, and World Spirituality. He is also actively writing, and has co-authored seven books and several "quick" books and audio products with Dr. Joe Slate and a new edition with commentary of *The Compete Magick Curriculum of the Secret Order G.'.B.'.G.'.* originally authored by Louis Culling in 1969. He is currently planning several books based on Tantra, Shamanism, and the Western Old Religion as *systems* of spiritual self-empowerment.

Creative Researcher, Author, and Magickian

Louis T. Culling, (1894–1973), Musician, Magickian, Southern California Avocado Rancher, Yi King Scholar, and Author. He was a theatre organist during the era of silent films, and a World War I veteran.

He was a man whose mind had a tremendous reach and vitality, whose life had been one of adventure and fulfillment, and whose contributions to modern occultism and paranormal work are unique.

In the early 1930's he joined that magical Order G∴B∴G∴, founded in the United States by C. F. Russell and fashioned after Aleister Crowley's A∴A∴. He was head of the Southern California section of the Order for a number of years.

Louis Culling was a recognized scholar of the Yi King, which he calls *the Pristine Yi King* to differentiate it from the more familiar I Ching, which espouses Chinese philosophy but ignores the more esoteric aspects of ancient Taoism.

Louis T. Culling, by Wanda Sue Parrot

I met Louis T. Culling while I was desperately trying to rise from the tomb of lost innocence resulting from my first devastating sexual love affair. My broken heart was again cracked from a date rape on August 1, 1960, by the first young man I tried dating after my boyfriend abandoned me in lieu of a Cadillac. I was 25. Lou was 66.

He deftly guided me through and out of the sleazy scumbag swamp that was and is Hollywood's dark side. When I was ready and able to search for the Greater Light, he pointed me north, wished me well, and I found the Rosicrucians in San Jose and joined. It was the best thing I ever did.

Lou was a unique gentleman, kind and definitely unique, a genuine mystic who was so innocently childlike in his joyful delving into the mysteries that his humanness colored him as a down-to-earth honest man who called dry water holes "dusters" and who was equally at home with a gladiola bulb and young Brit upstart with hair horns, but in spirit he shared the mystic's nature with Sir Francis Bacon (and me), inveterate experimenter. Bacon got sick from trying to find out if a bird was edible long after its death if it was kept chilled—in other words, frozen food before fridges were invented...or so the story goes. Lou was simply Lou. He gave me a Ph.D. because he became hypnotized by the wheel he invented and was using, in vain, to try to hypnotize me. He claimed I hypnotized him. Nah! He hypnotized himself.

And, for that, I got a free Ph.D. in Sex Magick!! Double Nah! It was from his 'Collegium Orthogenesis Nuit,' whatever that was. He referenced it in his book, so maybe that mystery will be resolved. Might you know the answer?

TO WRITE TO THE AUTHOR

If you wish to contact the author or would like more information about this book, please write to the author in care of Llewellyn Worldwide Ltd. and we will forward your request. Both the author and publisher appreciate hearing from you and learning of your enjoyment of this book and how it has helped you. Llewellyn Worldwide Ltd. cannot guarantee that every letter written to the author can be answered, but all will be forwarded. Please write to:

‰ Llewellyn Worldwide
2143 Wooddale Drive
Woodbury, MN 55125-2989

Please enclose a self-addressed stamped envelope for reply,
or $1.00 to cover costs. If outside the U.S.A., enclose
an international postal reply coupon.

Many of Llewellyn's authors have websites with additional information
and resources. For more information, please visit our website at
http://www.llewellyn.com

FREE CATALOG FROM LLEWELLYN

For more than one hundred years Llewellyn has brought its readers knowledge in the fields of metaphysics and human potential. Learn about the newest books in spiritual guidance, natural healing, astrology, occult philosophy, and more. Enjoy book reviews, New Age articles, a calendar of events, plus current advertised products and services. To get your free copy of Llewellyn's New Worlds, send your name and address to:

Llewellyn's New Worlds of Mind and Spirit
2143 Wooddale Drive, Woodbury, MN 55125-2989

CARL LLEWELLYN WESCHCKE

DREAM

ESP

The Secret of
"PROPHETIC CAUSAL DREAMING"
To Bring About Desired Change

As Derived from the Taoist I CHING

*Based on
the original Research and Writings of LOUIS T. CULLING*

Llewellyn Publications
Woodbury, Minnesota

FIRST EDITION
First Printing, 2015

Cover art by iStockphoto.com/18593861/©45RPM
Cover design by Lisa Novak
Intrior base figure on page 281 by Mary Ann Zapalac
Interior illustrations by Llewellyn Art Department
Proteus illustration on page 17 by Wen Hsu
Wanda Sue Parrot photo on page 287 by Bob Sadler of Lightmoment Photography Studios

Llewellyn Publications is a registered trademark of Llewellyn Worldwide Ltd.

Library of Congress Cataloging-in-Publication Data (Pending)
ISBN: 978-0-7387-4598-5

Llewellyn Worldwide Ltd. does not participate in, endorse, or have any authority or responsibility concerning private business transactions between our authors and the public.

All mail addressed to the author is forwarded, but the publisher cannot, unless specifically instructed by the author, give out an address or phone number.

Any Internet references contained in this work are current at publication time, but the publisher cannot guarantee that a specific location will continue to be maintained. Please refer to the publisher's website for links to authors' websites and other sources.

Llewellyn Publications
A Division of Llewellyn Worldwide Ltd.
2143 Wooddale Drive
Woodbury, MN 55125-2989
www.llewellyn.com

Printed in the United States of America

OTHER BOOKS BY CARL LLEWELLYN WESCHCKE

Weschcke, Carl Llewellyn (editor): *The Golden Dawn* by Israel Regardie, with revision, expansion, and additional notes by Israel Regardie, Cris Monnastre, David Godwin, Sam Webster, Mia Dhyan Anupassana, Hal Sundt, and George Wilson. Llewellyn, 2002

OTHER BOOKS BY LOUIS T. CULLING AND CARL LLEWELLYN WESCHCKE

Culling, Louis T., and Carl Llewellyn Weschcke. *The Complete Magick Curriculum of the Secret Order G.·.B.·.G.·.: Being the Entire Study Curriculum, Magick Rituals, and Initiatory Practices of the G.·.B.·.G.·.*. Llewellyn, 2010

OTHER BOOKS and AUDIOS BY JOE H. SLATE AND CARL LLEWELLYN WESCHCKE

Slate, Joe H., and Carl Llewellyn Weschcke. *All About Auras*. E-book, Llewellyn, 2011

Slate, Joe H., and Carl Llewellyn Weschcke. *All About Tea Leaf Reading*. E-book, Llewellyn, 2012

Slate, Joe H., and Carl Llewellyn Weschcke. *Astral Projection for Psychic Empowerment CD Companion: Past, Present and Future NOW (The Now Program)*. Llewellyn Audio CD, 2013

Slate, Joe H., and Carl Llewellyn Weschcke. *Astral Projection for Psychic Empowerment: The Out-of-Body Experience, Astral Powers, and their Practical Application*. Llewellyn, 2012

Slate, Joe H., and Carl Llewellyn Weschcke. *Clairvoyance for Psychic Empowerment: The Art and Science of "Clear Seeing" Past the Illusions of Space and Time and Self-Deception—Includes Developing Psychic Clarity and True Vision*. Llewellyn, 2012

Slate, Joe H., and Carl Llewellyn Weschcke. *Communicating with Spirit: Long Suppressed in Western Culture and Religions; Here's How You Can Communicate with (and Benefit from) Spritis of the Departed, Spirit Guides and Helpers, Gods and Goddesses, Your Higher Self and Your Holy Guardian Angel*. Llewellyn, 2015

Slate, Joe H., and Carl Llewellyn Weschcke. *Doors to Past Lives and Future Lives: Practical Applications of Self-Hypnosis*. Llewellyn, 2011

Slate, Joe H., and Carl Llewellyn Weschcke. *The Llewellyn Complete Book of Psychic Empowerment: A Compendium of Tools and Techniques for Growth and Transformation—*

Includes *Journey of a Lifetime, a Self-Directed Program of Developmental Actions to "Put it All Together.* Llewellyn, 2011.

Slate, Joe H., and Carl Llewellyn Weschcke. *PK: Moving Objects with Your Mind—The Power of Psychokinesis.* E-book, Llewellyn, 2011.

Slate, Joe H., and Carl Llewellyn Weschcke. *Psychic Empowerment for Everyone: You Have the Power, Learn How to Use It.* Llewellyn, 2009

Slate, Joe H., and Carl Llewellyn Weschcke. *Remembering Past Lives.* E-book, Llewellyn, 2011

Slate, Joe H., and Carl Llewellyn Weschcke. *Self-Empowerment and Your Sub-Conscious Mind: Your Unlimited Resource for Health, Success, Long Life, and Spiritual Attainment.* Llewellyn, 2010

Slate, Joe H., and Carl Llewellyn Weschcke. *Self-Empowerment through Self-Hypnosis: Harnessing the Enormous Potential of the Mind.* Llewellyn, 2010

Slate, Joe H., and Carl Llewellyn Weschcke. *Self-Empowerment through Self-Hypnosis Meditation CD Companion.* Llewellyn Audio CD, 2011

Slate, Joe H., and Carl Llewellyn Weschcke. *Self-Hypnosis for Success in Life.* E-book, Llewellyn, 2011

Slate, Joe H., and Carl Llewellyn Weschcke. *Vibratory Astral Projection and Clairvoyance CD Companion: Your Next Step in Evolutional Consciousness and Psychic Empowerment—An Audio CD companion to the book,* Clairvoyance for Psychic Empowerment. Llewellyn Audio CD, 2013

OTHER BOOKS BY LOUIS T. CULLING

L.R.I. I Ching: The Prophetic Book of Changes, by Louis T. Culling, Life Resources Institute/Llewellyn, 1966

The Incredible I Ching, by Louis T. Culling, Helios, 1969

The Complete Magick Curriculum of the Secret Order G.˙.B.˙.G.˙., by Louis T. Culling, Llewellyn, 1969

A Manual of Sex Magick, by Louis T. Culling, Llewellyn, 1971

Sex Magick, by Louis T. Culling, Llewellyn, 1993

Occult Renaissance 1972–2008, by Louis T. Culling, Llewellyn, 1972

The Pristine Yi King: The Pure Wisdom of Ancient China, by Louis T. Culling, Llewellyn, 1995

ACKNOWLEDGEMENTS

TO WANDA SUE PARROTT

As explained elsewhere in this book, Wanda has been a literary "life-saver" for this project, "translating" Lou Culling's impossible to read handwriting and copying his nearly impossible to see typed copy from the faded ribbon he used more than forty years ago, as well as understanding his preferred archaic language, British grammar and spelling, and his special humor.

I am very appreciative of her help and support. Read more about her in the Glossary.

TO JENNIFER ACKMAN

A special thanks also to Jennifer for taking on the job of identifying those words in the text to be listed in the Index, and providing me with a list of concepts and references needing a greater depth of explanation that I have provided in the Glossary.

LLEWELLYN PEOPLE

A special thanks also to everyone at Llewellyn. It's never just one or two or three people that contribute to the "process" that results in the book you hold in your hands, but rather the entire organization plays a role, or several roles, in doing so. I do thank everyone.

CONTENTS

FOREWORD
How This Book was Written

How This Book was authored by One Person, but written by Two People

As will be explained in the Preface, this book is written by two people, but it started with a first draft by Lou Culling who died before we could work together to finish it.

An Unfinished Manuscript, Badly Typed with Hand-written Notes, Faded by Time

Unfortunately, Lou had been ill and not only was the manuscript very rough, badly typed with a faded typewriter ribbon, and lots of even more difficult to read hand-written notes, it was incomplete. At first, I just put the work aside for a later time, and then time truly marched on and the manuscript remained in my file drawer until recently when I returned to nearly full-time writing.*

   *Please see the books co-authored by Joe H. Slate and myself at the end of the fore-
   word. More titles are forthcoming.

Our on-going Psychic Connection

Lou and I were great friends and—as he remarked to his daughter Georgine, he felt an immediate psychic connection between us when we first met, as did I. I still feel the connection after many years, and that is another reason I can comfortably say this book is co-authored by the two of us because I feel his presence as I write this first complete version. As I wrote in *Communicating with Spirit* (Slate and Weschcke) I do experience such connections—whether they may with a "surviving personality," a psychic guide, or my own Higher Self, I know I can direct my attention inward, form a question, and get a response.

Clarification of Who and Who

Commonly, in a co-authored work, no distinction is made as to who is writing what, but I feel a personal need to identify Lou Culling's voice when I feel it is pertinent, especially when he is relating a personal experience or judgment. Throughout the text of book, wherever you see the pronoun "I," do know that it is Lou 'speaking,' although I've had to fill in gaps where Lou's typing and his hand-written notes were difficult to decipher. Generally when you will see the pronoun "we" it is my voice, drawing upon my own resources including what may be Lou's presence—which could be *actual,* or reflect memories of our conversations and correspondence. All footnotes and glossary entries are my writing entirely unless I am quoting (and crediting).

Other than those passages specifically identified as Lou's, I have "modernized" and "smoothed out" the writing, up-dated dated "facts" that otherwise might have been confusing to today's reader, clarified references, but have fully preserved and developed Lou's unique contribution to the practice of Dream Work and specifically Dream ESP. You will find Lou's unique and *original* use of the *I Ching/Yi King* (Chinese "Book of Changes") in this book making it a virtual classic in its own right!

The Helpful Hand of Wanda Sue Parrott

However, despite our psychic connection, the manuscript remained nearly un-decipherable in many places. Thankfully, I remembered that Wanda Sue Parrot, who I've known for more than a half-century, had been a good friend of Lou's in Hollywood, familiar with his unique speech and writing. Wanda was available and delighted with this opportunity to renew friendship with both Lou's "spirit," and me and took on the task of "translating" the manuscript into readable English. And she contributed many valuable suggestions throughout the process.

As a result, we have fully preserved and developed Lou's unique contribution to the practice of Dream Work, and specifically Dream ESP and Prophetic Dreaming.

Now, I can't resist saying—because dreams are more important to our life and well-being than is generally credited—*Dream on! Dream on!*

Carl Llewellyn Weschcke. February 19, 2014
Newport (overlooking the Mighty Mississippi), Minnesota

PREFACE
How to Dream True
By
Carl Llewellyn Weschcke

The Author's "Assignment" and his commitment to "Higher Authority"

This book is the work of two people, one deceased and the other not. Louis Culling wrote a first draft of the manuscript some years ago, and died before we could work together to complete the "assignment."

Why do I use that word, **assignment***?*

Lou was a man who felt a personal commitment to "Higher Authority," that is, to his *Holy Guardian Angel* as an initiate and Chief of the Magick Order known as the **Great Brotherhood of God,** or simply, the G∴B∴G∴*

*Details about the G∴B∴G∴ can be found in the book by Culling and Weschcke, *The Complete Magick Curriculum of the Secret Order G∴.B∴.G∴..*

The Oath of Truth and Communication with the Holy Guardian Angel

Neophytes seeking initiation into this Order swore:

1. *I swear to tell myself the truth.*

2. *I swear to regard every event (or condition) as a particular dealing between myself and the Holy, Guardian Angel.*

Immediately, the wording of these two oaths and the earlier reference to "assignment" challenges us.

Words as <u>Symbolic Formulae</u> Working with the Sub-Conscious Mind

In these two areas of writing a book on a particular functioning of the Sub-Conscious Mind and entering into Advanced Magickal practice, we have moved from familiar objective reality into a special *subjective* reality common to *Dreams, Magickal Practice, and to Meditational (and prayer) Work.* In other words, we are 'switching gears' and using words as *symbolic formulae to initiate a Sub-Conscious process to explore and develop their meaning in a particular application and the consequences of action at both inner and outer levels.* The <u>operative words</u> here are to "explore and develop," and by that we mean we need to look for a deeper and larger meaning behind these words and then to develop them in application to our own Whole Being, *and* to that of others as may be pertinent.

Again, look at these words, or better, write them down on separate lines in a note-book or "magickal diary:" *assignment, truth,* and *a particular dealing between the personal self and the HGA.*

Assignment: *Writing a book about the Paranormal Power of Dreams*

An "assignment" is normally just a particular job or project on an objective *conscious* level that can be completed and put aside as "finished." That's almost never true of any book, and never true of a book of a Self-Help/Self-Improvement or of an esoteric nature. "Writing" is an *Art,* and all art is a subjective form of communication between two or more Whole Selves involving the multi-faceted and multi-dimensional "Truth" about an Object, a Person (or element of personal consciousness or other spiritual entity), or a Subject.

It is never finished!

Once something is "begat" in the subjective field, that seed gives birth to a metaphor-ical tree that grows, blossoms, bears fruit, and begets other seed forever. As a writer, you wake up in the middle of the night and know you have to go back to a particular page and change a word or add a sentence, and that you have to add a new chapter or insert a footnote, change the Index, add to the Glossary, etc. After the book is pub-lished and in the hands of readers and users, the writer thinks of things to change or add, and may start planning a new edition based on reader feedback, or a "new and improved" book. Even long after the book has gone "out-of-print," it lives on in the used book market, and calls out to other writers for recognition and use in reference and research, and it may become "born-again" in a new edition many decades later.

A Book as an Entity

A book, or other art form, is something more than a single physical thing: it is a human-seeded *incarnation* of both the Conscious Mind and the subconscious, call-ing on its creator's whole person of emotional, mental, and spiritual dimensions including some degree of a "Spirit to Spirit connection," drawing upon still Higher Resources. (That doesn't mean everything written is right, or "the whole truth and nothing but the truth" for the simple reason that no matter the source the communi-cation is filtered through a human psyche that is often far from being "perfect."

Subjective and Objective

When we say "subjective" we obviously mean something different than "objective," and when dealing with the Paranormal (and the Esoteric) we're involved with a con-cept much broader that the usual meaning commonly assigned to the word as "in the mind" of the perceiver or thinker vs. the "thing in itself" out in the "Real World." Often "subjective" is defined as personal *feeling* or an *interpretation* in relation to something objective—with objective being defined as impersonal *factual, measurable, universally identical to all viewers, replaceable, and repeatable*. "Object" is singular, whereas "Subject" is a comprehensive collective of many dimensions and facets sharing a common denominator. We simplify the matter by identifying Objective with the "Outer World" Subjective with the "Inner World."

Accepting an "assignment" to write a book on dreams as a paranormal process is therefore a commitment that the writer makes to some "higher" entity even if it is a for-hire, free-lance job. No matter how "objective" the project, it involves both objective and subjective skills and being of the writers.

The Role of the Trained Creative Imagination

There is another aspect to subjective working often overlooked in writing "job descriptions:" the involvement of the *Creative Imagination*. We all have an imagination, but there is a vast difference between the ordinary passively reactive imagination and the trained imagination intentionally and skillfully using the power of visualization and introducing into it "objective" elements to test and perfect alternative ideas. That's what makes the difference in the successful accomplishment of any creative project whether in science, art, psychology, business, dream interpretation, or "dreaming true."

The Reality of the "Paranormal"

"Paranormal" simply means *parallel* to normal but is often wrongfully interpreted as "other than Real" for the basic reason that most paranormal phenomena can't be objectively measured and duplicated in the same way that physical phenomenon can. To better understand "parallel to normal," we have to think in broader "cosmic" concepts beyond just the physical universe—even when including psychological and "spiritual" factors.

Cosmic Reality is inclusive of Other Dimensions

We place "spiritual" in quote marks simply because there is no room for spirit or spirituality in physical reality—it is simply conceptualized as "other worldly" and either accepted or rejected on that fact alone. The larger "Cosmic Reality," however, is inclusive of other *coincident* dimensions of a more broadly understood reality in which the *physical* is first joined with the *etheric* energy system and then paralleled with *astral, mental, causal,* and *spiritual*—which is understood to include several still higher dimensions of a different nature rarely encountered by any living individual.

What is important is that paranormal phenomena—as well the functions of dreaming, imagining, and magical operations including the invocation of the Holy

Guardian Angel—all occur in the astral dimension that is parallel and coincident with the physical and the mental, causal, and spiritual dimensions as previously mentioned. All are equally "real" but each dimension has its own substance, energy, and natural "laws" defining "the way things work" and how those things relate to the parallel dimensions.

The point is that "paranormal" can be defined as everything beyond the limited material dimension up to and including "the God factor."

Telling the <u>Truth</u> to one's Personal Self

In the physical world, truth is factual, and can often be verified by objective measurements (although their interpretation is often the subject of personal bias). In the astral world, truth is subjective but just as **REAL** as is objective physical fact. In other words, you know when you are lying to yourself. You *feel* the untruth and it hurts you as much as physically abusing your body. When you lie to yourself you impair the wholeness of your psyche and distort your perceptions of emotional, mental, spiritual, and even physical realities. *Be honest with yourself in all things!*

To regard <u>every event</u> (or condition) as a <u>particular dealing</u> between <u>myself</u> and the <u>Holy Guardian Angel</u>

Well, it isn't quite what the words seem to say. "I" (Carl) once challenged Lou about this. *How can everything be a particular dealing with the HGA?* He answered with an example that illustrates the Symbolic Formula in everyday practice. "Imagine you are driving down the freeway and, suddenly, something makes you look at the mileage indicator. Whatever it reads, three sequential numbers stand out. Remember them, and when you get a chance, interpret them numerologically. They contain a message for you from your Higher Self."

So, it really isn't every event, but events of any kind that suddenly stand our above all others. I (Carl) once brought a particular man and woman into proximity with each other, and you could see "time stop" for them. They were together for more than a half-century until her recent passing.*

*See *The Wizard and the Witch* by John C. Sulak, Oberon Zell, and Morning Glory Zell.

No matter the event, it requires some form of action to explore and develop its meaning and apply that accordingly. Even words when they are spoken or heard *inwardly* are never purely objective—they need interpretation if heard, and they need the addition of an Intentional, emotional energy charge, and goal direction if in a magickal or meditative operation.

Subjective and *Objective* are never quite the same. Action gives them meaning and direction. In either case that action should be intentional and carefully thought-out rather than merely (and dangerously) reacting to circumstance. "Road Rage" kills; Jealousy often leads to violence; "Haste makes Waste"; Envy can lead to crime; Greed for wealth can bring down an entire national economy, while Greed for territory and power can lead to meaningless war between nations.

Who, or What, is a Holy Guardian Angel?

The answer to that question is complex, and the detail is beyond the need of this book.*

　*Details about the HGA can be found in the afore mentioned book by Culling and Weschcke, *The Complete Magick Curriculum of the Secret Order G∴B∴G∴.*

However, unless you want to explore the higher forms of magickal practice and other esoteric systems of spiritual growth (see *Communicating with Spirit* by Slate and Weschcke), simply think in terms of what we call your Higher Self, or even the "Super-Conscious Mind." At its best, the Higher Self is the fully integrated personal psyche bringing together the Subconsciousness, Consciousness, and Superconsciousness under the WILL of your Whole Being. Such unity is the goal of personal evolution in each lifetime. It's what we are here for—that and to assume personal responsibility for all thought, feeling, and action in relation to the common good of Life and Planet. You, and each of us, are part of the Whole, and every action, and inaction, has an effect on the future health and well-being of every life and of our planetary home.

THE SYMBOLIC FORMULA IN DREAM WORK

A Seven-Step Practice in Dreaming True

This is a book about Dreams and the Paranormal, so we will only explore that aspect of the Symbolic Formula in practice. You will be aided in this with both a Dream "Dictionary" and examples.

To simplify the practice:

1. Immediately upon awakening, write down the elements of the dream (or dreams) that you recall. Also note (a) Date and Time; (b) whether you woke suddenly or naturally; (c) if suddenly, then any words or images that seem to have been actual factors in the waking process; (d) did you respond in any way (such as word or action, surprise or confusion, desire to awaken your partner if present and share); and (e) the concluding element(s) such as realizing that it was only a dream, a compulsion to get up and do something (other than using the

bathroom or dressing), your secondary feeling about any of the elements of (d) above.

2. When you do get up, but before your morning ablutions, look at your written notes and clarify any scribbles, abbreviations, references to people or obvious symbolic elements (such as birds, animals, archetypal personalities, or surprise appearances such as long-forgotten people or very strange images), and also note your feelings in relation to these notes.

3. The following evening, before sleep, look again at your notes, and write down what you now recognize as one or two (rarely more) symbolic elements—those that seem to stand out above any others.

4. Close your eyes, consciously relax, breathing rhythmically and more a little more deeply than usual. See the symbolic image or word in the "psychic window" before your brow, and ask it to complete its message to you.* Do that for each of the noted elements.

    > *This process may take *practice* to develop. Again, you are "switching gears" and engaging in new meditative process that make require several sessions to develop. Don't give up. Just go on to the next time.

5. When done, open your eyes, and write the messages and your feelings down.

6. Approximately one week later, at a fully awake and alert time, look at the entire set of notes, and analyze. What is the message, what is its intent, and what action—if any—are you supposed to take. Remember: you are to use these "*symbolic formulae to initiate a Sub-Conscious process to explore and develop their meaning in a particular application and the consequences of action at both inner and outer levels.* The operative words here are to 'explore and develop,' and by that we mean that we need to look for a deeper and larger meaning behind these words and then to develop them in application to our own Whole Being, *and* to that of others as may be pertinent."

7. At any time, you may recall these messages in relation to current happenings. Note them down in this same journal so that the connections are obvious. Give thanks for the positive value you now perceive.

A Lifetime of Experience and Devotion in Service to Others

We are now ready for the main text—as corrected, interpreted, and augments as necessary. The author, Louis Culling, brought a lifetime of experience and devotion in service to others. His methodology was unique in many ways, unexplored by others until this time. As in all subjective work, we are pioneers, sharing in the great evolutionary adventure of human growth and spiritual attainment. We are working to *become more than we are,* and *all that we can be.*

Suggested Reading:

Bailey, Alice A. *The Destiny of the Nations.* New York: Lucis, 2007.

Culling, Louis T., and Carl Llewellyn Weschcke. *The Complete Magick Curriculum of the Secret Order G∴B∴G∴: Being the Entire Study Curriculum, Magick Rituals, and Initiatory Practices of the G∴B∴G∴ (The Great Brotherhood of God) A Short-cut to Initiation and the Most Efficient Program for Union with the Holly Guardian Angel.* 2010, Woodbury: Llewellyn, 2010.

Slate, Joe H., and Carl Llewellyn Weschcke. *Communicating with Spirit: Long Suppressed in Western Culture and Religions—Here's How You Can Communicate with (and Benefit from)Spirits of the Departed, Spirit Guides and Helpers, Gods and Goddesses, Your Higher Self and Your Holy Guardian Angel.* Woodbury: Llewellyn, 2015.

Slate, Joe H., and Carl Llewellyn Weschcke. *Self-Empowerment and Your Sub-Conscious Mind: Your Unlimited Resource for Health, Success, Long Life, and Spiritual Attainment.* Woodbury: Llewellyn, 2010.

INTRODUCTION
Dreams and Our Secret Inner World

Dreams: how they have fascinated the mind and imagination of all Humanity! In our sleep they bring us secret advice, admonitions, warnings, prophecies, oracular, secrets, fantasies, inspirations, and the source of much of our creativity.

From the "World of Soul"

You've heard that expression: "Sleep on it" as formula for problem solving. It works, but the more you know about the actual "science" of dreaming the better you will be able to apply its marvelous powers to make your daily life richer. It's like forming a partnership with your Sub-Conscious Self and your Conscious Self.

Yet there are still many self-appointed experts as well as highly trained psycho-analysts who claim that dreams are nothing but wish fulfillments, adolescent sexual groping, or symbolic expressions of guilt and conflicted feelings.

One cannot quarrel with this if it is conditioned with "So it is with (this or that) percentage of the population," but what about the rest of the population? And what of those who learn to dream in a more significant and illuminating manner as you will be able to do even while reading this book and more so as you begin practicing the techniques you will discover?

There is No "One Size fits All" in the World of Dreams— Each of us is Unique

Nor is this promise only theatrical; it is based on real experience. It seems that any intelligent person should know that there can be no such thing as a worthwhile dream book that is only a simple *dream dictionary* filled with instant interpretations claimed to be universal—a "one size fits all" regardless of the dreamer's age, culture, life experiences, current hopes and worries, and such factors as post-traumatic stress disorder—unfortunately more and more common today as soldiers come home from recent wars. One can use some of these interpretations by putting in a bit of intelligent application. Be not dismayed: there is a system that does not heavily burden one, and it is clearly outlined in this book.

G∴B∴G∴, the Great Brotherhood of God

For four years, I had charge of the San Diego, California section of the G∴B∴G∴ (known both as the *Gnostic* Brotherhood of God and as the *Great* Brotherhood of God).* At the time there were almost one hundred people who had gone through the practice of learning how to dream and the way to record their of the dreams for the

1

purpose of personal growth and self-understanding that is the goal of all magickal work. It was my task to read all of their recorded dreams and to give any needed technical advice—but not an interpretation.

> *Why these two alternate names? We don't know as all the members I knew of are now gone. But logic suggests that they may have been used alternatively in relation to an Outer membership and an Inner one. "Great" for seeking initiation—*to become more than they are,* and "Gnostic" for those already initiated and striving to become *all they can be,* and thus "co-creators" of a better world. Another way to put is for the first usage to relate to personal evolution and the second usage in recognition that personal evolution accelerates the evolution of all humanity.

This generally covered a period of three months. You may therefore be assured that this is not just another valueless addition to the thousands of THEORIES about dreams that have been developed over the history of human life: rather it is based on EMPIRICAL EVIDENCE and ACTUAL EXPERIENCE in how to dream purposefully with real significance and value.

A Dream Cure of a life-long Allergy—the Case of Mary B.

Just one illustration is sufficient to show the small value of dream dictionaries: The Case of Mary B. You will not find either of the important elements in Mary's dreams in popular "Dream Dictionaries."

"I dreamed that I was between two long tall rows of blackberry vines, loaded with ripe fruit, "She immediately was reminded of an incident of ten years past. While picking berries, at the age of sixteen, she was seduced from her virginity by another berry picker. She then realized that she had been carrying an unconscious guilt fixation and that the dream was admonishing her to get rid of this "sin" fixation. The result was that she was able to salvage a happy marriage which had been close to going on the rocks. This same woman dreamed of seeing a tomato vine loaded with ripe fruit. She started to eat one and a bee which had been on the tomato stung her on the lip and her face swelled up and there was a torturing itch.

In a flash, she learned for the first time the source of her allergy: tomatoes. But let's see what the dream books say about fruit:

Freud really didn't say that Dreams are "All about Sex!"

It is well to clear up a misunderstanding about Freud's ideas on dreams. Quote: "I have never maintained the assertion which has been so often ascribed to me that dream interpretation shows that all dreams have a sexual content. The interpretation of dreams is the royal road to a knowledge of the unconscious activities of the mind."

The State of "Knowing" between the Unconscious and the Conscious Mind

Now there is a part of the 'Sub-Conscious Mind' that I call the 'Supra-Conscious' mind, meaning a factor that, in many ways, 'knows' more than the Conscious Mind. It is the work of this treatise to point out the way to greatly improve the content of one's dreams to a point that dreams become highly informative. There are those who would object to the term "supra-conscious" and, in this treatise, I am content to alternatively refer it the "Borderland Consciousness" which is neither 100% asleep nor 100% awake: the dream state.

There has been much scientific investigation, on brain activity during sleep. Electronic devices show a very slow rate of brain activity during full sleep, but then show a higher rate of brain activity during the dream state, and a still higher rate in the wake state—so it is not amiss to call it the "*Borderland Consciousness* between full sleep and fully awake."

The Inner World of Mind and the Outer World of Body

Can dreams be prophetic? But what does one mean by prophecy or prediction? Carl Jung writes about a dream that led him to the conclusion that a friend would soon die—unless there would be some radical changes. As Jung outlines the rationale of his conclusion, he had, on previous occasions, made a number of small observations, almost unconsciously, and the dream had sparked an intuitive conclusion from those observations. In short, the dream had brought focus to what had already existed in the 'world of mind.' It is my personal stand that all good prediction must be based on what is already existing in the world of mind, and as in the already existing potential in the 'world of body.' It is that potential that makes prophecy and prediction possible. (You will find more about this in Chapter Thirteen)

Why do some dreams appear to be so senseless, illogical, and weirdly distorted that we suppose that they do have meaning? This has never been sufficiently explained from a physiological standpoint, though empirical evidence does indicate that most such dream do have meaning—<u>sometimes more than ordinary meaning.</u>

We do know that when repressions and guilt are involved in dreams that the dream is sufficiently disguised to be acceptable to the dreamer. Even in the waking stage we veil our vices in virtuous words and acts! Unless we learn to probe their depths, their truth remains hidden from our conscious awareness while their repressed energies may continue to hinder our progress. 'Progressive Dream Work' can literally break the shackles of repression and un-real guilt.

But some dreams are so thinly veiled that the dreamer can divine their meaning by honest self-examination. There are also dreams which not disguised and have direct and exact import, and, typically have practical value. Too many people involved in creative work have testified to receiving the wanted clue in a dream for anyone to have doubts on this. This is the purpose of this book: to reveal how to have dreams of clear and practical value. In other words, to have dreams that are not so heavily disguised as to leave one in the dark.

The 'Borderland Consciousness'

As previously stated, the dream state is what this writer calls the 'Borderland Consciousness.' This can vary from 90% asleep and 10% awake to 10% asleep and 90% awake. The ideal would be approximately 50–50, but that will take effort and practice.

In any event, the development of the Borderland Consciousness requires more than 10% awake and the simple practices as outlined in this book will bring this result. More than this: _no longer need one to dream get into a state of inspired intuition_. The dream practices in the coming chapters lead to the gift of being able invoke inspired intuition in the waking state.

A CLASSIC DREAM
The Story of the Kewpie Dolls

Mariska (as her friends called her) loved to keep open house to people engaged in the arts. Almost always when Rose O'Neill was at the house, so also was Khalil Gibran who sat at her feet—worshipping her. When new people were at the house who hadn't heard Rose's story, Khalil always asked her to tell it again.

Briefly, here was her story:

"My father and mother and I were immigrants from Ireland to the United States. We were pitifully poor and there were times there was not much to eat. Then I had a dream. A number of the dear little doll-like spirits began to play around me, Then one of them spoke to me, saying: 'We are called 'Kewpies' and my name is 'Kew.' We have chosen you, and here is our promise to you. If you will give us life and expression then you shall have everything in this world that you desire—and more too.'

"I believed them, and I immediately began to draw them. More dreams gave me the plots of their playing and the names of more of them. There was 'Blunder Boo' who was always stubbing his toe on which there was a large bandage, and there was the 'Kewpie Dog' who also had Kewpie wings."

Some may remember that the Kewpie dolls sold by the millions, and they were copyrighted. But even before these dolls hit the Big Time, Rose had received a million dollars for the drawings of the Kewpies and their antics. Rose O'Neill was blessed with more than money. Her very soul was in her exquisitely beautiful face, and a personality of the rarest charm.

Years before, she had seen the 'Spirits' in the Kew Gardens in England—hence "Kewpies is my memory, but I can't completely vouch for it."

What have we here? A Dream come true? An emergence from the Sub-Conscious Mind in response to need? A clue from a Psychic Guide? A message from her Higher Self? An astral journey into the particular spirit world developed around Kew Gardens? All are possible in the 'World of Soul.' All are variations on the same theme—that the Creative Imagination rises through the Sub-Conscious Mind into the alternate reality of the Astral World to then manifest in the World of Body, the physical plane of 'material reality.'

Suggesting Reading:

Slate, Joe H., and Carl Llewellyn Weschcke. *Self-Empowerment and Your Sub-Conscious Mind: Your Unlimited Resource for Health, Success, Long Life, and Spiritual Attainment.* Woodbury: Llewellyn, 2010.

CHAPTER ONE
Learning How to Remember Dreams

We do dream every night, but need to learn how to remember them

In the neophyte's curriculum of the G∴B∴G∴ the first directive was to get a blank book and, upon awakening each and every morning, to record the dream in detail, "But," protests the neophyte, "I do not have a dream every night." He's wrong, and is told that he really does dream every night but he just has not learned how to recapture his dreams. Here's how:

1. *Every morning: Keep the mind still and only "half awake," and remember your dream*

It is not a technically difficult task, but the 'secret' is in the discipline. It is mainly a matter of a few tricks, as it were. Upon awakening, try to stay in the *borderland state* as much as possible. Do not stretch, yawn nor move. Do not think of the affairs of the day ahead but keep the mind still and only "half awake." There is only one thing to do: *to remember that dream*. Within a minute or so, you will remember that dream. If not, you should resort to the mnemonic method: Gently ask yourself, was there another person in the dream, man or woman, stranger or friend, or many people, in a building or in the open, travel or difficulty in travel, pleasant or challenging, any animals such as a snake, a dog, cat or horse, or any other possibilities that come to mind—but do not concentrate so hard that you become fully awake.

2. *Every morning: Record your dream in a Dream Journal*

When you finally hit a clue to your dream, think it out completely in detail before getting up to record it and all those details (and likely a few more) in your record journal.

Within one week of practice, if you are not able to recapture your dream almost every morning, then you are not sticking to all of the foregoing requisites, particularly that referred to previously: the discipline of UNFAILING REGULARITY. It is absolutely essential that you go through the practice each and EVERY morning, whether you get results or not. Missing one morning is exactly equivalent to cancelling out three-fourths of what progress you made on the preceding morning.

3. *Every evening: Tell yourself to remember your dream and visualize Khwan Pa Kua*

There is another aid to capturing the dream that is often effective. Just before falling to sleep tell yourself that you want to remember your dream and also visualize the **Khwan Pa Kua** which consists of a trigram of three broken lines.

====   ====
====   ====

It is the feminine symbol of RECEPTION and has often been proven effective in this and other forms of memory recall.

Another helpful technique is suggesting to oneself the general nature of the dream that one would like to have. This is also another developmental technique—though it most certainly will not conform exactly as one has pictured.

Another good help for dream recovery is, before retiring, to read a book which is truly in rapport with the dream world. For this, a most excellent book is "Fantasies" by George MacDonald.*

*George MacDonald, Scottish author and poet (1824–1905), has been called a "pioneering figure in the field of fantasy literature." He was a major influence on Lewis Carroll, J. R. Tolkien, C. S. Lewis, G. K. Chesterton, and many others. Some other of his novels and fantasy tales are *The Princess and the Goblin, At the Back of the North Wind, Lilith, The Light Princess, The Golden Key,* and *The Wise Woman.* He wrote many more books, both fiction and non-fiction, including works on theology.

After 9 to 14 days of consecutive dream discovery, one is recording at least one dream every morning—possibly more. While most of that time has been spent in recovering and recording the dream in some detail, now comes the time to give more concentration on exploring all those details of the dream to uncover their essential meaning and purpose.

The Power of Recall, and Command Control for Success and Achievement

The discipline of Dream Recall and recording your dreams in a dedicated journal or diary is only the beginning of a form of mind training that is at the core of most magickal curriculums. But expanding the practice of Recall and Recording to include all the major events of the day will lead to Realizations of the inner world processes that make the outer world "real."

Such mental training places the Mind and Will in command of the ranges of human consciousness. Such "Command and Control" is pertinent to personal success in most endeavors, and practical in business, art, writing, crafts, or in all forms of self-development, psychic empowerment, and spiritual attainment. A Trained Mind is the difference between a life of individual consequence and one of massive inconsequence.

There are many aids to Recall, such as the "Memory Palace" in which you create an imaginary castle of many rooms. Give each room a name, and place images of those things that should be remembered in those rooms whose names correspond to the nature of those things. It is really an "astral filing system" whose value extends beyond your personal memory to the entire inner (Unconscious) world of Correspondences that will give you "Command and Control" of archetypal knowledge and energies related to your accumulating experiences and thus the power to fulfill your needs and desires.

This is the Real World of Magick, but it starts with the simple practice of dream recall and recording, and can lead to success in every field of endeavor, personal growth, and achievement.

The following chapter, therefore, covers the subject of recovering and recording the dream in meticulous detail.

Suggested Reading:

Clement, Stephanie, and Terry Lee Rosen. *Dreams Working Interactive*. St. Paul: Llewellyn, 2000.

Culling, Louis T., and Carl Llewellyn Weschcke. *The Complete Magick Curriculum of the Secret Order G.·.B.·.G.·.: Being the Entire Study Curriculum, Magick Rituals, and Initiatory Practices of the G.·.B.·.G.·. (The Great Brotherhood of God)*. Woodbury: Llewellyn, 2010.

MacDonald, George. *George MacDonald's Fantasy Novels (Complete and Unabridged) Including: The Light Princess, Cross Purposes, Phantastes and Lilith*. Oxford, UK: Benediction Classics, 2013.

Slate, Joe H., and Carl Llewellyn Weschcke. *Psychic Empowerment for Everyone: You Have the Power, Learn How to Use It*. Woodbury: Llewellyn, 2009.

CHAPTER TWO
Probe the Details

"Try to think of every little detail . . . to solve this case."

Most people have read or watched television "who done it" mysteries where the detective tells the witness, "Try to think of every little detail. Just one little thing might be the single clue that we need to solve this case." This is not mere fanciful fiction, and the same thing applies to many dreams. Here is an example dream by a person I knew well.

The Case of the French Woman and her Mexican Lover

The Woman dreamer describes the dream:

> "I was in a two-seated plane being piloted by a man. We were flying over France. We were over a city which I was certain was Marseilles.
>
> The man asked me if I wanted to land there. I said 'no' and this made him angry but I was glad."

Two details are missing: (1) The description of the man. (2) Why she was certain that the city was Marseilles. Upon questioning, she described the man as a very handsome Mexican, but with 'hard eyes.' She was certain about the city because she knew the city, having been born and raised there.

I knew this woman had a remarkable memory of her dreams and I felt that there had been some inhibition which had caused her to gloss over some details of the dream. I asked her to concentrate on the dream for recovery of any points that she had failed to record. Suddenly she was smiling happily and told me the following:

> "I've been in this country (the United States) for twenty years, but it had always seemed an alien country and an alien people. Every year I would take a two-month visit to Marseilles, France. Maybe it was to find a good man friend. I had felt so alien that I could not feel sociable to Americans and because of this I had resorted to having a Mexican lover in this country."
>
> "I now remember that the man who piloted the plane was a Mexican. I see it all now and am so happy," she said. "I am cured. I now feel integrated with you people. No longer do I want to return to France. Of course the Mexican was angry when I said that I did not want to go down to Marseilles, I am through with him, and I am going with the American who has been begging me for a date."

The foregoing dream is an excellent example of the importance of recording details and also an example of an inhibition against recording some things.

The Case of the Man in the Snake Pit

Another example: A man dreamed that he was in a deep pit among about twenty snakes, He "knew" that some were poisonous and that others were huge constrictors which could have squeezed him to death. Fortunately he had included two details which makes the dream have meaning: Detail #1 "I felt that it was some kind of test or ordeal in relation to my work in the G∴B∴G∴." Detail #2 "I was certain that none of the snakes would harm me unless I stepped on one of them." This gave a clear interpretation as follows:

The Magickal Power of Sincerity

Quite rightly, he had been thinking about the psychological danger of the powerful practices of the G∴B∴G∴. The dream agreed with this but gave assurance that he was in no danger if he worked with sincerity, aspiration, and integrity—not stepping on a snake. The dreamer saw this clearly and had no more apprehensions.

From the two foregoing dream exemplars one can see the importance of persistently probing into the Borderland for all of the details of the dream.

The Importance of Recording the Dream, and of Later Reading

Certainly, at first, recording the dreams is the only really good method forcing a very necessary discipline upon the dreamer. The requirement of writing all possible details induces one to *probe* more deeply for details. As one reads records of past dreams one can see where and how details have been missed; also this written record serves two more purposes: (1) Reading past dreams show how much one is improving; (2) Reading a dream of ten days, or more, past reveals a meaning to the dream which one could not see at the time of the dream. Further, after reading and thinking about the dream and your subsequent realizations, *record those too, and—at any time—come back to your Dream Journal and add details of changes and happening that you can attribute to that dream.*

Let one not be impatient nor discouraged in the idea that recording the dreams takes up too much time. Certainly within twenty days of dream recording one begins to "remember" two or three dreams every morning. This indicates that one is now proficient enough that there is no necessity of writing down the dreams every morning. *However*, there will be a few dreams that are so outstanding that one records them—or should do so.

The Value of Making the Dream Journal into a Life Diary

And there are sound arguments for making the Dream Journal into a Life Diary. It not only has esoteric and magical values, but the added values of self-analysis, recording astral travel, and maintaining a health record.

There is one important point that runs throughout this chapter. You do not have a teacher in charge of your work: therefore you must be both pupil and teacher. What has been given in this chapter (if regularly and assiduously practiced) enables you to be your own teacher and also a good pupil. Do not argue with it. Keep in mind your ultimate goal. Your goal is to be able to function in the Borderland, more and more every day. What this does for you is given in later chapters of the book, in detail.

How Your Dreams will Become more Significant and Truly Meaningful

Briefly, you will dream more significantly and with clear meaning to the dreams. You will be able to direct the course of your dreams to a large extent. Further, it develops efficiency in the Borderland so that you can "see" or divine many things when not sleeping, or dreaming.

The Power of Immersion

The more you practice functioning deeper in the Borderland, the more orderly, coherent, and informative will your dreams become. This same principle applies to anything which involves coherency and understanding. One may read very much about, for instance, about Mexican people and think that then one understands them simply by reading or visiting—but not so. One must actually mingle with the common people to be able to have a good understanding of any people and their culture. To have understanding and feeling for them, one must live with them, and relate and function in their sphere.

In the following chapter you will learn a most excellent method and practice for attaining deeper union and functioning in the Borderland Consciousness.

Suggested Reading:

Cunningham, Scott. *Dreaming the Divine: Techniques for Sacred Sleep.* St. Paul: Llewellyn, 1999.

McElroy, Mark. *Lucid Dreaming for Beginners: Simple Techniques for Creating Interactive Dreams.* Woodbury: Llewellyn, 2007.

CHAPTER THREE
Union with the Borderland Consciousness
Conversing with a "God" named Proteus

Here is a metaphysical practice that is surely not 'just another boring chore.' Rather, it can be as entertaining as a good television episode, and is moreover both knowledge-growing and mind-growing. It's a form of "Communicating with Spirit"* to access spiritual resources

*See Slate, J.H. and Weschcke, C.L.: *Communicating with Spirit.*

This practice involves *imagining* yourself having a conversation with the mythic God, *Proteus.* First, we should learn something of the nature of Proteus. Proteus is the guardian of seals and all of the Cetaceans (dolphins, porpoises, and whales). These unique 'mammal/animals'* live in the ocean, itself the symbol of the vast 'Collective Unconscious.' As such, these ocean-living animals are symbolic of the 'Borderland' consciousness and Proteus is known as a God of Wisdom and hence, as a *channel* for *the 'wisdom' of the Borderland State,* and a connection to the Collective Unconscious.

*Fossil evidence suggests that cetaceans share a common ancestor with land-dwelling mammals that began living in marine environments around 50 million years ago. Today, they are the mammals best adapted to aquatic life. Cetaceans can remain under water for much longer periods than most other mammals, (ranging from seven to 120 minutes, varying by species) due to major physiological differences. Cetaceans use sound to communicate, whether it be groans, moans, whistles, clicks, or the complex 'singing' of the humpback whale. Besides hearing and vision, at least one species, the Guiana dolphin, is able to use electroreception to sense prey. Toothed whales, dolphin, and porpoises are generally capable of echolocation, and can discern the size, shape, surface characteristics, distance and movement of an object. This enables them to search for, chase, and catch fast-swimming prey in total darkness. In most cases, they can distinguish between prey and non-prey (such as humans or boats). Baleen whales can process sounds from low to infrasonic frequencies. These species have high intelligence. At the 2012 meeting of the American Association for the Advancement of Science, there was support for a cetacean 'bill of rights,' listing cetaceans as *non-human persons.*

The Challenge of Consulting with Proteus

What happens when one consults Proteus for wisdom on any subject is challenging and sometimes rather weird, and requires persistence, patience, and the intuitive ability to recognize when the answer is, finally, 'right.'

State the question simply and precisely, and Proteus will give an answer, but that first answer is likely to be garbled and tricky. When you persist, as you must, and ask again, Proteus will likely 'change form' and give another answer that's not quite 'right,' and then another, and maybe another. It is only upon single-pointed persistence, getting as many as a half-dozen 'not quite right answers,' that Proteus will finally come through with a really wise answer.

We will explore more of this process, the technique, and its value, as we progress in this chapter, but—for the moment—look back at the footnote about cetaceans. It is unlikely that the ancient Greeks or the even more ancient Egyptians for whom Proteus was also a 'mythic' deity knew these modern "scientific facts" about Whales, Dolphins, and Porpoises. But realize: *myth was the ancient science—a different kind of subjective (or Intuitive) understanding than the objective physical science we know today.*

The Necessity of "Wholistic" Knowledge

It was the "wholistic"* knowledge of things and processes that "seekers," shamans, entranced oracles, and priests intuitively acquired that led to the foundations of the various mythologies of the world in which specific "thought forms" were built up in the astral and mental worlds to become the particularized gods and goddesses of those ancient cultures.

> *"Wholistic" is not to be confused with "holistic" which relates to "holism," a thera-peutic system and philosophy that is not necessarily inclusive of the astral, mental, causal and spiritual dimensions considered in esoteric work. However, such inclusion is becoming more common in such "alternative" practices as Naturopathy, Homeopa-thy, Ayurvedic, and Chinese Folk Medicine.

These mythical systems and deities continue across the ages to this day and can function as an alternative system of knowing often more valid than current physical science.

The Secret Science of "Correspondences"

We must also understand that this kind of "subjective science" is a manifestation *downward* ("cosmically" speaking) of spiritual realities that "talk" to us through myth and symbol that we now systemize as the "secret science of correspondences." These are the vital elements behind all religious myths, all divinatory systems, all magickal knowledge, and what is commonly termed "the Ancient Wisdom."

The More We Know, the Deeper We Can Go

For people today, the more we know of Physical Facts <u>along with</u> Myth and Magick, the better are we able to efficiently and effectively communicate with Spiritual Sources and the Collective Unconscious (also considered by some as identical with the Akashic Records of occult lore). In other words, the more we know, the more connections we can make and the deeper we can go to benefit from these processes.

How to Converse with a God

Before starting your conversation, read about Proteus so he becomes imaginatively "real" for you. Look in books of Greek mythology for an artistic or sculptured rendition, or simply go online and look for an image and information.* Wikipedia is generally a good resource for this kind of information.

* In Greek mythology, Proteus was one of several deities that the poet Homer called the "Old Man of the Sea." Others called him the god of "elusive sea change," reflecting the constant changing nature of the sea and of the liquid quality of water itself. Proteus can foretell the future, but will change his shape to escape having to do so. Proteus will only give his predictions to someone able to capture and hold him until he gives in. From this elusive nature of the god comes the adjective "protean" meaning *versatile, mutable, flexible, adaptable, and able to assume nearly any form.*

A further attribute of Proteus comes from Egyptian mythology where he is described as one "who never lies" and "who sounds the deep in all its depths." This is, of course, the Unconscious Mind.

The great psychologist Carl Jung refers to Proteus as a personification of the unconscious, and because of his gifts of prophecy and shape-changing, has much in common with the central figure of alchemy, Mercurius.

The European alchemist, Von Hyleabschen, writes: "Mercury, by virtue of his fiery spark of the light of nature, is beyond doubt Proteus, the sea god of the ancient pagan sages, who hath the key to the sea and . . . power over all things."

Illustrastion based on
Proteus as envisioned by Andrea Alciato

With this understanding of the mythic god, we are not only better prepared to discourse in the borderland state of consciousness but better able to understand the ways in which dreams function to answer our questions and give guidance about the future.

When conversing with Proteus in your imagination, you should be seated comfortably in a quietly passive state and giving Proteus some 'magical reality.' Do not speak with a deity out loud but silently within mind and imagination 'where Spirit lives.' Talking out loud would 'break the spell' and take you out of the borderland state. Start the conversation lightly at first—no depth of thought—such as: "How are you, Proteus? Are you in the mood to dispense some wisdom?"

Then Proteus might answer, "Only to those who have sense enough to ask a coherent, sensible question, and to those who do not expect to have it handed out on a platter without sincerely and persistently working for it."

Then one might say, "How do I work for it?" and Proteus answers, "By having brains enough to know what you are asking about, and by using your mind to make sense of the answer."

The Active Imagination

After such an introduction, you should be in the subjective mode of Active Imagination* and ready to proceed to the question in hand. Remember, a sloppy question brings nothing but a sloppy answer. Always carefully and explicitly state the question (mentally) and imaginatively see Proteus pondering before he gives his answer. In other words, *enter into the Spirit of the exchange.*

*The "Active Imagination" (also called *Moving Meditation*) is a powerful technique using the imagination as an *organ of understanding*. It is heavily used both in Jungian psychology and in such magickal practices as Kabbalistic Path Working, Dream Analysis, and Psychic Research. Other practices using the active imagination are used in many religious, metaphysical, and spiritual traditions, including visualized rituals of Wicca, forms of Invocation and Evocation, the "Assumption of God Forms," and "Ritual Dramas" in magical and spiritual systems of Self-Initiation.

In early Islamic mystical writing the trained imagination is empowered to mediate between human reason and the divine creative being. First, reason must rise above itself to the level of active imagination in the astral and mental 'space' shared with the lower spiritual forces of the divine realm; Second, to manifest in the material world, the trained imagination must access the "non-spatial fabric" between the sensory world and the spiritual realms to perceive or act within the spiritual dimension.

Following the Renaissance, the active imagination played a large role in the mystical works of Böhme, Bacon, Blake, and Swedenborg, with the active imagination serving as an "organ of the soul," by which we can establish a cognitive and visionary relationship with the intermediate world of spiritual beings and forces.

In modern psychological practice, Carl Jung explicitly developed the active imagination's therapeutic values as a meditation technique wherein the contents of the unconscious become images, described or personified as separate entities. The imagination is then used to bridge between the Conscious Mind and the unconscious to see the enactment of a drama. The technique includes working with dreams and creative fantasy, and some degree of purposeful creativity in business, science, and art.

In the initial work with the active imagination one must assert as little influence as possible on the images as they unfold. Observe the scene, watch for changes, record them but do not consciously fill the scene with your own desired changes. Then respond honestly to these changes, and note any further changes in the scene, letting the unconscious express itself without controlling influences from the Conscious Mind. At the same time, Jung insisted that some form of participation in Active Imagination was essential: "You yourself must enter into the process with your personal reactions … as if the drama being enacted was 'real.'"

Active imagination is a visualization technique similar to shamanic journeying. It can also be done through automatic writing, or such artistic activities as dance, music, painting, sculpting, ceramics, crafts, etc. Jung linked the Active Imagination with the processes of alchemy in that both strive for oneness and inter-relatedness from a set of fragmented and dissociated parts.

Now for an actual exemple—a personal experience of this writer. I had known of a rather unusual phenomenon about people's reactions to the first part of the second movement of Prokofiev's 'Second Violin Concerto.' Many people, upon hearing this particular music, unabashedly cry real tears. My question to Proteus was, "There are many other musical compositions with a similar sad or plaintive strain to which most people do not usually respond with tears. Why do they cry when hearing this music?"

After some half-dozen exchanges, Proteus finally said, "What most surely brings tears is the loss to finality of what has been precious, as for instance, the death of a loved one." Not exactly a definitive answer, but enough to precipitate further understanding through a subsequent dream experience.

The Dream of Happy Childhood Playmates

I was in bed at the time and soon drifted to sleep, but not for long. I woke from a dream of seeing some of my childhood playmates happily wading in a small creek. *Then I knew the answer!*

In childhood, we live in simple, happy, and carefree union with nature in which death has no reality and there is no sense of finality. It is, in fact, an enchanted world in which time has no dimension. But as we reach puberty, or sooner if "reality" darkens our sky, the enchanted world and the enchanted state of consciousness is lost and gone forever.

True, in later life some people may create another sort of enchanted world, but it is never the same as that in childhood. Even from a physiological standpoint it would be impossible to bring back that childhood state—with the possible exception of a few psychopathic cases in mental institutions.

Yes, it is the remembrance, and the loss, of the enchanted world that brings tears to the eyes.

It was then, after this dream, that I could see that the music of this concerto was a musical description of enchanted children in their enchanted world. Having been a theatre organist in the days of silent motion pictures when I had to play suitable music for the hundreds of nuances of different emotions, I could then recognize what was in this music. I double-checked with a dozen different people, asking, "Does not this strain of music remind you of your childhood?" The answer was "yes" from all those who were truly responsive to music.

Now the quibbler can rightly say, "Yes, but in the dim recesses of your mind you already knew this."

Agreed! But what is required to bring it to the waking-day consciousness? Some of it may arise from that thing called 'instinct,' some from 'intuition,' or *prosper chance*, from the *supersensual* mind or from other little understood aspects of the world of mind—but to bring it to the Conscious Mind, that bridge is needed which I have called the "Borderland" state.

"Well, what good did it do to find out about that music?" demands the scoffer. Two examples are then in order where money and practical value resulted.

The Dream Inventing of Plastic Cement

First is the dream of the inventor, Hans Olson, as he told it to me: He read in a chemistry journal that the addition of 15 percent of oleaginous substance to cement would make it plastic, but that this would weaken the cement too much. He spent considerable time in testing different additives to the oiled cement to try to strengthen the cement, to no avail. *Then he had his dream!*

Hans told me, "In my dream I saw myself adding only about 5 percent of oil to the cement, and it came out plenty plastic—sticky as clay. When I woke up, I said to myself: 'Those birds did not try a smaller percent of oil!' That dream told me that 5 percent was enough for stickiness and not enough to weaken the cement. I gobbled my breakfast and went to work in my lab. You know the result, Lou. My invention of Portland plastic cement has brought me a small fortune. Sure, I probably knew in the back of my mind that 5 percent would be enough, but it took that dream to bring it to my Conscious Mind."

The Dream Leading to the Perfect Well

The second example is a dream of my own. I had settled on forty acres of land in the mountains of Southern California. For two solid months I dug in many places showing possible signs of water, but they all turned out to be dusters. The last place that I dug was only two hundred feet from my cabin. After digging four feet in depth, and not seeing any signs of hoped-for water, I gave up in despair and decided to turn the place back to the packrats and ground squirrels. *Then came the dream!* Two more feet of digging and there came copious water of remarkable purity.

Again the admission: Yes, this spot, I had noted as having the best water signs on the land, but I had given up, and, without that dream, the ground squirrels and the gophers would still have exclusive tenancy, along with a few coyotes.

We have now seen some fine examples showing that what exists in the borderland state can appear in dreams accessed by the Conscious Mind. Indeed, one is inclined to the opinion that even prophetic dreams first exist in that vast vibrant sphere which we call the "World of Mind," which, perforce, includes the borderland state of consciousness.

This writer knows of one case, which at first sight seems to be downright miraculous, but with due examination shows that the dream had a definite source in the world of mind *before* the person had the dream.

The Dream Meeting of Brother and Sister at the Golden Gate Bridge

I knew this person, J. Kelsoe, very well when we were members of the Southern California Gladiola Growers Association. In his dream, he was speaking with his sister who was living in Oregon, and whom he had not seen for over twenty years. They both agreed that twenty years was just too long, and that they must meet for a reunion. Kelsoe's work permitted him to take time off pretty much as he chose, and before the week was over he and his family headed for Oregon in his automobile.

He told me, "When we arrived at the Golden Gate Bridge, 'something' told me not to cross the bridge immediately. I had waited at the bridge for perhaps a half hour when, to my amazement, I saw my sister coming out of the bridge in her automobile—and she saw me at the same time!"

When he told his sister about the dream, she said that she had decided to visit him on the same night as he had the dream. Kelsoe's dream and also his 'feeling' to wait at the bridge, are fine examples of thought transference via the borderland.

It remains pure speculation to explain the meeting at the bridge: we do swim in an ocean of unknown possibilities in which anything can trigger movement into manifest realities. Ah, but we can learn to become aware of those possibilities through dream experiences, and we can consciously determine to turn possibility into reality. That's what this book is about.

Suggested Reading:
Andrews, Ted. *Sacred Sounds: Magic and Healing through Words and Music.* St. Paul: Llewellyn, 2002.

Jung, C. G., and Joan Chodorow, ed. *Jung on Active Imagination*. Princeton, NJ: Princeton University Press, 1997.

Farrell, Nick. *Magical Pathworking: Techniques of Active Imagination*. St. Paul: Llewellyn, 2004.

Slate, Joe H., and Carl Llewellyn Weschcke. *Communicating with Spirit: Here's How You Can Communicate (and Benefit from) Spirits of the Departed, Spirit Guides & Helpers, Gods & Goddesses, Your Higher Self and Your Holy Guardian Angel*. Woodbury: Llewellyn, 2015.

CHAPTER FOUR
ESP in Relation to Dreams

The Failure of Statistical Research in Relation to the Paranormal

Unknown to the general public, the old type of quasi-scientific parapsychological investigation has long ago lost standing in scientific circles. In just one example, in 1938, the scientific world was shaken by the revelation that the highly touted ESP cards used by Dr. J. B. Rhine at Duke University could be *read from their backs under certain lighting conditions*. Although it was never proven that all the earlier research results were erroneous, and the cards were later changed, that type of statistical research conducted under "laboratory conditions" were henceforth viewed with doubt and even with suspicion.

The Problem of a "Negative Definition"

Dr. Edwin Boring, professor emeritus at Harvard University, pointed out that Extra Sensory Perception has only a *negative* definition, which is: "Communication without the intervention of ordinary sensory channels." He continues: "A universal negative of this sort can be neither proven nor disproved."

ESP in Dreams and Emotion

Then suddenly ESP investigations have taken on a new turn and changed the rules of the game, such as in the work of the pioneering Dr. Montague Ullman at the Maimonides Medical Center in Brooklyn, New York. Where the earlier researchers attempted complete objectivity with machines, buttons, switches, screens, and printed cards, Ullman began to relate ESP to dreams and emotions.

A sudden surge of new knowledge in dreams opened the way to approximate the emotional content of apparent paranormal experience, thus bypassing the past critics of ESP.*

*Throughout this book one can see the implied importance of intense emotion in relation to good manifestations of ESP.

Emotion as the "Initiator" of ESP

Dr. Ullman testified that during his twenty years of psychoanalytic practice, he had many patients bring in dreams that reflected events in *his* (Ullman's) own life, events unknowable to his patients. Other analysts have reported similar experiences. Here we can see clearly that it is *the patient's emotions toward the analyst that initiate the ESP experience between the two involved individuals*. One can also see that factoring in these emotional states in relation the ESP experience is a tough one to duplicate in the emotional-chilling atmosphere of the laboratory.

We can now see that it is NOT ESP that is the great validator of dreams. It is the other way around. The Dream 'Borderland state' is the validator of ESP.

The Borderland State of Consciousness

Throughout this book are many references to what I call the "Borderland." *What is this "Borderland?"* It is the particular state of consciousness which bridges waking consciousness into that vast sphere known as the "World of Mind." *The World of Mind* is a name conceived by my good friend Dr. Marc Edmund Jones, the eminent astrologer and perhaps the greatest occult writer of the twentieth century (as distinct from the magickal writings of Aleister Crowley and others, and from other Mystical, Esoteric, and Paranormal subjects often mixed into a confusing and confused array of personal ego projection by self-proclaimed "masters" and founders of "Scientific" Religion).

With the exception of hypnotism, reliable occult tradition has not viewed thought transference and thought reception as 'quasi-radio mechanism' taking place directly between two people, but rather was understood as follows: Thoughts, feelings, and emotions were absorbed in a vast never-ending reservoir of 'Ether,' (now called the *World of Mind* and otherwise known as the Astral Dimension), then these ideas and emotions could be received by another person—particularly by a person attuned to the content.

> While emotion always involves a physiological response, emotion itself operates at the astral level which is not limited by the physical boundaries of body or geography. The astral dimension is accessible to all and is, in fact, the "Psychic World."
>
> "Attention" and "Intention" connect both individuals and phenomena. "<u>Pay attention to me</u>" and we are emotionally and psychically connected. "<u>Intend" (or Desire) to cause physical actions</u>, and the emotional *substance* of the astral world becomes a Thought Form that translates astral energy into physical manifestation.
>
> The astral dimension has many levels, at which—emotion guided by a trained mind—different "transactions" are carried out as empowered by love or hate, desire to heal or harm, to discover and learn, to grow and become, to share or deny, etc.
>
> Emotion is Energy-in-Motion. It is always moving, but can be shaped and directed by Mind and Will. Emotion, guided by a trained mind, is the power behind so-called miracles.

"Things" vs. Thought and Feeling

While the major content of this chapter refers to thoughts, ideas, feelings, and emotions, *it does not refer to things*. It is really quite silly to equate those boringly repetitive ESP *statistical tests* conducted in a *sterile* laboratory atmosphere in which the receiver is put to guessing what thing (an uninteresting object) the sender has in mind—a cup, a pipe, a pencil or paper. There is no place in the world of mind for mere dead objects or things. Of course, a "thing" may be a <u>symbol</u> for some vast idea or emotion, and I have seen this demonstrated by Professor Albert Mogul, a good friend of mine. He told the sender to think of a thing that was the object of veneration and hate by thousands of people. Albert easily captured the heavily charged idea-symbol, *the Nazi Swastika.*

In this thing called ESP, the necessity of the theory of the World of Mind (or its equivalent) is well attested by the experimental investigation of ESP by H. Richards, a professor of science, in Iowa. Professor Richards had been having discouraging results with the Rhine method. He was impressed by some points of value in my small book, *The Incredible Yi King,** published in England. There ensued a series of correspondences between us on the "Borderland Consciousness" in which I elaborated upon investigations of ESP in conjunction with the postulated "World of Mind."

*See also Culling: *The Pristine Yi King.*

The results of Prof. Richards' tests that he shared with me show a far higher percentage of true ESP sending and receiving, both in the dream state and also in the quasi-normal state of consciousness. Also, the reports are almost equaled by my nephew, a teaching professor of psychology in Kansas—all based upon the theory of the World of Mind.

*"Theory" and "the Proof is in the Pudding!"**

Now there is nothing wrong with objecting to a theory upon the grounds that it is mere theory, but let us heed the words of Dr. Carl Jung: "I do not hold for the validity of my theories. All that I can say is that they work for me."

*"The proof of the pudding is in the eating," which basically means that the quality of something is uncertain until it has been tested directly, sort of like: "You don't know whether you like it until you've tried it."

Perhaps the best evidence for the World of Mind is demonstrated in all animal life.

What animals "instinctively" do can be best understood as the inherited *cumulative* experience of evolution based on trial and error, step after step over eons of time, from the ancestors as transmitted both by the physical DNA and Causal, Mental, Astral, and Etheric composite matrix guiding the individual form.

But now let us refer to Van Nostrand's Scientific Encyclopedia: "Science knows of no method whereby the learned experience of ancestors can be transmitted genetically to the offspring. What is called instinct may well be some sort of directive capacity."

This is nothing less than saying the "instinct" (and intuition?) is part of what we now call the World of Mind.

The "World of Mind"

The World of Mind also includes Jung's Collective Unconscious. This dream book is based upon such a concept, and I further state that this is the only basis upon which a dream book can be based in order to be worth more than the paper and printer's ink.

In closing, I hope that I have not left the impression that one cannot receive "thought" from some known person, friend, or loved one—or about them. The simple point is that thought and emotions are taken up first in the medium of the World of Mind, and then he or she may receive the original if attuned mentally or emotionally to the sender or to what is sent.

One may well ask, "Why this quibbling?" The point is that when the mechanics of this medium is admitted in theory and understood, then one does not go by a "Tomfool" method of testing another person by saying, "What am I visualizing or thinking about?" and it is nothing but a pair of uninspiring chopsticks upon the table. The World of Mind neither accepts nor respects such fool trivia.

Suggested Reading:

Crowley, Aleister. *Magick Without Tears.* St. Paul: Llewellyn, 1973.

Culling, Louis T. *The Pristine Yi King.* St. Paul: Llewellyn, 1989.

Slate, Joe H., and Carl Llewellyn Weschcke. *The Llewellyn Complete Book of Psychic Empowerment:A Compendium of Tools and Techniques for Growth and Transformation—Includes Journey of a Lifetime, a Self-Directed Program of Developmental Actions to "Put it All Together."* Woodbury: Llewellyn, 2011.

Slate, Joe H., and Carl Llewellyn Weschcke. *Psychic Empowerment for Everyone—You Have the Power, Learn How to Use It.* Woodbury: Llewellyn, 2009.

Slate, Joe H., and Carl Llewellyn Weschcke. *Self-Empowerment through Self-Hypnosis: Harnessing the Enormous Potential of the Mind.* Woodbury: Llewellyn, 2010.

Slate, Joe H., and Carl Llewellyn Weschcke. *Self-Empowerment through Self-Hypnosis Meditation CD Companion Audio CD.* Woodbury: Llewellyn, 2011.

CHAPTER FIVE
The Submerged Sub-Conscious Dream

The Memory of the "Unremembered Dream"

The "Submerged Sub-Conscious Dream" relates to that kind of dream which is mostly remembered as only a mass of unrelated seeming nonsense, yet it has induced impressions in the sleeper's 'mind' that often prove to be of great utilitarian value—even though not remembered as a dream. But while it is commonly believed that, with practice, all dreams can be recalled, as can other mental activity that goes on while we sleep—that is not completely factual.

For example, the sleep-walker does not typically remember what was happening while walking in his sleep, nor does one remember talking in his or her sleep unless suddenly awakened in its midst. Yet, upon investigation, it is commonly found that during such sleep-walking or talking, there is often some dreaming of apparently un-related content that can be remembered. All of this may be obscure to the reader's understanding and both the clarification and the value is perhaps much better presented in actual case history dreams, as follow:

The Case of Richard Wagner's Inspired Dreams

Case History #1: The great music opera composer, Richard Wagner, has testified that, on several occasions—even after long concentration—he could not capture certain character and incidental themes needed for his composition. Then he would have a dream, a worrisome dream of trying to work out some unrelated problem not even about music. Yet, on the following day, he was finally inspired with the desired music theme.

(Note: The reader must take note of the importance of 'the following day' in the above example. One must concentrate on the problem or project, or visualize whatever is in the mind before going to bed on the following night; if this is not done, it is lost. One must seize upon it while it is still "hot off the griddle" as the expression goes.)

The Case of Richard Strauss and the "Dragnet" Theme

Case History #2: The case of Richard Strauss, the music composer of "Electra," is like that of Wagner. He had worked long and hard on the assassination scene with the inexorable denouement against the criminal. After a dream of trying troubles, he awoke inspired the following day, capturing the missing theme he had struggled so mightily for all the previous day. The enduring genius of this theme is testified to by the fact that it was used as the theme for Jack Webb's famed "Dragnet" TV detective series.*

> *Notes from Wikipedia: Dragnet* was an American radio, television, and motion picture series, enacting the cases of a dedicated Los Angeles police detective, Sergeant Joe Friday. The show's title relates to the police term "dragnet", a system of coordinated measures for apprehending criminals. *Dragnet* remains a key influence on subsequent police dramas in many media.
>
> *Dragnet* is perhaps the most famous and influential police procedural in history. The series revealed the boredom and drudgery, as well as the danger and heroism, of police work, earning praise for improving the public opinion of police officers.
>
> The show's cultural impact is such that after a half century, elements of *Dragnet* are familiar to those who have never seen or heard the program:
>
> The ominous, four-note introduction to the brass and tympani theme music (titled "Danger Ahead") is instantly recognizable.
>
> Another *Dragnet* trademark is the show's opening narration: "Ladies and gentlemen, the story you are about to hear is true. Only the names have been changed to protect the innocent."

Another cribbing of this overwhelming powerful musical theme was its use by radio station KLAC of Los Angeles. On their Talk Radio show they had the rule that no listener could call in more often than once every four days. To merely say to a violator, "You are a repeater; hang up" was not very effective, so the station instead blasted forth with the Electra assassination theme. This really shriveled those rule violators trying for their moments of fame!

The Case of Frater∴ A of the G∴B∴G∴ and the Meaning of the Star Card

Case History #3: Frater∴ A of the secret magick order, the G∴B∴G∴ (the Great Brotherhood of God). This 'Master' of the Order had spent long hours trying to divine the true meaning of the major Tarot trump called the "Star." Then he had the aforementioned type of dream in which he was trying to resolve or solve dozens of worrisome things and getting nowhere. He did not have to burn much night oil on the following night before the whole solution came like a flash. This important card shows a nude woman pouring water from one vase into the ocean, and from the other hand she pours water on the land, which trickles back into the ocean. Correctly, she should be taking water from the ocean (instead of pouring into it) and she also pours water onto the land, which runs back into the ocean. Therefore, correctly interpreted, it is the symbol of the continuity of spiritual existence.

In only two among the many hundreds of Tarot decks available today is the "Star" correctly drawn,* i.e., with seven points which symbolize the highest aspect of Mother Nature. Strict empirical observation has proven this interpretation to be eminently correct, and with other cogent implications.

*It is increasing believed that many of the esoteric "masters" in the late nineteenth century, and earlier, deliberately planted false information and misleading trails as *occult secrets* were made public in regard to the Tarot, Magickal practices, techniques for Psychic Empowerment, Kabbalistic Correspondences, Alchemical processes, and more, in the belief that such knowledge could not safely be given to the public and should only be revealed to carefully screened and trained students in the Secret Orders—*"when the time was right!"*

In the same manner, we've come to realize that only about sixty percent of the Yi King Hexagram meanings as given in the standard texts upon which Legge and Wilhelm base their translations are correct. How and why they are correct in some cases, and incorrect in other cases, is discussed in my book, *The Pristine Yi King.* (See reading list at end of this chapter for further information.)

The Case of Frater ∴ Zeus Turned Warrant Officer

Case History #4: Frater ∴ Zeus of the G∴B∴G∴, as written in his dream record: "I joined the navy with the idea of making it my life's work, but I was later dubious about this, being only a first-class machinist, and I became dissatisfied. I had a dream in which I was being compelled to surmount a number of difficulties and problems; they made no sense—not even enough for me to remember them. Still, they worried me so much in trying to accomplish senseless things that I spent a very fitful night. On the following day, I set myself to concentrating, trying to extract some sense from the dreaming. It hit me suddenly, like a flash out of the blue: "Shoot the moon; shoot the works—all or nothing." I wasted no time in putting in for an examination as machinist warrant officer." (Note: In most ways the warrant officer is a higher position than the commissioned officer of second lieutenant is.)

Conclusion: Within two months Zeus was in the uniform of warrant officer. (Note again: the inspiration came to him on the day following the jumbled dream.)

The Case for Frater ∴ A—Discovering the Calypso "Moon" Language

Case History #5: For several months, Frater ∴ A had worked far into the night with the idea of finding and solving some magick mystery in Egyptian hieroglyphs. One night, after working until 2 a.m. on the problem, he fell asleep and within a few minutes a stately Egyptian in full ancient regalia appeared before him and said, "It is of no avail. The doors of the temples of Egyptian Magick have been sealed forever." The vision was so vivid that it awakened him and he immediately set to work on his problem again. Within a few minutes the word "Calypso" made a strong impression upon him. This led him to make a serious investigation into the *Calypso* "Moon" language along with the *Enochian* language. Details on both are given in a latter chapter on symbols and in the book, *The Complete Magick Curriculum of the Secret Order G∴B∴G∴* by Louis T. Culling and Carl Llewellyn Weschcke.

The Case of the Atheist J. P., and the founding of the Kerista Religion

Case History #6: This is the case of the skeptic, J. P., who had reluctantly reached the stage of being a hopeless atheist because of a deep-seated skepticism. As he told it to me, he was even contemplating suicide. Then, he had a dream in which some invisible "intelligence" was asking silly questions and giving equally silly answers. On the following day, in thinking about this dream, he had a "vision" in which a man said, "You have been chosen to found a new religion." This seemed to be so ridiculous to Bro Jud (as he was better known) that he said, "Why choose me?" The reply was, "Because you are so gullible." A rather contradictory seeming answer, but one that led to the birth of the quasi religion called "Kerista."* Scattered over the country are only about five thousand self-styled Keristans, but, as a code of belief and conduct, Kerista has made no small impact. The following note illustrates just one example of how a seemingly strange dream can become a reality with many permeations.

Notes from Wikipedia: Kerista was founded in 1956 by John Peltz, also known as "Bro Jud" Presmont. Kerista centered on the ideals of polyfidelity and intentional communities. From 1971 until 1991, the group headquartered at the Kerista Commune in San Francisco's famed Haight-Ashbury district from which the movement developed a lighthearted polytheistic mythology revolving around a pantheon of benevolent and technologically adept goddesses and gods. The group also promoted a World Plan to establish a functional Utopian society on a large scale.

The Keristans shared income and could choose whether or not to have outside paying jobs or work within the community (which operated several businesses, a legally incorporated church and an educational non-profit organization). The most successful of the businesses was Abacus, Inc., an early Macintosh computer vendor in San Francisco selling computer hardware, training, and services. At its height, Abacus had annual sales of $25 million, employed over 250 people with offices in five major California cities until 1992 when Apple pulled the plug on Value-Added Resellers.

The commune functioned as a religious order and was an important focal point for a larger community of people in San Francisco interested in alternative lifestyles, and maintained a very active program of social events and Gestalt-o-rama rap groups. In 1998, Robert Furchgott, the father of Eve Furchgott also known as Even Eve, who worked with Bro Jud and Susan Furchgott won the Nobel Prize in Medicine for a scientific breakthrough that was important in the creation of Viagra and several other drugs. Eve Furchgott is an active professional artist, as are some other former members of the commune.

In 1966, Science-fiction author Robert A. Heinlein learned that his 1961 novel *Stranger in a Strange Land* was considered the "New Testament" and compulsory reading for Kerista members. This same novel led to the founding in 1962 of the influential neo-Pagan Church of All Worlds, by Oberon Zell-Ravenheart, and to Discordianism by Carole M. Cusack in her book *Invented Religions: Imagination, Fiction, and Faith.*

The Case of Departed Relatives' Dream Message

Case History #7: The Departed Relative Dream Case. A director of the Los Angeles Dream Society said that she had a "secret" to tell me about dreams; however, it is secret only because import of the Departed Relative Dream is understood by only a surprisingly few people.

In these dreams, the dreamer's experience is with a departed close relative, particularly the father and/or the mother. Otherwise it differs little from the other six cases in this chapter in that there is nothing in the dream containing any clue about the real import of the dream (with the exception of wish fulfillment dreams).

The "secret" of such dreams is the dreamer is actually, but indirectly, receiving information of direct importance via the Supra-Conscious Mind. The importance of the information is only revealed through applied mental exploration the following day. Even then, it may not be consciously understood but instead functions through the Sub-Conscious Mind leading one to "intuitively" respond advantageously. The big point is that, after dreaming about being with a departed father or mother, one should make the effort on the following day (never later) to discover what very probably is the advice, help or direction that is or was beyond the power of the Conscious Mind.

One may very well ask why it is that such dreams are so obscure—almost beyond recovery. First, take note that, in most cases, one remembers nothing about one's sleep-walking and also sleep-talking. The simple fact is that within the sleep world of mind, there are different grades of obscurity in relation to the Conscious Mind—from thin gossamer veils to the heavy opaque—and even theories of the "why" and "how" may be misleading. However, be assured that the simple practices for dream remembering given in this book will wear down the thick obscuring quality of these veils.

In this case history of departed parents, Mr. H., a building contractor, faced a deadline foreclosure within thirty days which, if not paid, would wipe out his business. He saw three procedures which would at least salvage portion of his assets. There was a fourth alternative in which he could save everything, but he figured that it would not meet the deadline and, therefore, it would be better to focus on what seemed to be the sure thing.

Then he dreamed that he was visiting his mother and father. It was a short visit because he had a deadline to get to a certain place. He met three insurmountable difficulties in three different methods of travel—by bicycle, by auto, and by bus. Thus he desperately ran to the station to catch a train. Ten seconds later and the train would have left the station.

Now I had informed him that when dreaming of departed parents it is a strong probability that he is getting some kind of help. On the day after the dream, he concentrated on how he could handle that fourth alternative. He figured it out by a rare "intuition" how to manage it and meet the deadline. He managed it by a bare twelve-hour margin and saved his entire business.

(Note: Is not the word "instinct" more accurate than "intuition"?* We should note that all wild animals do marvelous things through the supposed instincts inherited from their ancestors. However, I make no claim of solving anything by using the word "instinct".)

Resorting to a quotation from the great psychologist Carl Jung, "I am far from knowing what 'spirit' and 'instincts' are; they are beyond my understanding. They are terms that we allow to stand for powerful forces whose nature *we do not know*."

*Instinct, or Intuition? There is a difference. Lou indicates a preference for "instinct" in his case example of Mr. H. even though it involved a human person and Lou describes instincts in wild animals. Animals do have instincts, but we have no way of knowing it they also have intuition. We know that humans have both.

"Instincts" are successful behavior patterns inherited from the long line of ancestral choices, that are perhaps transmitted through the generations both by physical DNA and animal consciousness of which we know very little.

Humans likewise have "Instincts" operating at more or less "animal levels" of consciousness, although we recognize that human instinctual levels of behavior have both good and bad results. Instinctive *reactions* in social situations are generally irrational and often disastrous. Jealous rages often lead to serious crimes. Hormone-driven behavior often leads to unfortunate pregnancies. Road Rage accounts for a variety of accidents involving both cars and sometimes guns. The ready availability of any kind of weapon can lead to injuries and crimes of passion, anger, frustration, depression, and hate.

But, instinctive actions can also prevent crimes, avoid accidents, and save lives; liberate great physical strength when and where it is needed; and sometimes even provide the right answer to a question beyond knowing.

"Instinct" derives from the Past. Instincts, in humans at least, (and perhaps in animals) arise in the Sub-Conscious Mind and yet involve emotional energies and mental know-how and memories passed from previous lives or through the Collective Unconscious.

"Intuition" functions at levels beyond instinctual patterns and past memories, and arises in the Supra-Conscious Mind. Even when it is expressed with "references" to personal or universal memories, it is *new* and seemingly with an "eye to the future." It is the "smart decision" by a business man, a doctor of lawyer, a politician or diplomat, even a general in the midst of battle. It is the "flash" that leads to a new scientific discovery or an innovative breakthrough in technology. It may be called "a Leap of Faith" but involves no faith other than one's own belief in its rightness.

"Instinct" is largely physical in nature; "Intuition" is non-physical and perhaps "spiritual" in origin.

As Jung wrote, there are "powerful forces whose nature *we do not know*."

We all dream, both humans and animals. The "Dream World" involves both Astral and Mental dimensions and is *energized* from both physical and spiritual levels. Dreams mostly include references to past experiences, but dreams themselves are *Messages from the Future.* When treated with "respect," they will answer questions, solve problems, forecast the future, and guide us to growth, success, and happiness. Dreams are Doorways to Other Dimensions and to our *Becoming More than We Are,* and to *All we Can Be.*

Dream on, Fellow Traveler. Dream on. <u>The Greatest Adventures are Yet to Come.</u>

Suggested Reading

Clement, Stephanie, and Terry Lee Rosen. *Dreams Working Interactive.* St. Paul: Llewellyn, 2000.

Culling, Louis T. *The Pristine Yi King.* St. Paul: Llewellyn, 1989.

Culling, Louis T., and Carl Llewellyn Weschcke. *The Complete Magick Curriculum of the Secret Order G.˙.B.˙.G.˙.: Being the Entire Study Curriculum, Magick Rituals, and Initiatory Practices of the G.˙.B.˙.G.˙. (The Great Brotherhood of God).* Woodbury: Llewellyn, 2010.

McElroy, Mark. *Lucid Dreaming for Beginners: Simple Techniques for Creating Interactive Dreams.* Woodbury: Llewellyn, 2007.

CHAPTER SIX
Three Pioneer Geniuses:
Creative People Ahead of Their Time

(Please note that short, updated biographies of each of these pioneer and prophetic persons are provided at the end of this chapter. In addition, suggested reading resources for each are included.)

———

Paschal Beverly Randolph, Dr. J. Rhodes Buchanan, and Ida C. Craddock were great Initiates* in understanding the "Borderland Consciousness" concept and how it applies in making dreams serve and do things for the dreamer, and then how to actually employ this esoteric *technology* for both practical and spiritual benefit. All three of these people were genuine "masters" of this particular technique and of the "Borderland" concept, but it was actually Ida C.** who coined the specialized term, the "Borderland."

> *Culling is using this word to mean that these people were "masters" of this particular manner of esoteric working rather than being formal initiates of any occult or masonic order, although Dr. Randolph was indeed an initiate of the Rosicrucian Fraternity. Culling was also an advocate of "self-initiation" as described in his as yet unpublished book, *A Shortcut to Initiation*.

> ** Ida Craddock (Aug. 1, 1857–Oct. 16, 1902) was known only as "Ida C." for the purpose of anonymity because of the nature of her writing on sexuality, her advocacy of Free Speech and Women's Rights for which she was both prosecuted and persecuted.

Paschal Beverly Randolph—A Pioneer of Occultism in America
Paschal Beverly Randolph (October 8, 1825–July 29, 1875)—A "Free Man of Color" in a time of Slavery in America, an active Abolitionist, a Medical Doctor, a "stage" Spiritualist Medium, a noted Occultist and prolific author, a Rosicrucian and founder of the first American order, a known Sex Magician in a time when "such things were unheard of," a world traveler at a time when most people's "worldviews" rarely extended beyond their birthplace, and a close friend of President Abraham Lincoln.

Randolph was a great initiate who had received a dispensation to found a Rosicrucian Fraternity in the United States, which is still operating (under later headships) in Quakertown, Pennsylvania. Although a prolific published writer, some of his works were privately distributed to a select few individuals. Fortunately, I have original copies in my library. (Note: today, all titles are again available—see list at end of this chapter.)

Randolph traveled extensively in foreign countries and among primitive peoples, and there gleaned valuable insight and guidance from secret rituals of several African tribes in making dream-working serve one in valuable and practical ways. He lectured and published these same teachings he'd learned from African "medicine men" who used them with astounding results.

Magick Mirror: Construction and Use

Another technique taught by Randolph was his so-called "Magick Mirror." Here's how to make it:

Use a small piece of glass three or four inches square.

Mix thoroughly one teaspoon full of black India ink with a teaspoon of "Will-Hold Glue" (or other liquid glue).

Lay the glass flat and paint this mixture on the top side with a small watercolor paint brush. Let this get completely dry (two or three hours) and cover with another coat. Let this dry for two or three days and your Magick Mirror is ready for use. Randolph says that this is better than the crystal ball for clairvoyance. He particularly recommends it for stimulating good dreaming by just gazing into it for a couple of minutes before going to bed.

An alternate way to produce a very nice mirror is by removing the mirror from a cosmetic powder compact, carefully scrape all the material that is on the back of the mirror with a single-edged razor blade, and then treat the glass as above.

Joseph Rhodes Buchanan—A Pioneer of Alternative Healing

Dr. Buchanan was best known in the world of medicine as the great exponent of "Zone Therapy" which was given in his book titled "Sarcognomy." Long ago this book was a rare and out of print collector's item. His privately printed material on dreams is largely unobtainable but, by pure fortune, I have copies of these.

Buchanan's Dream Technic method

Upon retiring, tie a small strip of cotton rag on one of the toes, tight enough to be felt, but not tight enough to impede circulation.

Which toe?

1. Small toe pertains to Mercury: mental activities, plans, writing, contracts, conversations, resourcefulness, trickiness.

2. Second toe pertains to the Sun: high or brilliant position of authority, dominant roles, realization.

3. Third toe pertains to Saturn: materialistic, stable, fixed, depth of mind, destiny.

4. Fourth toe pertains to Jupiter: generous, bountiful, good natured, lucky.

5. Fifth (big) toe pertains to Venus: the feelings, good friendship and love, good growth and also physical development, good help, associations or partnerships.

6. Ankle: for high spiritual development, place around ankle so that it touches the ankle bone.

Which foot? The right foot is for projecting, sending out, and aspiration, initiating or starting. The left foot is for reception and developing.

My personal inspiration: The left foot is for receiving intelligence, and the right foot is for sending or using intelligence.

As a special relaxation technique for some people to release the day's stress and facilitate sleep and dreaming, Buchanan recommends that a person should hold the palms of the hands on the fleshy part of the back shoulders for about five minutes. Once in bed, rest the temple in the palm of the opposite hand.

All these things WORK and should not be passed over as invaluable nonsense.

Ida C. Craddock—A Pioneer of Free Speech, Women's Rights, and Sexual Liberation

Before we meet Ida C., I want first to introduce Dr. MacDonald. The good Doc was eighty-seven years old when I met him back in 1937. He was a dedicated occultist and Theosophist, and had intimately known both Dr. Buchanan and Ida C. He was the one who gave me the rare manuscripts issued by the three of the triumvirate. Without the private manuscripts put out by Ida C., much that is in her "Heavenly Bridegrooms" would remain cryptic, to say the least.

Doctor MacDonald insisted on the importance of maintaining what he called the "positive phase of psychic magnetism." His formula for this is not only simple and practical, but also serves to keep the metabolism of the body and the nervous system at the peak healthy condition.

The MacDonald Formula for Positive Psychic Magnetism

Upon arising and allowing a considerable time before breakfast, drink a cup of hot water into which has been squeezed the juice of one-half a lemon—no sugar. In the evening, before going to bed, drink one-half of a cup of Sarsaparilla brew made as follows: Put four full cups of warm water in a cooking pan and then add two heaping tablespoons of grated sarsaparilla root, and stir until the root becomes fully saturated. Let this stand overnight and on the following dawn, gently simmer the brew for ten minutes. Then drain the liquid off into a glass container and place in the refrigerator. This makes a week's supply of one-half cup nightly. Doc, hale and hearty at the age of 87, maintained that the foregoing formulae, taken every day for the previous twenty years, accounted for his remarkably good health.

Ida C.'s "Heavenly Bridegrooms"

Ida C. wrote a series of short manuscripts under the general title of "Heavenly Bridegrooms" in which she gave instructions on developing the "Borderland Consciousness" and attaining valuable dreams in and by the sexual relationships. She circulated copies of these manuscripts among her friends, acquaintances, and others whom she considered to be ready and worthy. In those days, a *"nice woman"* did not even utter the word "sex." Moreover, since she had never been married, there came the public uproar: *"How then can she know these things about sex? She is a shameless, sinful woman."* Overnight she became a social pariah, shunned by friend and stranger alike. Deeply grieved and disillusioned, she sickened and died—a tormented suicide.*

*Note: Please see an updated and more complete biography at the end of this chapter.

Dr. Theodore Schroeder, a specialist in what he called "The Erotogenesis of Religion," had published "Heavenly Bridegrooms" by Ida C., intended for circulation among fellow psychologists, but such was the puritanical climate of the times that it added still more fuel to fires that eventually consumed her.

Incidentally, Dr. MacDonald was the only remaining friend of Ida C. and he revealed her name: Ida C. Craddock—the first time in print.

Union with the Divine Genius

Here follows the essence of Ida Craddock's teachings for attaining proficiency in the borderland, for closer union with the Supra-Conscious (the Divine Genius) source of wisdom and guidance and, of course, bringing the dreams to a great value and utility, both materially and spiritually.

1. That phase of sexual union called "Dianism,"* which at its most basic level is sexual union without climax. To be realistic, it obviously requires the partners to be in agreement that there is to be no climax even though sexual pleasure is allowed. But instead of being the goal, it is to be the fiery engine that feeds and energizes each person's aspiration and pre-determined goals. This union must extend to the point where the parties gradually slip over into the Borderland

Consciousness. This may take one hour and, even better, extend into several hours. The partners should continually keep their high aspirations in mind, constantly energized by unmitigated sexual ecstasy rather than sexual pleasure and the culmination of climax.

*Please also see the Glossary for further information on both Dianism and Qodosh.

2. After the partners have become proficient in Dianism, they can proceed to number two, "Qodosh." In this, the partners decide upon a single specific Magickal Goal and give a specific name. Examples: beauty, wisdom, resourcefulness, opportunity, valuable dreams, money, spiritual enlightenment, inspiration, clairvoyance, etc. While there is no limit to the names that can be used to define the magical goals, i.e. they can be symbolic or code words, words in other languages or that have meanings within magickal or divinatory systems, the chosen name must have specific meaning to the user. (Note: Some people known to this writer have used the proper hexagram of the 64 figures of the Yi King as a symbol for the "name word" and, upon retiring, instead of thinking the word for dream direction, they visualize the particular hexagram. In any event, the whole operation should lead to valuable dream information, direction or illumination.) One should be sufficiently experienced in Dianism to keep the name in mind long enough, say thirty minutes, for it to be impressed upon the subconscious. The net result is, metaphorically, a psychic offspring which has the nature of its name in a very intensified phase of your supraconscious—your Genius—your Daemon.

In Qodosh, unlike Dianism (defined as sexual union without climax), and unlike Alphaism with its emphasis on complete abstinence (for a specified time period), here the partners should be warm and ardent, but controlled. It's like a surfer riding the crest of the wave forever. There should be no feelings of frustration, no "lust for result." Rather than allowing oneself to be submerged in the full flow of pleasurable sensation, one should allow the ecstasy to feed the fires of aspiration and inspiration.

Dianism is not an end in itself but rather is the means to a greater end than orgasm, which is fleeting. *One comes, and then it's gone!* Here, Dianism uses the energy of sexual ecstasy to feed the fire of concentration—which we will learn to project in the attainment of our magickal goal.

To become a manifestation of the Holy Guardian Angel

The aim of the highest magick of Dianism lies in continuing the union until such time as one slides into the "Borderland" consciousness in which a hallucinatory meditation may be achieved in which one is submerged in spiritual inspiration and aspiration.

Both concentration and meditation disciplines are involved in the practice of Dianism. The role of the male is the more challenging, and he should withhold from consciousness any awareness of the known personality. Each partner must constantly perceive the other as god or goddess. In the beginning work it is only natural for the known personality to intrude, but continually suppressing it until the partner finally becomes the *visible manifestation of one's own Holy Guardian Angel.*

All things require time, regularity and persistence for results. Experience indicates that one or two hours, or even more, are required to attain the Borderland state. And it takes time to build up the energized enthusiasm of the Magickal Imagination which gives one's thoughts *subjective* reality. It might take thirty minutes or it might take hours to build up a satisfactory force.

Individuals are different, and each must work out his and her own individual technique. Dianism is not an end in itself, but the means to greater ends. In time one will learn through practice to *concentrate* on a chosen point, while at the same time riding the wave of sexual ecstasy. The fire of concentration will replace the preoccupation with sexual sensation. What seems difficult at first will become greater pleasure with accompanying spiritual realization.

Your Innate Dream Power

Dear reader, do not pass too lightly over the dream techniques given in this chapter for they have great efficiency and power. Among all the dream aspirants that I have known, I have never seen failure when the desires and aspirations were consistent with the potential of the particular individual. Every individual is endowed by birth with certain specific potentials—not all of the potentials of all living things. Here follows an example of a case where the desires and aspirations were not in the potential of the individual.

The Case of the Unfortunate Miss X: who had an overpowering desire to be an opera singer. However, she was not born with the very necessary kind of vocal cords nor the high palate required for such singing. True, at the expenditure of much time and money on the best of singing lessons, she became a fair night club singer, but not the lead opera singer of her desire.

The Case of Over-Indulgent Mario Lanza: There are also cases where even a high potential is ruined by the individual. Mario Lanza was hailed as having the voice of a second Caruso, but he ruined his potential with too much spaghetti, wine, and wild living.

The Case of Over-Straining Ferruccio Tagliavini: A more poignant case is that of the opera singer Ferruccio Tagliavini. As a heart-throbbing opera idol he was shoulders above all of them; yet, despite repeated warnings, he overstrained his voice by continually singing to those way up in the gallery. Take a warning from this: Yes, let your dreams direct you to your highest potentials, but also temper your dreams to direct you in not hampering or ruining your potentials. The following example is particularly relevant to this chapter.

The Case of Overly-Ambitious Wilfred T. Smith: For thirty years, starting at age 30, Smith had been an assiduous worker in the secret order O∴T∴O∴ (Order of Oriental Templars) headed by the noted magician Aleister Crowley. Smith was the head of the small Southern California group and was a 9th Degree initiate in the Order. The Ninth Degree holder was the "Keeper of the Secrets," which are the same secrets given in this chapter as revealed by Ida Craddock. Dr. MacDonald said Ida C. told him that she had received these secrets in a series of dream initiations. During the Middle Ages, the Catholic Church sponsored the Crusades (from the year 1095 to 1291) to wrest control of the "Holy Land" from the native Muslim people. During this same time, the Order of Templars fraternized with the old secret sect of Sufis of Arabia and received the secrets of what is now in the 9th Degree of the O∴T∴O∴.

For ten years Smith was almost obsessed with the desire to have a large piece of land within commuting distance from Los Angeles. He said that he wanted this for the O∴T∴O∴ headquarters where many members could live and congregate, and also where they could raise vegetables in communal gardens. After ten years, all that he had to show for this ambition was $1,000 in the bank. I suggested that he start to perform the 9th Degree rites and to then follow the guidance of his borderland intuition and his dreams.

This is the first recorded dream: "I dreamed that I was in a large old-fashioned house. Somehow I knew that it was in Hollywood. A voice came to my mind (not to my ears) and said: 'You should first buy a house like this in order to get your large piece of land.' I then said that I did not save enough money. Again the voice: 'There are a few places like this which can be bought for a small down payment and very soon there will be a chance to sell it at a big profit.' It was convincing to me; I believed it."

Smith immediately asked three acquaintances to keep an eye out for a place which would require only a small down payment. Such a place was soon found and bought on contract, price $12,000. Now, Smith noticed that there were large apartment buildings on each side of his place, both under the same ownership.

Just three months later, a man offered him $16,000 for the place. *(Reader, please note that these prices were substantial back in the mid-twentieth century.)*

Smith's borderland awareness was working and he had a suspicion that the offer came from the owner of the two apartment buildings. He immediately had a dream which confirmed this and told him that the apartment people wanted his property in order to build another apartment. In full confidence in this, he held out on repeated raised offers until he was offered $30,000. Then another dream told him to hold out for a trade. The apartment people knew of five acres with ocean frontage, about twenty miles north of Santa Monica. They told him the truth when they said that it was a steal at $18,000 (Smith's profit on the sale) for land on both sides of this acreage was selling at double that figure.

A small short-term mortgage upon the land financed the building of the house, which contained a large assembly room, an important stated objective for O∴T∴O∴ activities in their headquarters. This had been 75 percent of Smith's outwardly stated purpose. However, instead of carrying out his avowed aim, Smith began to play the part of the country gentleman on his landed estate. Worse yet, he reneged, in a more culpable manner, in his dealings with Carl Germer, the head of the O∴T∴O∴ in the United States.

Carl Germer made the following proposition to Smith: "Deed over one acre to the O∴T∴O∴ and I will build the large national headquarters here. There will be one large building for the Los Angeles lodge which you can take over and build it to something big." Smith turned this down, later on explaining to me that Germer would have too much to say and that he, Smith, would not have free rein.

Six months passed and still Smith had made no sincere move toward fulfilling his stated goal of providing for O∴T∴O∴ activity.

That was when I told Smith in words here given almost verbatim: "Smith, you have violated your oath to tell yourself the truth. You have sworn that your dedicated aim was to have a fine O∴T∴O∴ headquarters and that a large piece of land was merely the means to that end. But the real truth was that having your own landed estate was the real goal and the O∴T∴O∴ lodge was merely a sugared-up means toward that attainment. You have told yourself the truth that you wanted to be the big O∴T∴O∴ boss, and that is why you turned down Germer's offer. You are wise enough to know that one cannot fool the supra-conscious, the Great Genius, the Daemon, the Guardian Angel."

I did not see Smith again until he was getting ready to cross the border with an incurable sickness. He said, "You were right. The first taste of success was sweet as honey, but it turned bitter as gall in my stomach. Tell people about this ensnaring trap." He then said, "I am asking you, as my best and sincere friend, do all that you can to keep the O∴T∴O∴ alive."

(Note: At first glance, one might come to the judgment that too much space has been devoted to the Wilfred T. Smith case; however, it is a most excellent example of the specialized dream technique described to bring about the end result. And, also, warning both violating the stated goal and about what can happen if one violates the oath to tell oneself the truth and never to try and fool one's supraconscious.)

Dr. Carl G. Jung—A Pioneer of Esoteric Psychology

This work on dream interpretation follows the line of Dr. Carl Jung, although it may not readily appear so. Here follows a quotation from one of Jung's lectures:

"The view that dreams are merely imaginary fulfillments of suppressed wishes has long ago been superseded. True, there are some dreams which embody wishes and fears, but dreams, on occasions, can embody most anything. Dreams may give expression to ineluctable truths, to philosophical pronouncements, illusions, fantasies, memories, plans, anticipations, irrational experiences, even telepathic visions, and heaven knows what besides.

"One thing we ought never to forget: almost half of our lives is passed in a more or less unconscious state—and the dream is specifically the utterance of the unconscious. It is highly probable that the unconscious psyche contains a wealth of contents and living forms equal to or even greater than does consciousness in which concentration brings limitation and exclusion."

It is well to add more to the foregoing paragraph by a quotation from another Jung lecture, as follows:

"Investigations of animal instinct, as for example in insects, show that if man acted as certain insects do, he would possess a far higher intelligence than at present. It cannot, of course, be proven that insects possess conscious knowledge, but we cannot doubt that their unconscious action patterns are psychic functions. Man's unconscious likeways [sic] contains all the patterns of life inherited from his ancestors. The unconscious perceives, has purposes and intuitions, feels and thinks as does the Conscious Mind."

(Note: The reader will see the application of this paragraph to what is termed the Borderland Consciousness in this book, and the "Daemon"—but more particularly on the Daemon as referenced in the following paragraph quotation).

"If it were possible to personify the unconscious, we might call it a collective being, combining the characteristics of both sexes, transcending youth and age, birth and death, and having at its command a human experience of one or two million years—next to immortal. Such a being would be exalted above all temporal change; the present would mean no more than any year or two thousand years; owing to its immeasurable experience, it would be an incomparable prognosticator."

(Note: All of this is an apt reminder of what Jung wrote about what he called his "Daemon" which, at times, acted as a sort of super director general and led him into ways other than what he had planned—for his own good. As the reader will note, in this book there are frequent references to the "Supra-sensual of the Borderland" or the "Daemon".)

It is not amiss to mention here a few comments on Freudian psychoanalysis regarding dreams. Upon telling a Freudian psychologist what I had written about the subject "Mouse" in the dream dictionary (see Appendix A), he said, "But the mouse in dreams has a particular sexual implication." I replied that this dream book is being directed to people who do not have such a warped psychopathic personality that they relate such a thing as a mouse tail to a 'male sex organ'; and, anyway, that I had small regard for Freud's book *Interpretation of Dreams*. My psychologist friend then took refuge in a tricky and not outstandingly sincere argument by saying, "You do not understand Freud at all."

My reply to this is that if I understood ten times as much of Freud as I do now, I would still take the word of such a great authority as Dr. Carl Jung. So let us see what Jung has to say about Freud in the business of dream analysis.

Quote: "It is a pity that Freud turned his back on philosophy, i.e., rules of logic. Not once does he criticize his premises or even mere assumptions that underlie his personal outlook. Had he critically examined his assumptions, he would never have put his peculiar mental disposition so naively on view, as he has done in his 'Interpretation of Dreams'."

From what Jung has said as in the foregoing paragraph, let one not assume that Jung fails to give Freud credit where credit is due, as we can see in the following:

"What Freud has to say about sexuality, infantile pleasure, and their conflict with the 'principle of reality', as well as what he says about incest and the like, can be taken as the exact and truest expression of *his own psychic makeup*. He has given adequate form to what he has noted in himself. No experienced psychotherapist can deny having met with dozens of cases which answer in all essentials to Freud's descriptions. By his avowal of what he has found in himself, Freud has assisted at the birth of a great truth about man. But Freud's teaching is definitely one-sided in that it generalizes from facts that are relevant only to neurotic states of mind; its validity is really confined to those states. In any case, Freud's is not a psychology of the healthy mind."

Typical of Jung, he is not confined to one side of the coin. One short quote from the other side is quite sufficient. "For my part, I look at man in light of what in him is healthy and sound. The unconscious is not a demonic monster, but a thing of nature that is perfectly neutral as far as moral sense, aesthetic taste and intellectual judgment go. It is dangerous only when our conscious attitude towards it becomes hopelessly false." Jung then continues along this line in speaking about the value of dream assimilation:

"As soon as one begins to assimilate the contents that were previously unconscious, any danger from the side of the unconscious diminishes. As this process of assimilation goes on, it puts an end to the dissociation of the personality and to the anxiety that inspires the separation of the two realms of the psyche."

In combing through a number of Jung's dream case histories for a dream which is a good exemplar of the determination of the future outcome of something by the Yi King system of divination, we have an excellent exemplar in one of Jung's lectures on dream analysis.

(Note: In the Yi King system of divination, the formula is that if one proceeds in accordance with the positive nature of the particular "Hexagram," then the future "prediction" is [A plus a] and if not doing this, the predicted result is [A minus a].)

The dream and outcome given by Jung: "In Zurich, a colleague of mine often teased me about my interest in dream-interpretation. One day when I met him, he called out to me, 'Are you still interpreting dreams? By the way, I've had another idiotic dream. Does it mean something, too?'"

"He had dreamed as follows: 'I am climbing a steep snow-covered mountain. The higher I climb, the better I feel. I think: *If only I could go on climbing like this forever.* Upon reaching the summit, my elation is so strong I feel I could mount right up into space. And I discover that I can actually do this. I go on climbing on empty air. I awake in a real ecstasy.' "When he told me his dream, I said, 'My dear man, I know that you cannot give up mountaineering—never—but let me implore you not to go alone from now on. When you go, always take two guides and follow their directions.'"

"Incorrigible!" he said, laughing.

"I never saw him again. Two months later he was buried in an avalanche and was dug out in the nick of time by a military patrol which happened to pass. Three months after this, the end came. He again went climbing without guides. An Alpinist from below saw him literally step out into thin air as he was letting himself down a rock wall and he was dashed to pieces far below. That was his *'ecstasis'* in the full meaning of the word."

There is another beautiful point about this dream. Even though our mountaineer was a deviate from the "Normal," nevertheless, the average intelligent reader could have hazarded the same interpretation as did psychiatrist Jung. Be not brainwashed in and by this common propaganda that "normal" people who are working at self-understanding and self-integration have any need for outside psychological analysis. *Any person who is working at discovering one's own true self and to express one's true Individuality is one's own best psychologist.*

The *Life Goal* of every healthy adult is to "grow" as a person, and thus to become more than they are and all they can be. This "growth" involves both the continued development of the individual person and of humanity as a whole through the instrument of each and every one of us.

This "growth" requires both self-sufficiency and self-responsibility as well as devotion to the "communal all "at whatever level of our participation. This "growth" further means awareness of, and the continuous integration of all the "selves" and dimensions that make up the totality of the person. This "growth" extends to awareness of the effect of every thought and action in acknowledgement that all the Cosmos in a unity.

We need to acknowledge that each is both a "spark" of the Divine and a "god/goddess" in the making.

There is no other person (no matter how great) who knows as much about your own self as you alone can. Naturally, this does not apply to "sick" people; their own sickness is the proof that they need the aid of a psychiatrist. Certainly it must be stated that the non-sick man has a Lingam and the non-sick woman a Yoni, but it is only the sickly disturbed man and woman who relates, in any way whatsoever, mouse tails, elephant trunks, fish, circles, pools, pencils, cigars, gun muzzle, mother, father, etc., to Lingam and Yoni. Let the reader be not timid and feel a self-sufficiency in interpreting the dreams, with the aid of the hints given in this book; and let not the two oaths be neglected—practiced daily and unceasingly.

Short Biographies and Suggested Reading Lists:

Joseph Rhodes Buchanan (1814–1899) was an American scientist, academic dean and professor of eclectic medicine, and a research pioneer in psychometry. It was he who, in 1842, came up with the term "psychometry" as meaning the "measuring of the soul."

Dr. Buchanan launched an experimental program in which students of a Cincinnati medical school registered distinct and different impressions from disguised medicines held in their hands. Buchanan concluded that some type of emanation radiates from all substances, including the human body, and that certain people had greater sensitivity to these emanations and could readily distinguish and interpret these emanations. Considering the possibilities of these abilities, he stated:

"The past is entombed in the present, the world is its own enduring monument; and that which is true of its physical is likewise true of its mental career. The discoveries of Psychometry will enable us to explore the history of man, as those of geology enable us to explore the history of the earth. There are mental fossils for psychologists as well as mineral fossils for the geologists; and I believe that hereafter the psychologist and the geologist will go hand in hand, the one portraying the earth, its animals and its vegetation, while the other portrays the human beings who have roamed over its surface in the shadows, and the darkness of primeval barbarism. Aye, the mental telescope is now discovered which may pierce the depths of the past and bring us in full view of the grand and tragic passages of ancient history."

He called the subtle emanation given off by the human body "nerve aura." In the *Journal of Man,* one of the first Spiritualist monthlies, he published a complete exposition of his system of neurology and anthropology.

Psychometry, for Dr. Buchanan, was essentially a human psychic faculty and does involve the intervention of spirits. However, Mrs. L. A. Coffin, in her preface to Dr. Buchanan's *Manual of Psychometry* (Boston, 1889), stated that she often felt the presence of spirits while performing psychometry.

In the course of his investigations, primarily through the mediumship of Mrs. Hollis-Billing, Dr. Buchanan received direct writing, purportedly from St. John. After being held in privacy for 17 years, these communications were published in 1897 under the title of *Primitive Christianity: Containing the Lost Lives of Jesus Christ and the Apostles and the Authentic Gospel of St. John.*

An invention of Dr. Buchanan is the "Sarcognomy."

Buchanan claimed that Sarcognomy solved the mind-body dualism problem. He wrote that the soul occupies the brain as a master occupies the mansion. The soul leaves the brain "when invited by a congenial season of pleasure" and occupies "the body to the apparent neglect of the brain." A telepathic connection to the body not only establishes a sympathy between the brain and body parts including those recognized in the practice of phrenology.

Buchanan said that knowing which character traits are located in which body parts would be of vital use in diagnosing and treating disease. See Dr. Buchanan's book *Therapeutic Sarcognomy.*

Books by and about Joseph Rhodes Buchanan

(Works by this author published before January 1, 1923, are in the public domain worldwide because the author died at least 100 years ago)

Buchanan, Joseph Rhodes. *Therapeutic Sarcognomy: A Scientific Exposition of the Mysterious Union of Soul, Brain, and Body*. Whitefish, MT: Kessinger Publishing, 2003.

Buchanan, Joseph Rhodes. *Manual of Psychometry*. Boston, 1889. (No publication information is available.)

Buchanan, Joseph Rhodes. *Journal of Man*. (No publication information is available, though several volumes are available from Amazon, Barnes and Noble, and other resellers.

(Note: the following information was selected mainly from Wikipedia and various published sources.)

Ida C. Craddock (August 1, 1857–October 16, 1902) was a nineteenth century American advocate of free speech and women's rights, and—for lack of a better term, "Sexual Ecstasy." For much or her life, she was simply known as "Ida C." to provide anonymity as protection from both prosecution and persecution for her outspoken advocacy. Even her own mother sought to have her institutionalized because of her well-known sexual writings and teachings at a time when such things were judged as proof of depravity and criminal behavior.

She was born in Philadelphia of Quaker parents. Her father died when she was just four months old. Her mother raised her and homeschooled her with an extensive Quaker education. In her early twenties, she qualified for admission to the University of Pennsylvania, and would have been the first female undergraduate student had not the Board of Trustees blocked her entrance. She then wrote and published a textbook on stenography and taught the subject at Girard College for women.

Later, she left the Quaker community and became a Unitarian and joined the Theosophical Society in 1887, developing a wide academic interest in the Occult and began her writing career. As a freethinker, she was in 1889 elected Secretary of the American Secular Union Philadelphia Chapter.

After a run-in with her mother over her teachings of religious eroticism, Craddock moved to Chicago and opened an office offering "mystical" sexual counseling to married couples. Although unmarried, she dedicated herself to "preventing sexual evils and sufferings" by providing a sexual education to adults.

A gifted writer, Craddock achieved national notoriety for her defense of a controversial belly dancing act by performer "Little Egypt" at the 1893 World's Columbian Exposition in Chicago. She wrote many serious instructional books on human sexuality and appropriate, respectful sexual relations between husband and wife. Among her works were *Heavenly Bridegrooms, Psychic Wedlock, Spiritual Joys, Letter to a*

Prospective Bride, The Wedding Night, and *Right Marital Living.* Of *Heavenly Bridegrooms,* Aleister Crowley wrote: "This book is of incalculable value to every student of occult matters. No Magick library is complete without it."

However, her "sex manuals" were considered obscene by the standards of her day and led to numerous confrontations with the law, some of them boldly initiated by Craddock herself. She was held for months at a time on morality charges in five local jails as well as the Pennsylvania Hospital for the Insane—such was the attitude of those times.

Her writings on supernatural topics also continued throughout her life. Mass distribution of *Right Marital Living* through the U.S. Mail after its publication in a medical journal, *The Chicago Clinic* led to an 1899 Chicago Federal indictment of Craddock to which she pleaded guilty and received a suspended sentence. A subsequent 1902 New York Federal trial on charges of sending *The Wedding Night* through the mail resulted in her conviction. Refusing to plead insanity as a condition to avoid prison time, she was sentenced to three months in prison, much of which she served in the notorious Blackwell's Island workhouse. Upon her release, the infamous Anthony Comstock immediately re-arrested her for violations of the federal Comstock law and on October 10 she was tried and convicted. During the trial, the judge declared that *The Wedding Night* was so "obscene, lewd, lascivious, dirty" that the jury should not be allowed to see it during the trial. At age forty-five, she saw her five-year sentence as a life term and so committed suicide on October 16, 1902.

A century later, Ida C. is honored as a pioneer for free speech and women's rights. In 2010, Vere Chappell wrote and compiled *Sexual Outlaw, Erotic Mystic: The Essential Ida Craddock* which he describes as "an anthology of works by Ida Craddock, embedded in a biography." The book reprints *The Danse du Ventre* (1893), *Heavenly Bridegrooms* (1894), *Psychic Wedlock* (1899), *The Wedding Night* (1900), *Letter from Prison* (1902), *Ida's Last Letter to Her Mother* (1902), and *Ida's Last Letter to the Public* (1902).

Books by and about Ida C. Craddock

(Works by this author published before January 1, 1923, are in the public domain worldwide because the author died at least 100 years ago.)

Chappell, Vere, and Mary K. Greer. *Sexual Outlaw, Erotic Mystic: The Essential Ida Craddock.* San Francisco: Red Wheel/Weiser Books, 2010.

Schmidt, Leigh Eric: *Heaven's Bride: The Unprintable Life of Ida C. Craddock, American Mystic, Scholar, Sexologist, Martyr, and Madwoman.* New York: Basic Books, 2010.

Craddock, Ida. *The Heaven of The Bible*. Nabu Press, 2011. (No publication information is available.)

Craddock, Ida: *Lunar and Sex Worship* (Introduction by Vere Chappell), 2010, Teitan Press

Craddock, Ida. *Heavenly Bridegrooms: An Unintentional Contribution to the Erotogenetic Interpretation of Religion*. Whitefish, MT: Kessinger Publishing, 2010.

Craddock, Ida. *Right Marital Living*. (Self-published by the author in 1901.)

Craddock, Ida. *The Wedding Night*. (Self-published by the author in 1902.)

Books Mentioning Ida C. Craddock

Culling, Louis T. *Sex Magick*. St. Paul: Llewellyn, 1993.

Peiss, Kathy, ed. *Major Problems in the History of American Sexuality: Documents and Essays*. Boston: Houghton Mifflin, 2001.

Sachsman, David, S. Kittrell Rushing, and Roy Morris Jr., eds. *Seeking a Voice: Images of Race and Gender in the 19th Century*. West Lafayette, IN: Purdue University Press, 2009.

Strub, Whitney. *Obscenity Rules: Roth v. United States and the Long Struggle over Sexual Expression*. Lawrence, KS: University Press of Kansas, 2013.

Wood, Janice Ruth. *The Struggle for Free Speech in the United States, 1872–1915: Edward Bliss Foote, Edward Bond Foote, and Anti-Comstock Operations*. Abingdon, UK: Routledge, 2012.

Paschal Beverly Randolph

(Note: the following information was mainly selected from Wikipedia and various other published sources.)

Paschal Beverly Randolph (October 8, 1825–July 29, 1875) was an African-American "free man" at a time when most Africans were slaves in the American South. He became a medical doctor, occultist, Spiritualist, trance medium, and writer. He was perhaps the first person to introduce the principles of sex magic to North America, and, accordingly established the earliest known Rosicrucian order in the United States.

His father was a nephew of John Randolph of Roanoke and his mother was Flora Beverly, whom he later described as a woman of mixed English, French, German, Native American, and Malagasy ancestry. She died when he was young, leaving him homeless and penniless; he ran away to sea in order to support himself. Due to his work aboard sailing vessels he traveled widely as a teen and young man. His travels took him to England, through Europe, and as far east as Persia, where his interest in mysticism and the occult led him to study with local practitioners of folk magic and varied religions. On these travels he also met and befriended occultists in London, England, and Paris, France.

After leaving the sea, Randolph embarked upon a public career as a lecturer and writer. By his mid-twenties, he regularly appeared on stage as a trance medium and advertised his services as a spiritual practitioner in Spiritualist magazines. Returning to New York City in September 1855, after "a long tour in Europe and Africa," he gave a public lecture to African Americans on the subject of immigrating to India and became a spokesman for the abolition of slavery. In 1865 he was the principal of the Lloyd Garrison School in New Orleans, teaching literacy to freed slaves.

In 1851, Randolph had become acquainted with Abraham Lincoln. Their friendship was close enough that, after Lincoln's assassination in 1865, Randolph accompanied the President's funeral procession to Springfield, Illinois. However, when some passengers objected to the presence of an African American in their midst, he was asked to leave the train.

In addition to working as a trance medium, he became medical doctor and wrote and published more than fifty books, both fiction and non-fiction, on health and medicine, sexuality, Spiritualism, magic and occultism, established an independent publishing company, and was an avid promoter of birth control during a time when it was largely against the law to mention this topic.

In his 1863 book *Pre-Adamite Man,* written under the pseudonym of Griffith Lee, he concluded that humans existed on earth long before the Biblical Adam. He traveled to many countries as he wrote different parts of the book and drew upon a wide range of sources from many different world esoteric and religious traditions. In the book, he claimed that Adam was not the first man and that pre-Adamite men were civilized and existed on all continents around the globe 35,000 to 100,000 years ago.

Having long used the pseudonym "The Rosicrucian" for his Spiritualist and occult writings, Randolph eventually founded the *Fraternitas Rosae Crucis*, the oldest Rosicrucian organization in the United States, dating back to the American Civil War. This group, still in existence, today avoids mention of Randolph's interest in sex magic, but his magico-sexual theories and techniques are incorporated into the teachings of the *Hermetic Brotherhood of Luxor.*

Randolph married twice: first to an African-American, second to an Irish-American. He lived in many places, including New York, New Orleans, San Francisco, and Toledo, Ohio, where he died at the age of 49. According to biographer Carl Edwin Lindgren, many questioned the news story, "By His Own Hand," in *The Toledo Daily Blade* which claimed that Randolph had died from a self-inflicted wound to the head. However, his own writings taught against suicide, and court record listed the cause of death as accidental. R. Swinburne Clymer, a later Supreme Master of the *Fraternitas*, stated that years later, in a death-bed confession, a former friend admitted that he had killed Randolph in a fit of jealousy and temporary insanity. Randolph's successor as Supreme Grand Master of the *Fraternitas,* and in other titles, was his chosen successor Freeman B. Dowd.

Randolph's published works include:

1854 *Waa-gu-Mah*

1859 *Lara*

1860 *The Grand Secret*

1860 *The Unveiling*

1861 *Human Love* and *Dealing with the Dead*

1863 *Pre-Adamite Man*

1863 *The Wonderful Story of Ravalette*

1863 *The Rosicrucian Story*

1866 *A Sad Case; A Great Wrong!*

1868 *Seership! The Magnetic Mirror*

1869 *Love and Its Hidden History*

1870 *Love and the Master Passion*

1872 *The Evils of the Tobacco Habit*

1873 *The New Mola! The Secret of Mediumship*

1874 *Love, Woman, and Marriage*

1874 *Eulis!: The History of Love*

1875 *The Book of the Triplicate Order*

Books About and By Paschal Beverly Randolph

(Works by this author published before January 1, 1923 are in the public domain worldwide because the author died at least 100 years ago.)

Clymer, R. Swinburne. *Paschal Beverly Randolph and the Supreme Grand Dome of the Rosicrucians in France*. Whitefish, MT: Kessinger Publishing, 2013.

Deveney, John Patrick. *Paschal Beverly Randolph: A Nineteenth-Century Black American Spiritualist, Rosicrucian, and Sex Magician*. Albany, NY: SUNY University of New York Press, 1996.

Randolph, Paschal Beverly. *After Death: Or Disembodied Man* (Classic Reprint), 2012, London: Forgotten Books, 2012.

Randolph, Paschal Beverly. *Dealings with the Dead: The Human Soul, Its Migrations, and Its Transmigrations.* London: Forgotten Books, 2012.

Randolph, Paschal Beverly. *EULIS!: The History of Love.* Whitefish, MT: Kessinger Publishing, 2010.

Randolph, Paschal Beverly. *Hermes Mercurius Trismegistus: His Divine Pymander.* (No publication information given.)

Randolph, Paschal Beverly. *Magia Sexualis: Sexual Practices for Magical Power.* Rochester, VT: Inner Traditions, 2012.

Randolph, Paschal Beverly. *Pre-Adamite Man: Demonstrating the Existence of the Human Race Upon the Earth 100,000 Thousand Years Ago!* William White, 1869.

Randolph, Paschal Beverly. *Seership and the Magic Mirror: Cool Collector's Edition.* CreateSpace Independent Publishing Platform, 2008.

Randolph, Paschal Beverly. *Sexual Magic.* Magickal Childe Publications, 1988.

Randolph, Paschal Beverly. *The Immortality of Love: Unveiling the Secret Arcanum of Affectional Alchemy.* Beverly Hall Corp., 1978.

Randolph, Paschal Beverly. *The Realms Beyond.* Kindle Edition, 2012.

Randolph, Paschal Beverly. *The Rosicrucian Dream Book.* London: Forgotten Books, 2013.

Randolph, Paschal Beverly. *The Wonderful Story of Ravalette.* Kindle Edition, 2014.

Randolph, Paschal Beverly. *Tom Clark and His Wife, Their Double Dreams, and the Curious Things that Befell Them Therein; Being the Rosicrucian's Story.* Kindle Edition, 2011.

Randolph, Paschal Beverly. *Soul!: The Soul World:The Homes of the Dead.* Confederation of Initiates, 1932.

Books mentioning Paschal Beverly Randolph

Alexander, Skye. *Sex Magic for Beginners: The Easy and Fun Way to Tap into the Law of Attraction.* Woodbury: Llewellyn, 2010.

Augustus, Jason. *Sexual Sorcery: A Complete Guide To Sex Magick.* Boston: Red Wheel/Weiser, 2006.

Barrett, David V. *A Brief History of Secret Societies: An Unbiased History of Our Desire for Secret Knowledge.* Philadelphia: Running Press, 2007.

Clifton, Chas S. *Her Hidden Children: The Rise of Wicca and Paganism in America.* Lanham, MD: AltaMira Press, 2006.

Culling, Louis T. *Sex Magick.* St. Paul: Llewellyn, 1993.

Culling, Louis T., and Carl Llewellyn Weschcke. *The Complete Magick Curriculum of the Secret Order G.'.B.'.G.'..* Woodbury: Llewellyn, 2010.

D'Aoust, Maja, and Adam Parfrey. *The Secret Source: The Law of Attraction and Its Hermetic Influence Throughout the Ages.* Port Townsend, WA: Process Media, 2012.

De Naglowska, Maria. *Advanced Sex Magic: The Hanging Mystery Initiation.* Rochester, VT: Inner Traditions, 2011.

Farber, Philip H. *Brain Magick: Exercises in Meta-Magick and Invocation.* Woodbury: Llewellyn, 2011.

Frater, U.'.D.'.. *Where Do Demons Live?: Everything You Want to Know About Magic.* Woodbury: Llewellyn, 2010.

Gehman, B. Anne, and Ellen Ratner. *Self Empowerment: Nine Things the 19th Century Can Teach Us About Living in the Twenty-first.* Cleveland, OH: Changing Lives Press, 2011.

Goodrick-Clarke, Nicholas. *The Western Esoteric Traditions: A Historical Introduction.* Oxford, UK: Oxford University Press, 2008.

Greer, John Michael: *The New Encyclopedia of the Occult.* St. Paul: Llewellyn, 2003.

Greenfield, A. H. *The Roots of Modern Magick: An Anthology.* Lulu.com, 2004.

Hanegraaff, Wouter J., and Jeffrey J. Kripal. *Hidden Intercourse: Eros and Sexuality in the History of Western Esotericism.* Bronx, NY: Fordham University Press, 2010.

Harms, Daniel, and John Wisdom Gonce III. *The Necronomicon Files: The Truth Behind the Legend.* Boston: Red Wheel/Weiser, 2003.

Heimbichner, Craig, and Adam Parfrey. *Ritual America: Secret Brotherhoods and Their Influence on American Society: A Visual Guide.* Port Townsend, WA: Festal House, 2012.

Horowitz, Mitch. *Occult America: White House Séances, Ouija Circles, Masons, and the Secret Mystic History of Our Nation.* New York: Bantam, 2010.

Kripal, Jeffrey J. *Mutants and Mystics: Science Fiction, Superhero Comics, and the Paranormal.* Chicago: University Of Chicago Press, 2011.

McIntosh, Christopher, and Colin Wilson. *The Rosicrucians: The History, Mythology, and Rituals of an Esoteric Order.* San Francisco: Weiser, 1998.

Pineda, Daniel. *Book of Secrets: The Esoteric Societies and Holy Orders, Luminaries and Seers, Symbols and Rituals, and the Key Concepts of Occult Sciences Through the Ages and Around the World.* San Francisco: Weiser Books, 2011.

Smoley, Richard, and Jay Kinney. *Hidden Wisdom: A Guide to the Western Inner Traditions.* Wheaton, IL: Quest Books, 2006.

Valiente, Doreen. *Natural Magic.* Blaine, WA: Phoenix Publishing, 1985.

Webb, Don. *Overthrowing the Old Gods: Aleister Crowley and the Book of the Law.* Rochester, VT: Inner Traditions, 2013.

Magic Mirrors:

Clough, Nigel R. *How to Make and Use Magic Mirrors.* San Francisco: Weiser, 1977.

Kraig, Donald Michael. *Llewellyn's Truth About Calling Spirits.* Woodbury: Llewellyn, 2013.

Slate, Joe H., and Carl Llewellyn Weschcke. *Communicating with Spirit.* Woodbury: Llewellyn, 2015.

Tyson, Donald. *How to Make and Use a Magic Mirror.* St. Paul: Llewellyn, 1990.

CHAPTER SEVEN
Using Symbols in Dreams as a Powerful Technique to Direct Desired Dreams of Value

The "Language" of Dreams is that of Symbols, Signs, Analogies, and Archetypes

In his great classic work, *Problems of Mysticism and Symbolism* Dr. Herbert Silberer (1882–1923), has convincingly proven that the vision and language of dreams is closely related to the language of symbols, analogies, and the presence of living archetypes as also seen in the writings on Alchemy, Magick, and other related mystical writings: each deriving from the unconscious via the Borderland State. His work makes a great case for the use of symbols in *purposeful dream induction*. In this chapter, we are not concerned with deductive theory, but rather in presenting actual case histories of dreams, and the method in which they are used.

Also, in this chapter I have provided a number of symbols which have proven to be of great value in intentional dream induction leading to the desired outcome of these dreams in resolving problems. Our first symbol exemplar is probably the most universal symbol resident in the collective unconscious of man.

The Use of Symbols in the Language of Magick

SYMBOL—CROSS WITHIN CIRCLE

In the ancient Egyptian hieroglyphs, this symbol, *the cross within the circle,* was the symbol for the planet Earth. The four points symbolize the Four Great Powers of Fire, Air, Water, and Earth, represented by the Bull, the Lion, the Eagle (or Dragon), and by Man.

However, we are not concerned with ideas about the symbol; instead our interest is with the actual practices which are involved or pictured in the symbol. For thousands of years, great magicians and the priests of the older, non-Abrahamic religions, have followed the principles of *empowered symbol employment* in an essential part of their Magick rituals.

The Procedure to form the Magick Circle

Here is the procedure: At the beginning of the ritual, the magician paces around the room to establish a "Magick Circle," and then <u>forcefully</u> announces (silently or aloud) that all alien forces shall stay outside of the circle, and all of the intended good and powerful forces are to stay within the enclosing circle. He then goes to each of the four "corners" and invokes the four physical elemental (directional) powers to aid and support him. Always we start with Air in the East, Fire in the South, Water to the West, and end with Earth to the North before returning to the starting point to complete the Circle.

Example of such an Elemental Invocation: ***Oh, thou great power of Fire, come thou forth and aid and guard me in this work of art.*** (Note: further examples of such elemental invocations, opening and closings of the circle, banishing rituals, and other magickal techniques are provided in the suggested reading materials listed at the end of this chapter. Also note that there is considerable value to composing your own invocations and rituals once you have fundamental understanding of the technology involved. Outside of participation in magickal or religious orders for their "High Magick" ceremonial work, all magick is personal and copying of other rituals and spells—particularly those employed for "Low Magic" (i.e., *practical magic, or "spellwork")* can dilute their value in personal applications as described in this chapter.

One may well wonder about what value this may be to the dream practice. *Wherein lies any potency?* Hundreds of great ritualists, in using the foregoing practice, have endowed this symbol system with great force and power which now exists in the sphere called the World of Mind, and which is available to those who now employ the procedures applying such symbol science.

The Procedure to Banish Undesired Influences

The value represented in this planetary earth symbol is here limited to the "banishing" of alien or undesirable forces or influences, and also to seal in or contain all that is desirable within one's inscribed circle—the True Self. But this symbol is not specific in nature; rather, it is the *procedure* (or magickal operation) used to achieve specific goals of desire and aspiration. Therefore, it is used in the banishing procedure in conjunction with some other symbols specific to the particular operation. The valuable use of this symbol is illustrated in the following case histories of other symbols.

The Procedure to Trace the Sigil of Babalon, the Earth Goddess

Name: Babalon*—Her symbol: the Seven-pointed Star*
Name: Babapanlon

*Note: Please refer to the Glossary for detailed entries on Babalon and the Star.

This symbol is to be made by tracing it in one continuous line, first practicing with paper and pencil and then tracing it out of imagination—i.e., firmly and without hesitation, visualizing it in the mind.* It is the Sigil of the Goddess (under Her many names) of this planet which has nourished and developed all life on this earth beginning from the simple single-celled life form to the many particularized celled complex being called "Man" but meaning *male and female She created them*," the Crown of Earth—growing, adapting, surviving and changing through all of the environmental disasters and opportunities of earth evolution.

> *All works of magick, religious ritual and prayer, and mystical procedures begin in the mind guided by will, are given form in the imagination, energized with emotion and purpose, and empowered and brought into reality by physical acts. They can be "ensouled" through the invocation of appropriate deity, and given further definition at all levels by identification with established correspondences.

In present times, when Man has needs for other ways of protection and development, Her rulership is on a different plane:

1. To protect man and woman from what is called "psychic attack," or adverse influence on the psyche.

2. Protection from the attempts by other people to dominate individuals or the masses, or to assert undue bad influences by whatever means—whether material, psychological, or psychic. (Note: it is at the human level that life is individualized, and any attempt to treat the individual as part of a "flock," "herd," "mass" or other *imposed* "collective" is a contradiction of the Prime Directive

and is True Evil whether under the pretense of Church or the State, *which in the New Age exists to serve people, not vice versa.*

In all of the cases I've known, where the protection and benefice of *Babalon* was sincerely invoked for worthy purposes, I have not known of a single case where there has not been some result.

The Case of Mary V., Freeing Herself from Psychic Attack

Mary V. wrote as follows: "Many nights when I go to bed, there is a huge Evil thing that forms at the corner of the ceiling. It seems to have a life of its own and gets bigger and bigger until it almost fills the room, and it sucks away all the good air. I feel that I am suffocating for lack of air, and have to go to the other room and sleep on the couch. It is what you call a 'psychic attack.' Please help me at once, or I shall go crazy."

Accordingly, I sent her the basic instructions for using the "Banishing Ritual", telling her to perform it and speak the words upon going to bed, explaining that she could do all of this mentally while in bed; and then to visualize tracing the seven-pointed star of Our Lady Babalon, calling her name and asking for her protection. (Note: This case continues in the fifth paragraph below.)

Adapting the Banishing Ritual

Refer back to the previous instructions on Forming the Magick Circle and on Tracing the Sigil of *Babalon*. (At this point I should interject there are several variations for spelling the Goddess' name, and there are many variations of Banishing Rituals. Some of these are specific to particular magical orders while others relate to the purpose of the banishing.)

In all cases, we have the instruction to first form a Magick Circle for the purposes of a) the focus and concentration of specific psychic or divine energies as—in this instance—associated with the feminine and beneficent power of Babalon; and b) the exclusion of energies opposite to the character of the deity being invoked. The second instruction relates to the means of invoking a specific energy. This can become very complex, or kept rather simple. In this instance, and in the other examples given in this book, simplicity has its own value. Rather than calling for the pronunciation of many names and words in exotic languages, long and repetitive speeches, many circumambulations, movements and gestures, the participation of many supporting people, and so on, ("all serving mainly the ego-gratification of the ritual leader") we need only to call the name of Babalon and trace her symbol physically and mentally.

When you look at the instruction for these cases, you will see that each calls for a first action at the physical level, and then the second action at the mental level.

In these simple cases, there is no need to specifically act at the emotional level in between physical and mental because the people involved are already strongly motivated and that emotional energy automatically empowers the physical application.

Finally, in all cases there should be acts of closure. Here closure was by the simple acts seen in the dream and the physical acts of sending a last letter. It is also desirable to simply end the sessions with a mental "thank you" or a "so mote it be!" When the actions are more complex, then the closure should be a reversal of the opening of the magick circle, thanking the powers at each quarter for their presence.

Continuing the Case of Mary V.: Two weeks later, I received the following letter: "I practiced this for three nights and there were no dreams, but I had a strong feeling that something happened while I was asleep." (Note: this is often the case.) "The morning after the fourth night, I remembered a dream in which I had received a letter. In my hand it felt sinister and evil. Now, about six months ago I had lived intimately with a man for two weeks, and since that time we have been writing to each other. Well, that four nights of dream practice gave me an intuition, or whatever you call it, and I knew for sure that the evil letter of my dream referred to this man. I wrote to him that from now on it was to be as though we'd never known each other. Now, I am now happily back to normal, thanks to your help."

Notice the specific closure actions in which Mary, the victim of psychic attack, strongly stated that the *affair* was over "as though we'd never known each other." And, then in her final letter to me she affirms that she is "now happily back to normal," and then, "thanks to your help." Closure is important in magickal operations: *When you open a door, you must also close the door!*

The Case of Emelio X., Securing Psychic Protection

I received the following letter from Emelio X.: "There is a man who breaks into my restaurant about four times every month and steals food. Worse, he always wrecks the door. I am certain who he is, but I have no proof. *What can you do to stop this?* I have small faith in this magick stuff, but because you do not charge money, you may really have something."

In my reply, I sent him the "Basic Banishing Ritual" guidance and instructed him to first perform it once around his restaurant and, second, later, to perform it while in bed, before sleep. Six symbols were also sent which were to symbolize the mentally and magickally projected "message" to the thief. He chose the Yi King Symbol illustrated here.

The Yi King Symbol representing Incompetence and Restriction
as Projected to protect against Theft

Two months passed before I received any word from him. This is the letter:

"I followed faithfully your instructions. On the first four nights, I did not have any related dream." (Note: usually the case, as previously stated.) "But on the fifth I saw myself in front of a jail because I felt guilty about something. I figured that this was one of those transference things where I was feeling what that thief was feeling. Sure enough, when I went to the restaurant, I saw signs that he had started to tamper with the door, but not much. In the afternoon, this fellow dropped in for a cup of coffee. After a few minutes, he said, 'This coffee tastes like witches' brew. Say! *What are you? Are you a* brujo?' (Spanish for witch.) Two months have passed and no break-in. It sure worked. I knew it was working when I had that dream."

The points made in this case history example are most valuable in making the dream and concomitant Borderland Consciousness serve one in a valuable, practical way.

The Unusual Case of the Truth-seeking Lawyer

In this Case of the Truth-seeking Lawyer, a prominent lawyer in San Diego asked me to outline a technique for inducing adverse witnesses to tell the truth. I sent him a dozen symbols relating in one way or another to "the truth", and told him to try to dream about these symbols in hope that the best one for him would be indicated in such an induced dream. It was not until the sixth night that the dream came to him in which he saw the "Eye of Horus." (Note: He was not certain whether it was an ordinary dream or whether it was a vision given to him while he had drifted into the state of the Borderland or an ordinary dream or vision of no importance.

The Eye of Horus in the Triangle

It is now necessary to explain the meaning of the Horus symbol. The Goddess Isis symbolizes the Matriarchal Age where humanity lived in simple union with "Mother Nature". Then came the advent of the Patriarchal Age symbolized in the god Osiris. He promulgated codes and laws of conduct for people to follow. Now, to the New Age of Horus. There are not many people who are exemplars of Horus. The Horus individual is a superior one. He (or she) has attained to self-integration. Unlike the Osirian, the Horus person has no need for such outside patriarchal guidance; he/she goes by his own INNER guidance of true wisdom. He/She goes by his own light, by his own TRUTH. He/She is the New Age Individual—not a sheep to be herded and led about by the bishop's crook.

Here are the instructions given to the lawyer.

1. First physically perform the "Banishing Ritual" (forming the Magick Circle) and then, using your *physical* thumb (Step 2 below) and, thereafter, to perform it in mental imagination each night before the second procedure.

2. For the first time, physically trace with the thumb the Horus Eye in the triangle symbol on the forehead. After this first tracing, and upon going to bed mentally imprint the symbol in intense imagination upon the forehead.

3. In the courtroom: Mentally trace the circle of the Banishing Ritual so that the circle includes all witnesses; then, intently print the Horus Eye upon your forehead in golden light.

Before testing the foregoing in court, the lawyer had a dream. He first saw a dog and a man. The dog had a high respect for the man as its superior and the dog was not apprehensive nor frightened. Then he saw another dog and man. In this case, the dog feared the superior power of the man and, as a result of the fear, was savagely attacking the man in self-defense. The lawyer interpreted this dream as giving good advice that he take care that a witness should not be overawed and so frightened at the superior power and truth of Horus that he would panic into desperate self-defense and speak lies in a fighting mood.

After using this symbol for some six months, the lawyer stated that the technique was producing results beyond both his expectations and hopes.

There are perhaps hundreds of good symbols which one can use, but one should remember that a good symbol must have occult power, i.e., of initiated wisdom and used by many initiates and high aspirants. Furthermore, the symbol used should very specifically apply to the intended purpose of the operation. *Don't use an axe for a delicate surgical operation!*

Astrological symbols are generally not of good magical value because each symbol alone covers too broad a territory. Their value is descriptive and interpretive.

The Yi King "hexagrams" are more appropriate to dream working. This writer knows of three of these hexagrams which have been used and proven to be particularly effective:

As a relief from insomnia; also in developing the Borderland Consciousness.

To bring about forces to produce a higher transformation in one's spiritual nature.

To attain favors from some person or institution. To receive guidance and help from one's Daemon or one's higher wisdom and intuition

The use of Tarot symbols in purposeful dream work is not recommended unless you have considerable understanding in the Tarot. With solid knowledge and experience, that Tarot can become an excellent tool in purposeful dream work and interpretation.

This chapter is closed with the advice that all serious students and workers in dreams should give some study to symbolism for, after all, symbols and analogies are the language of dreams.

Suggested Reading:

Buckland, Raymond. *Signs, Symbols, and Omens: An Illustrated Guide to Magical and Spiritual Symbolism.* St. Paul: Llewellyn, 2003.

de Biasi, Jean-Louis. *Secrets and Practices of the Freemasons: Sacred Mysteries, Rituals, and Symbols Revealed.* Woodbury: Llewellyn, 2011.

Gillentine, Julie. *Tarot and Dream Interpretation.* St. Paul: Llewellyn, 2003.

Kraig, Donald Michael. *Modern Magick: Twelve Lessons in the High Magickal Arts.* Woodbury: Llewellyn, 2010.

Lo Scarabeo. *Dream Enchantress Tarot.* Torino, Italy: Lo Scarabeo, 2012.

Marchetti, Ciro. *Legacy of the Divine Tarot.* Woodbury: Llewellyn, 2009.

Regardie, Israel, Chic Cicero, and Sandra Tabatha Cicero. *The Tree of Life: An Illustrated Study in Magic.* St. Paul: Llewellyn, 2000.

Silberer, Dr. Herbert. *Problems of Mysticism and Its Symbolism.* 2012, London: Forgotten Books, 2012.

Silberer, Dr. Herbert. *Hidden Symbolism of Alchemy and the Occult: Problems of Mysticism and its Symbolism.* Mineola, NY: Dover, 1971.

Silberer, Dr. Herbert. *Alchemy and the Occult Arts.* CreateSpace Independent Publishing Platform, 2012.

Skinner, Stephen. *The Complete Magician's Tables.* Singapore: Golden Hoard Press, 2007.

CHAPTER EIGHT
The Use of Symbols in Dreams (continued)

The Ankh

Most Symbols have More than One Meaning and Application

Before continuing with this discussion on the *purposeful* use of symbols in Dream Induction, forms of Invocation, Magick, and *Active* Meditation—all of which are "projective" in contrast to the "receptive" use as in dream interpretation and other systems of divination and analysis—we need to point out that most symbols have more than one meaning and more than one application.

The Ankh—the Key of Life

In addition to representing the ankle strap of a sandal as discussed below, hence suggesting "self-directed going," in contrast to a barefoot suggesting the status of a slave who is "other-directed," the Ankh (literally a *Cross with a Handle*), was also known as *the Key of Life* (representing the concept of eternal life), *the Key of the Nile* (representing the life-sustaining river), *the planet Venus* (representing the goddesses of love), *the Biological Source of Life* (representing semen believed to be created at the base of the spine), and *Power and Domination* (representing the head and tail of the god Set). Yet, all of these variations still symbolize "empowered life" and it is the reason many gods and goddesses were portrayed carrying the ankh, held by the "loop" and directing Life into things touched by pointed end. The obvious significance is that the loop is the vagina—the *feminine* source, and the pointed end is the penis—the *masculine* source. Their union is the gift of life, as *from the gods*.

Note the resemblance of the Ankh to the Egyptian musical instrument, the Sistrum, which when shaken from the pointed end produces a hypnotic sound that *projects* life force in ritual and magical operations.

Know What You Need to Know!

The Ankh is a good example of why one should know as much as possible about any symbol used for dream induction. The Ankh is the Egyptian pictograph of the ankle strap of the sandal. Even the English word "ankle" is descended from the Egyptian word "ankh". This ankle strap carries with it the idea of "going." The implication of the power "To go" led to the idea of "Life" in the sense of *movement, growth, evolution*. It is equivalent to the word "Lama" of Tibet, which means "he who goes" of his own volition.

Now, there is a special concept of "going" connected with the ankh. It means that one does not "go" by the rules, guidance and dictums of "leaders," but rather one has attained to a sufficient point of self-integration and has enough higher intuition to go entirely by one's own self-determined direction. This, then, is the aim of using the ankh symbol: for attaining dreams leading to good-willed self-direction.

The Case of Soror Nova Dreaming her True Self

An example dream case history seems to be the best way of explaining the above in a more lucid and concrete form. Taken from the record of Soror Nova of the "New Aeon Experiment" later incorporated as the "Orthogenesis Assembly of Nuit," Soror Nova was a teacher in a private school for children. Her record:

"A very wealthy man asked me to marry him and for the honeymoon, a trip to the Panama Canal, and from there what would become our family home. He insisted that I give up teaching and be a part of his social activities.

"I concentrated three nights on the Ankh for dreaming to get some clue as to my true unique self for my own true going. The dream came to me on the third night.

"I dreamed that I was talking with a very beautiful woman who seemed to have the understanding of a Goddess. She said, 'I am your true self and what I am telling you is what your true self knows but your conscious self knows not.'

"She then told me that if I married the wealthy man that I would be completely diverted from my true path and which is also my true self. She then said, 'You already know a man who knows your true path. He awaits only for you to recognize yourself and to give him recognition.' I knew the man to whom she referred; he was the owner of the school."

Within four months she married the school owner. Together, they increased the size of the school and Soror Nova became well-known as no less than a genius for teaching and training "difficult" children. To this day, she will say to friends, "I had a dream which led me to the true path of my true self."

(Author's note: It is my experience that her true self led her to her true path and that the dream was merely the mechanism of knowing.) But all of us have need for an aiding "mechanism" to know our true self and our true path!

PROCEDURE TO INVENT THE NEEDED SYMBOL

There are times when one does not have a ready-made symbol to concisely fit the objective in mind. Here is a case where the suitable symbol had to be devised—and it was well done.

The Case of Atta-Turk, son of Aleister Crowley

Name of dream subject: Aleister Atta-Turk, bastard son of the noted Magician, Aleister Crowley, the Beast 666.

Nearing the age of twenty, he was allowed entry into the United States under the conditions that various O∴T∴O∴ members would sponsor him and see that he did not become a public charge. He lived with me for a long period and I vouch for the truth of all that is here given. Atta-Turk was, at the outset, enough of a tricky weirdo that we soon learned to call him "The Terrible Turk."

The Turk had copied one of his father's styles. He had shaved his head but had left two horn-like small tufts of hair above the forehead. He confided in me that he wanted to be the kind of magician that could travel all over the country, doing no work at all, and living fairly well by his own "Magick Wits." Nothing daunted, I suggested that we devise a suitable symbol to be used for dream guidance.

The demigod *Loge* of Wagner's Ring opera series was chosen for the basis of a symbol. As Wagner conceived *Loge*, he is the god of Western Magick. *Loge*, being a past master at meeting the "exigency of the moment," *tricky and resourceful,* was chosen as the basis for the Terrible Turk's personal symbol. The main symbol was the averse pentagram, so often used in magick. Inside the pentagram was inscribed the number 44, which cabalistic number is explained at the end of this case history.

Forms of Invokation

While living in England Atta-Turk had put in considerable practice in concentration and in imaginative visualization. His dreams started with a bang. His first dream had told him to always start something at an unexpected time and in an unexpected manner.

Two days later he was in a room with an ex-soldier who had learned Judo. The Terrible Turk, who knew next to nothing about Judo, announced that he was also a Judo expert, and he challenged, "Come outside and we shall see who is the better man." The challenged man started for the door first, and his back was towards The Turk, and, at that moment, the Terrible Turk gave the fellow a terrific rabbit punch which stunned the man.

When the fellow had recovered enough to listen, The Turk declaimed, "See, that's the highest Magick secret of Judo—let them have it when they don't expect it and aren't looking for it." Later, The Turk used this in many other ways, not always of physical force.

It would be tedious to recount the substance of all of The Turk's dreams. The big point is that he was meticulously guided by his dreams in all outstanding details of his incredible journey across the United States.

The Turk went from city to city, rooking people out of money in a manner which, although not actually illegal in end result, bordered on the illegal in intent. His dreams enabled him to always be one jump ahead of the Law, even evading the police hold-orders from towns that he had left.

The Turk had an obsessive desire to work as an informer for the FBI. He got an audience with the mayor of Cleveland, Ohio, where he told the tale that a gang of vicious Communists (this was during "the Red Scare") had taken him into their confidence and had appointed him for a very special job of criminal sabotage and also for espionage.

The mayor pretended to be intensely interested and told The Turk that he would arrange an interview with the FBI. That night, The Turk's dream was of a kind that told him to get out of Cleveland fast.

Two FBI men visited me to try to get some information as to where The Terrible Turk could be picked up. They viewed The Turk's escapades in high good humor and laughed about it. What they wanted was merely to locate him to send him back to England. But he even eluded the FBI.

It was a ruptured appendix that put an end to his adventure. Having no money, he had to go to a charity hospital and that is how he was located and deported back to England.

It should be mentioned that Atta-Turk had developed the ability to induce the borderland dream state of alert consciousness without going to sleep and dreaming. In fact, most people, if consistently using the symbology technique of dream induction, should finally attain to this ability. Atta-Turk's father, Aleister Crowley, was particularly adept at this. I am personally acquainted with one Crowley case.

The Case of Aleister Crowley vs. Frater 132

In the early 1940s, some twenty O∴T∴O∴ members lived together in a large three-story mansion in Pasadena, California. Wilfred Smith, otherwise known as Frater 132, was the head of this "Abbey of Thelema." Members became displeased with the way 132 handled the members, and Crowley, then in England, received a flood of complaints from the members.

Crowley, using the number 132 for his symbol, went into the self-induced borderland dream state. The result of this was that Crowley wrote an eight-page document entitled "Liber 132." Liber 132 contained an astoundingly profound analysis of Smith. The summation of analysis was that Smith was an unconscious embodiment of a demigod or demiurges.

Smith was ordered to take a "Magick Retirement" until he had made identity with his demigod—an extended retirement even if it required six months. To lose no time for starting the retirement, Smith was immediately put in "Coventry," (a term which means that no person speaks to a person in Coventry). I alone was allowed to speak to 132 because I furnished the place in the mountains for his retirement.

Now, here is the final point about Crowley's use of the symbol (132) for the borderland dream state. I personally testify that 132 did, indeed, finally identify with this Demigod.

On this point of whether there are Gods and Demigods, I am forced to again quote psychiatrist Carl Jung, who wrote:

"It is unintelligent to spend one's time denying the existence of Gods when one should be busied in learning about those 'forces' which act just as the Gods are said to act."

USING THE CABBALA OF NUMBERS

For those who may want to use the Cabbala of Numbers for obtaining a number symbol, here is the table of number values for the letters by the Cabbala system:

Table of Number Values

1	A	20	K
2	B	30	L
3	G	40	M
4	D	50	N
5	H-E	60	S
6	V-F-W	70	O
7	Z	80	P
8	C	90	X
9	T	100	Q
10	I	200	R
		300	Sh
		400	Th

Example:	L	O	G	E	
	30+	6+	3+	5	= 44

The Case of Miss M. A., aka I V A = 17 = the Tarot Star = her True Self

Miss M. A. had taken the name Iva as the ideal symbol of her true individuality—for her dream symbol. Sometime later, she applied the Cabbala of Numbers:

I   V   A

10+   6+   1   = 17

She was both astounded and overjoyed to find that the Tarot card number 17 (called the Star) was in a most beautiful correspondence with what she had been dreaming many times. The most beautiful part has been saved for the last, i.e., in the beginning she had dreamed the name "Iva."

This is a classic example of the astounding potentials in good dreaming.

Suggested Reading:

Almond, Joyce, and Keith Seddon. *Egyptian Paganism.* St. Paul: Llewellyn, 2004.

Christopher, Lyam Thomas. *Kabbalah, Magic, and the Great Work of Self Transformation: A Complete Course.* Woodbury: Llewellyn, 2006.

Clark, Rosemary. *Sacred Magic of Ancient Egypt: The Spiritual Practice Restored.* St. Paul: Llewellyn, 2003.

DeTraci, Regula. *The Mysteries of Isis: Her Worship and Magick.* St. Paul: Llewellyn, 2002.

Forrest, M. Isidora. *Isis Magic: Cultivating a Relationship with the Goddess of 10,000 Names.* St. Paul: Llewellyn, 2001.

Marquis, Melanie. *A Witch's World of Magick: Expanding Your Practice with Techniques and Traditions from Diverse Cultures.* Woodbury: Llewellyn, 2014.

Morris, Peter J. *The Power of the Ankh: How to Use the Ancient Symbol of Life to Transform Your Wealth, Health, and Destiny.* Devon, UK: Kinsett, 2012.

Page, Judith, and Jan A. Malique. *Pathworking with the Egyptian Gods.* Woodbury: Llewellyn, 2010.

Page, Judith, and Ken Biles. *Invoking the Egyptian Gods.* Woodbury: Llewellyn, 2011.

Schueler, Gerald, and Betty Schueler. *Coming into the Light: Techniques of Egyptian Magick.* St. Paul: Llewellyn, 1989.

Schueler, Gerald and Betty Schueler. *Egyptian Magick: Enter the Body of Light and Travel the Magickal Universe.* St. Paul: Llewellyn, 1997.

Trobe, Kala. *Invoke the Goddess: Visualizations of Hindu, Greek, and Egyptian Deities.* St. Paul: Llewellyn, 2000.

CHAPTER NINE
The Symbol and Nature of the God Proteus

Persistence in the Pursuit of Wisdom is Wisdom Itself

We've already introduced the god Proteus back in Chapter Three, but I suggest there is value in going back and reviewing what it has to say.

The World's Ocean is a universal symbol of the vast "ocean of the unconscious," and Proteus is described as the God of the "Wisdom of the Subconscious." The sight of a seal or dolphin rising into view from the ocean symbolically represents the wisdom of the unconscious and the subconscious brought to manifestation and, therefore, this is a most excellent symbol of the wisdom of Proteus.

From the foregoing, it can be seen that our understanding of the wisdom of Proteus is pertinent to our ability to apply this wisdom to one's own psychology. This is valuable to all people, for who is the man or woman that cannot profit with a greater knowledge and understanding of one's own psychological processes!

All Learning is Progressive, and Never Finished

When questioned, Proteus is said to give his answers in a progressive fashion. The first answer from Proteus is superficial. His answers become progressively more profound, and wise only if one persists in receiving the sum total of wisdom that one is capable of recognizing and understanding. Those who accept the early answers of Proteus as final are comparable to those of whom it can be said: "A little knowledge is a weak or misleading or dangerous thing."

The point really is that we are never finished learning. True knowledge is as deep or deeper than the ocean itself, and its potential applications are as far-reaching as the depths of space, and as extensive as the ever-increasing reach of consciousness itself.

The Protean Case of "Vulgarian," George X

Again, a case history seems to be the best elucidation. George X had a problem which he recognized as psychological. He could put on a brand new suit and within six hours he looked like a sloppy dresser. Although a master of English, he habitually lapsed into vulgar English: "you was" and "they was" were some of the milder examples. In short, his relatives said, "He looks, talks, and acts like a *Vulgarian*."

George knew that his recalcitrance and flair for nonconformity was the psychological factor in not only making him look and act like a "Vulgarian," but that it was communicative to other people. He, therefore, decided to post the question to Proteus: "*How can I keep my character and convictions, and still appear and relate to other people in an acceptable and favorable way?"* He used the dream symbol of a seal lifting its head above water.

For three straight nights, George dreamed that he was in a huge cave, and that the "silent" voice of Proteus came from the deep recesses of the cave.

It is obvious, from what George received, that he did not press Proteus even near to the limits of the applicable wisdom, but it was enough to make George become acceptable to even those whom he called "Aristocrats." I have not found any psychologist who could see why and how the dream worked, but again the big point is that it did work. Here follows the record of what George got from the dream invocation of Proteus:

1. Vulgarian Apophasis—You must stop being bugged by the perpetrations of the "Aristocratic Institutions" to regiment and dominate the "Vulgarians."

2. Dogmatist—Be not dogmatic in expressing your nature; also, your dogma defines the abyss of your unfitness.

3. Let the recalcitrant nonconformist truly love "I" and the love for "You" will thrive.

4. Many "top level" and "summit" conferences are held in dank murky basements, but a worthy Vulgarian must get out of the murk into the sun.

5. Do not try to crush big balloons—prick them.

6. Do not work hard at being yourself—let your true Nature do it.

7. Do not try to violate Nature by trying to make a plant thrive with roots vainly seeking some soil.

8. Do not double-cross yourself by saying that this or that is an illusion and then being hung up with illusions.

George received illumination. He opened up a restaurant in the outskirts of San Diego and named it "Café Vulgarian for Aristocrats." He had signs on the walls, such as

"True Vulgarians do not flaunt vulgarity" and "Dress in fine apparel, eat rich foods, drink fine wines, but to the glory of Life." Maybe a few of the soup and fish class came to his place as a lark—at first, but many became habitual patrons. It was a kick to see George call the bejeweled ladies by their first names—and from the way that they ate it up, George had become an aristocratic vulgarian.

In the vision that Proteus gave to George, the Vulgarian, in a dream, two aquatic mammals meet. One is a Vulgarian and other is an Aristocrat. Both say simultaneously, "You are not like me." The actual sketch George drew after he had this dream appears below.

The Vision that Proteus gave to George, the Vulgarian:

Be True to Oneself

Suggested Reading:

Connor, Janet. *Writing Down Your Soul: How to Activate and Listen to the Extraordinary Voice Within.* San Francisco: Conari Press, 2009.

Estes, Clarissa Pinkola. *Seeing in the Dark: Myths and Stories to Reclaim the Buried, Knowing Woman.* Louisville, CO: Sounds True, 2010. Audio CD.

CHAPTER TEN
Awareness

Wake Up, and Become More than You Are!

By now, the astute reader has already divined that mental awareness is necessary for both more coherent dreams and for their interpretation. It's a common understanding that the average person is mentally alert for only a small fraction of the day, or we can say that a person is aware in only one limited groove of mental activity. Yet, *there is no known limit to the potential for human awareness!*

Is there a method to increase the intensity and scope of awareness that is simple and easy? Indeed, there is such a method, not widely known, but nevertheless tried and proven.

True <u>Self-Awareness</u> is Two-Way Communication with your Higher Self

The method: Many times throughout the day, silently remind yourself: "I vow to regard *every incident of which I am conscious* as a particular dealing between myself and my soul or psyche."*

*Words such as Soul, Higher Self, Spirit, Psyche, Inner Self, the *Atman,* the Whole Personality, Causal Self, *Chiah, Neshamah,* Higher Manas, Higher Ego, Holy Guardian Angel, Spiritual Soul, Intuitional Self, *Buddhi,* Higher Causal Self, Super Conscious Mind, and many more in all languages and cultures have been used variously with little definition other than a presumed meaning of "other than physical consciousness," and "that which survives physical death," and "that which is immortal."

In modern psychological and esoteric terminology these same words and related concepts have been associated with the Personal Unconscious, the Collective Unconscious, the Archetypal Mind, the Subtle Bodies making up the complex structure of the whole person, and more.

For our purposes here, we see a basic psychological model that parallels a similar esoteric model as follows:

The Psychological and Esoteric Model of the Whole Person
TABLE OF THREE LEVELS OF SELF, MIND, BODY AND CONSCIOUSNESS

PSYHOLOGICAL MODEL	ESOTERIC MODEL
Lower Self, aka Sub-Conscious Mind	Astral Body and Consciousness (Self)
Middle Self, aka Conscious Mind	Mental Body and Consciousness (Self)
Higher Self, aka Super-Conscious Mind	Causal Body and Consciousness (Self)

In both models, at each level, there is more complexity than shown. Generally, and in relation to their multiple functions, each level in both models is further divided into seven sub-levels. Our focus is on the highest sub-level of Level 3, simply called the Higher Self and the Causal Self. Essentially, they are the same, but because our focus in this book is magickal and esoteric, we will target the Causal Self.

The Causal Self is not the Soul, nor is it the Spirit, but it is magickally called the "Holy Guardian Angel" and is the highest aspect of <u>personal</u> consciousness in *the incarnating personality*. Understand that *the Soul, itself, does not incarnate,* but abstracts the life lessons from the incarnated personality through the Causal Self, which then "dies" along with that personality. The Soul then creates a new "Causal Seed" with the abstracted memories of many life times and a new life plan which generates a new incarnating personality, step-by-step, following the Esoteric Model into physical incarnation from which new levels of psychological consciousness develop as the physical body grows and matures to work side-by-side with the esoteric selves through a new life time.

If the Higher Self communicating with the Causal Self that is our aspiration in what we call the "Knowledge and Conversation with the Holy Guardian Angel" which is the goal of all High Magick, the purpose of all Self-Development, the ultimate accomplishment of all Meditation. It is the fulfillment of this process that fully transfers "command and control" of the entire personality from the reactive emotional-centered Lower Self and the more-or-less brain-centered mental Middle Self to the Spirit-centered Causal Higher Self. That the state of self-mastery we call "adepthood." (The chances of you encountering such an adept—whether in this world or the next—is very slight. No real adept will ask for your obedience, devotion, or your money—*so don't give it!)*

Living the Awareness: Practice Every Day in Every Way
Also, take note that this vow is quite different than affirming "I am filled with awareness," which is most probably a self-told bald-faced lie. Also, take note that this silent vow, pronounced no matter how many times daily, does not rob you of one single minute of your time in your various tasks. Here, is given an example of the result of the awareness practice, as follows:

The Example Case of the Black Crow Messenger
This occurred at the time of eleven people performing their weekly Magickal ritual. One regular performer, Brother Pan, was absent. He, by the way, was not yet practiced in the awareness vow. During the ritual, suddenly a black crow flew through the skylight ventilator into the room. Immediately, Brother Zeus cried, "There is something wrong with Brother Pan. Let's go to his room immediately." All of the performers were in accord.

"This is Wotan's crow," said Sister Isis. "We can't get there too soon."

(Note: In mythology, Wotan's crow was an omen of impending death of some hero.)

When the group arrived at Pan's room, they saw that he had red streaks running up his arm almost to the shoulder. He was immediately taken to the doctor. The doctor said that if Pan had waited until the next day, it would have been necessary to amputate the arm; he was even in danger of losing his life from the blood poisoning.

The "mechanics" involved in this example should be explained. First, the crow is brought to the awareness; second, the awareness has some kind of "particular dealing;" third, being trained in closer function in the "Borderland Consciousness," the "message" in the world of mind was received that the significance pertained to Brother Pan because he was absent from the meeting.

At some other time, what might be the significance of one's awareness of a crow? It might be nothing more than the beauty of something black. Or, one might be reminded, in particular, that the crow being the "Genius of the Skies,"—one of the most resourceful of all birds—hence signifying the need to exercise one's genius for something.

The point is that the crow could be, by the very nature of one's vow, significant of something small or to something big—but SOMETHING. But what is that "something?"

Well now, this vow "To regard it as a particular dealing" magickally gives more and more intuitive ability to divine the significance if one has continually felt the vow.

Here is another example in the files which excellently illustrates the point:

The Example Case of the 333 Message

After belonging to an occult order for three years, a change in their working caused me to decide to disaffiliate very soon. It was at this time that I became "aware of the particular dealing" on this question. It was when I suddenly felt the need to look at my speedometer at the end of a trip. The registered mileage was 33,333, exactly. It so happens that the kabalistic number of the Order was 333. This "message" caused me to remain with the Order for another year. I give undying thanks for the great value to me for remaining with the Order for another year.

Now this case is a beautiful example of unawareness and, on the other hand, awareness. The clue to this is the solution of why I had looked at the mileage register at the end of the trip. The obvious solution is that I had "seen" the mileage gauge at times as it was approaching the 33,333 figure, but I had not been aware of it. It had registered in the mind, even though there was no awareness; any awareness was lurking in the borderland. However, having been trained in Borderland Consciousness, there remained the subconscious urge to finally look at the mileage gauge in a state of awareness.

In the foregoing example, the reader should grasp an excellent lesson: A more intimate union in the borderland (involving the subconscious) can and does lead to conscious awareness which can well be of great practical value to one. The great gap between non-significance and significance is bridged more and more as one progresses in the practice. So keep it in awareness, every day and every hour: "I vow to regard every incident as a particular dealing between myself and my higher self."

The reader should easily see that the practical value of a greater faculty for awareness is not limited to dreams. Experts tell us that most people who are truly aware for only scattered moments of the day cannot take advantage of very much that they could and should do. On the other hand, let us observe those who are alert and "on the ball" so that they see and take advantage of all possible opportunities. These opportunities pass unnoticed and unseen, and without evoked and seized interest, by most people. The strange thing about it is that it requires only a small effort to develop one's awareness; more than that, it is interesting—not a chore.

The Awareness PAC, and our failure to use it

Yes, we have the **POWER**, and fail to use it.

Yes, we have the **ABILITY** for Greater Awareness, and fail to pay Attention.

Yes, we have the **CAPACITY** for far greater Attainment, and fail to make the effort.

We have only ourselves to blame for remaining as we are. Don't look to others to tell you what to do when you already know it—so just do it. We have only ourselves to blame for not becoming more than we are—so just know and do it. We have only ourselves to blame for passivity in the face of opportunity—so just move ahead and become all you can be. There are no limitations except for those you accept—so accept none. There are no "overlords" holding you in bondage—so shake off those invisible shackles and join the race to the top. There is no "grand conspiracy" preventing human progress—so open your eyes and know that the Truth will set you Free!

Nothing is greater than the Power of the Conscious Mind joined with the Sub-Conscious and the Super-Conscious in Fullness of Self under Will—so take control and become a *Master of the Universe!*

Suggested Reading:

Slate, Joe H., and Carl Llewellyn Weschcke. *Doors to Past Lives and Future Lives: Practical Applications of Self-Hypnosis.* Woodbury: Llewellyn, 2011.

Slate, Joe H., and Carl Llewellyn Weschcke. *Psychic Empowerment for Everyone: You Have the Power, Learn How to Use It.* Woodbury: Llewellyn, 2009.

Slate, Joe H., and Carl Llewellyn Weschcke. *Self-Empowerment and Your Sub-Conscious Mind: Your Unlimited Resource for Health, Success, Long Life, and Spiritual Attainment.* Woodbury: Llewellyn, 2010.

Slate, Joe H., and Carl Llewellyn Weschcke. *Self-Empowerment through Self-Hypnosis: Harnessing the Enormous Potential of the Mind.* Woodbury: Llewellyn, 2010.

CHAPTER ELEVEN
Incredible Examples of Borderland Functioning

The two exemplars given in this chapter are not only remarkably great, but also there is no room for that thing called the "Credibility Gap"—they are authenticated in all directions, leaving no room for doubt in any sense.

The Incredible Dream of the Drunken Reporter
who saw Krakatoa as it happened

The case of Ed Samson, an alcoholic reporter, who had an incredible dream on the night of August 28, 1883, which was printed for real on the following day, August 29, 1883, in his paper, the *Boston Globe*. Ed Samson, after being at a bar and getting plenty looped, wandered into the newsroom and flopped on a couch, about midnight. At 3 a.m., a terrible dream jolted his befuddled brain into a state of fair consciousness. "Wow! What a dream," he said to himself. "Could be a great feature yarn for some dull day." So he immediately sat down at his typewriter and typed the entire story as he had seen it in his dream.

The "Important" Accident, or "the Truth is Out There!" Somewhere?

Ed thought enough about the yarn that, when he put the finished script on his desk, he scrawled on the top page "Important," and then he left the office for an eye-opener. When the *Boston Globe* office opened that morning, the editor saw the "important" script and, thinking that it was something that had come in from the night wire service, he sent it down the line for printing.

> *The Real Story: One of the most massive volcanic eruptions in history—an explosion four times greater than the most powerful nuclear device ever detonated, the sound was heard 3,000 miles away, 165 villages and towns were destroyed and as many as 120,000 people died.*

The Globe came out with a two-column banner news story—for real. There was the account about a small island near Java which Ed had named "Pralape." There was the vivid account of the natives being trapped between the sea and the flowing molten lava of an erupting volcano, and how nearby ships at sea were badly buffeted and damaged by vast tsunami-like waves generated by a continuing series of volcanic explosions.

Then the final climax: a tremendous explosion of the volcano, sinking the entire island into the ocean depths, and blackening skies around the world.

No Verification in Boston of Globe's Scoop

Now, in those days, there was no wire communication from Java and no other newspapers had received the story, even if it was a true story, so on the evening of the twenty-ninth, the editor of the *Globe* fed his scoop to the Associated Press wire. Then the editor was in a jam, for newspapers began asking for more details. The *Globe's* publisher finally found Samson in his favorite gin mill, where Ed wailed, "What? You printed my dream for real?"

Demands for Confession, and Retraction . . .

Worse yet, in the meantime, some of the newspapers had made a "searching investigation" and determined that there was no island named Pralape close to Java, nor in any other place. This resulted in the members of the Associated Press (including the Boston Globe) having a conference where it was decided that the *Globe* was the culprit and the *Globe* agreed to publish a front page confession and retraction.

True—after all!

However, by this time, a few ships from Java had weathered the great ocean disturbance and had limped into port in Australia. They brought with them the terrible story of the vanished island Krakatoa (not Pralape), near Java. There was wire service from Australia and this news came in time for the *Globe* to consign their apology type setup to the melting pot, and to run a bigger and better story.

And—more amazing yet!

Ed Samson became a noted Associated Press phenomenon, but there was still the problem of the island's name: Krakatoa versus *Pralape*. Was Ed's dream an incredible coincidence—almost as amazing a story in itself? But a few years later came the final clincher: the Dutch Historical Society sent Samson the information that the island's true native name was actually "Pralape" but had been officially changed some hundred years previously to "Krakatoa."

Ed dreamed the "story" <u>as it was happening!</u>

Now, we must take note that Ed's dream took place at the same time of the island happening—not before—not after. From this, there seems to be only one possible explanation for the "mechanics" of Ed's dream.

A Powerful "Thought Wave"

The terrified natives must have sent out a terrific emotional thought force, into the "World of Mind," of what they saw and felt. Furthermore, the natives knew the island name *Pralape* better than they knew the changed name of Krakatoa.

The Thin Veil between the Conscious Mind and the Borderland State

But there also comes the question of why Ed Samson was the receiving vehicle. For one thing, it is well-known that many alcoholics have worn that dividing veil between the conscious and the borderland down to a very ragged or thin condition, and that this would put him into a better state of "reception" than that of more "normal" people. But there are other "sensitives" than alcoholics. Again, why Ed Samson? For one thing, drunks are prone to "see" frightening or hideous things, and what the natives of Pralape felt and saw was frightening, horrible, and hideous beyond measure.

The Incredible Case of the Ancient-Egyptian speaking English woman

In the following exemplar, a so-called normal sociable woman who probably had never even heard the words "occultism" or "mysticism," begins the condition by dreaming, and then later, she fully functions in the Borderland, no longer dreaming. The point, here, is that the attainment of dream efficiency gives ability to have psychic ability and valuable information when not asleep or dreaming. In other words, you can learn to access the knowledge which dreams can give—and even better—without dreaming with an ability developed from dream practice.

In 1931, Rosemary, a young woman from Blackpool, England had a series of dreams in which an invisible person spoke to her in a "silent language." At first she regarded the sounds of the language as pure gibberish. However, this "gibberish" was later proven to be pure Ancient Egyptian. Later, she could hear and speak the strange sounds in her conscious waking state simply by getting into the mood. This is a clear example of being able to continue the dream sequence on into the waking state is particularly valuable for those really interested in controlled clairvoyant ability.

More than a "Paranormal" Phenomenon

There are many examples of *xenoglossia* (speaking in a language not acquired by natural means) and of *glossolalia* (speaking in tongues, or unrecognizable words), and there are many divergent claims and explanations offered about the experiences involved.

Commonly, speaking in foreign or ancient languages is associated with reincarnation, i.e. of past-life memories. Less commonly, it is associated with some access to universal consciousness. Other offered explanations include a sharing of consciousness between individuals or an individual and a group by means of hypnosis or ecstatic states of consciousness.

Speaking in tongues is generally associated with ecstatic religious experience, sometimes called "Baptism of (or in) the Holy Spirit." It is a phenomenon of intense religious experience found in Charismatic movement of Pentecostal and Mormon churches.

The *Interpreter's One-Volume Commentary on the Bible* defines it as: *"the ecstatic utterance of emotionally agitated religious persons, consisting of a jumble of disjointed and largely unintelligible sounds. Those who speak in this way believe that they are moved directly by a divine spirit and their utterance is therefore quite spontaneous and unpremeditated."*

Some claim it as the language spoken by God and the angels. It is also observed in some tribal religions and in the African-derived religions of Voudoun, Candomble, Santeria, and others, and in shamanic traditions worldwide.

Spirit and Consciousness are Universal

The Human Spirit and Mind have unlimited power—unlimited, that is, except for the limitations imposed by ignorance, false assumptions, and lack of training and development. Spontaneous phenomena such as described in this chapter are just examples of human potential. Other examples from around the world that include forms of healing, of walking on fire, of great strength, encyclopedic knowledge, scientific discoveries during sleep, Out-of-Body travel, Clairvoyance, Telekinesis, and other Psychic Powers.

Conscious and Dream access to the Borderland state are available to anyone, and should be developed and practiced by everyone. *It's your obligation to grow, to become more than you are, and all you can be.*

Suggested Reading:

Clark, Rosemary. *Sacred Magic Of Ancient Egypt: The Spiritual Practice Restored.* St. Paul: Llewellyn, 2003.

———. *The Sacred Tradition in Ancient Egypt: The Esoteric Wisdom Revealed.* St. Paul: Llewellyn, 2000.

Lo Scarabeo: *Egyptian Tarot: 22 Grand Trumps Cards.* Torino, Italy: Lo Scarabeo, 2006.

Page, Judith, and Jan A. Malique. *Pathworking with the Egyptian Gods.* Woodbury: Llewellyn, 2012.

CHAPTER TWELVE
Developing the Dream Dictionary

Why old-fashioned Dream Books fail

I have examined all of the dream dictionaries that I could come by. They all bear one common stamp: while there is indeed a substantial demand (and, so we suppose, a real need) for such a book, what I find is completely without conscience and filled with fanciful nonsense. And, whatever the price, they're all the same: they all show a disregard for the psychology of the subconscious, which cannot be ignored in any worthwhile analysis of dreams. There are some good books on how to analyze one's dreams, but such books do not assay a really functional dictionary of dreams meeting today's challenges.

Good conscience seems to demand that we look at a few examples from these dysfunctional dream dictionaries and show some of the fundamental errors common to the genre of those "old fashioned" *Dream Books.* These exemplars were taken at random, and not specially selected, so I see no need to credit the sources.

"FALCON—to see: signifies honor." In case you didn't know, a "falcon," a species of predator chicken-hawk, and a hawk is both cunning and swift and could advise one to be the same in something, or beware of it from another.

"FEEDING—to feed animals foretells a journey" How ridiculous can one get? Psychologically, this dream implies friendliness, compassion, or assurance of simple needs, either by or to one.

"FAVOR—to ask a favor of someone predicts loss of social standing." How does the person respond? That is the key.

"DISTRESS—to dream of you will have a period of good luck"! Actually, the dream indicates that one is either already in distress about something, or else has anxieties about the bad outcome of something which could be a completely unfounded fear, or just the opposite—one that is well founded.

"Each individual person is different."

It is only the other details and conditions of the dream which can give the correct clue. It is well to hearken to the words of Dr. Carl Jung: "There is no overall psychology, for each individual person is different." Each person is unique in heredity and experience. Human beings are as varied in their physical, emotional, mental, and spiritual "composition" as is the total population on this planet.

However, there are universal psychological principles of association in dreams, and we also have many details or elaboration of these associations in the dream, which give the dreamer the clue to determine the significance and import in one's individual case within an historical context. *Dreaming of a <u>horse</u> today is likely to have different meaning than it would have in ancient Greece or Medieval Europe or the nineteenth century American "cowboy" West.*

Let us take the word "FRUIT" from one of the typical popular Dream Books as a good example of a wide principle which is conditioned by various incidentals.

Each Fruit is different

"FRUIT—to eat or be offered: You will have visitors or receive an invitation; beware of temptation." Now, this suggest that—with the exception of special associations of different individuals—all edible fruits should logically have the same implications, but see what the "book" says about the different fruits. It proceeds with unabashed devil-may-care inconsistencies, as follows:

"PEAR—to eat: You will hear scandalous news."

"PEACHES—Your friend is taking a love affair too seriously."

"APPLE—to eat: Presages sadness."

"GRAPES—to eat: You will be offered a better position."

"FIGS—to eat: Your financial situation will improve."

(Note: All dream dictionaries that I have seen are equally worse than useless: they mislead with equal nonsense.)

"One thing leads to another"—the Importance of Association

Now, what is the real psychological association with eating fruit, when it's not just a wish fulfillment? It is enjoyment in a pleased satisfaction; metaphorically, it is delicious. Any "wish fulfillment" could derive from memories of the past when the family was too poor to afford the luxury of fruit—or even of the present; and this could also lead to some unrelated wish for pleased satisfaction. But do not be over-ready to think that it is merely a "wish fulfillment," for it may very often "be for real."

The Magick of "Prepared Awareness"

Here is a "secret" for you. It is given in the following dream as an example of a wish fulfillment leading to something that became real by 1) the magick of prepared "awareness" and 2) by the oath of "regarding every (alerted) event as a particular dealing . . . " Understand that *prepared awareness* is a state of consciousness that responds to that sudden "alert" that calls your attention to an event that would otherwise be passed over and shrugged off.

I dreamed that I met a woman on the street; she was very beautiful and seductive. She had a dog on a leash. She was dressed entirely in green and the dog was green in color. The dog said to me, "Good morning," while the woman smiled. The dog again spoke. "We have your number and you are promised the most joyous time of your life by my mistress." She smiled an assurance. The dog then said "Good-bye" and they disappeared in a green mist.

This is very clearly a wish dream; even the dog doing the speaking adds the clincher.

But remember: There is an inherent magick potential in all dreams. If one gets the opportunity—*and is ready to relate the dream to the opportunity when it occurs*—one can very often bring the dream to objective realization.

So here is what happened. Two days after the green dream dog talked, I was among about a dozen people waiting for the bus. There was one beautiful woman; no, not dressed in green nor with a dog. She had the purest green eyes that I had ever seen. It was only the dream which urged me to brave a possible "drop dead" look and to say to her, "Good morning." As the popular expression goes, "One thing led to another." What a beautiful enchanting love affair this turned out to be!

Solving the Problem—Connecting the Dots

I've been working on this book for some time, and for almost a year I'd been trying to solve the problem of a format for the dream dictionary section which would adequately cover most of the subjects of dreaming, and still not require long interpretations of each subject. My answer came by a "chance" meeting with an Arabian mystic who had a dream book written in Arabic. He claimed that it was two hundred years old and that it was the only existing copy. When he translated the interpretations of some of the dream subjects, I noticed that he would flip the pages to an extra reference volume. Upon questioning him on this, he explained that there were 32 principles that covered all dream subjects and that each dream had one (or even three) references to the appropriate section of the 32 principles.

I immediately saw that 32 is exactly one-half of the number of hexagram figures of the Yi King.* The 64 hexagrams would be even more concise than the 32 Principles in my friend's ancient Arabic Dream Book. I felt that I was on the edge of a momentous insight. Then I remembered an almost completely forgotten point I had received when being a ember of a highly secret Chinese Order, named the "Order of the Singing Fan." This was the format that I had been looking for. In the back part of this book is a complete and extended analysis of the 64 Yi King figures.

How this is used is explained in the following chapter.

*Better known today as the *I Ching*, or *Book of Changes.*

Suggested Reading:

Fox, Dr. Steven. *Dreams: Guide To The Soul: 40 Ancient Secret Keys to Healing, Renewal and Power*. Create Space Independent Publishing Platform, 2013.

Garrard, Ana Lora. *Your Dreams: Spiritual Messages in Pajamas*. Woodbury: Llewellyn, 2010.

Johnson, Robert A. *Inner Work: Using Dreams and Active Imagination for Personal Growth*. New York: Harper and Row, 2009.

McElroy, Mark. *Lucid Dreaming for Beginners: Simple Techniques for Creating Interactive Dreams*. Woodbury: Llewellyn, 2007.

Taylor, Jeremy. *Dream Work: Techniques for Discovering the Creative Power in Dreams*. Mahwah, NJ: Paulist Press, 1983.

Taylor, Jeremy. *The Wisdom of Your Dreams: Using Dreams to Tap into Your Unconscious and Transform Your Life*. New York: Tarcher, 2009.

CHAPTER THIRTEEN
The Secret of
"PROPHETIC CAUSAL DREAMING"
and How to Do It

How to Use the Dream Dictionary with the Trigrams and Hexagrams
of the Ancient Yi King

An Introduction by Carl Llewellyn Weschcke

I want to confirm something I anticipate many readers have already perceived—but something I doubt that even Lou Culling himself fully recognized at the time of his writing. More than Dream Interpretation, more than a technique of "Dream ESP," Culling invented a form of *"Prophetic Causal Dreaming."*

It is common that many pioneers and great innovators fail to recognize all the future ramifications and applications of their "discoveries" and "inventions," but Time reveals the Truth and future generations benefit, or—in some unfortunate cases—suffer.

Prediction vs. Prophecy

First I must distinguish between "Prediction" and "Prophecy." Both deal with the <u>future</u>, but predictions deal with "tomorrow" as it already exists "as the shadows cast by coming events" that most <u>probably</u> will see the light of day as the completion of on-going processes and happenings. To paraphrase a popular television commercial (itself paraphrasing Newton's First Law of Motion): "It's a simple law of physics that a body in motion tends to stay in motion."

Prediction is a Vision of the Future as it exists

Mostly, we can say that the majority of tomorrow's news will just be the completion of events already set in motion, like the weather, or an announcement of government compiled statistics. Even though less certain, tomorrow's stock market closing is not likely to bring much of a surprise.

Predictions based on "real" astrology (not newspaper sun-sign readings) applying complete astrological data to an individual horoscope will be a continuation of planetary bodies already in motion.

Accidental Change

However, it does happen that a "body in motion" can abruptly crash into some other unforeseen body or object, or be deflected from its intended path into a new direction, or speed up or slow down because of some other force.

Intentional Change through Applied Divinatory Practices

Sometimes such alterations, or their possibilities, may be foreseen and noted in a prediction. It is within the realm of possibility that an expert astrologer or trained psychic can give an individual a warning of the potential for an accident, but those alterations will not have been intentionally induced.

<u>Intention</u> mobilizes Mind Power to direct and accomplish <u>Change.</u>

Such intentional induction is enabled through forms of traditional mind-training, the practice of magick and native shamanism, techniques of invocation derived from ancient Taoism and pre-Hindu Tantra, as well as the application of technologies developed from new scientific understandings in psychology, parapsychology, and quantum physics. Even more dramatic is to realize the wide-scale results attained in progressive government and political thinking, of progressive education and business management, of personal growth and self-improvement, *and sometimes it is within the role of the prophet to shape change and alter the future.*

Causal Prophecy is Applied Mind Power <u>shaping</u> the Future

But all prophetic action is not on the grand scale of the Biblical Prophets of old, or such far-seeing inventors and innovators like Thomas Edison or Nikola Tesla and Bill Gates or Steve Jobs. The same intentional altering of the future for personal improvement is possible for anyone to accomplish, and that's the potential application of "Prophetic Causal Dreaming" in your life. <u>You can induce desired change yourself.</u>

A True Prophecy, esoterically speaking, may look at the probable *coming event framed as a question seeking an answer or as a problem seeking resolution. In either case, we must look beyond the* probable tomorrow *to envision an "alterable future" in the bits and pieces of developing trends and logical sequences, and interrupt that assumed inevitability through a projection of* **<u>Mind Power*</u>** *intended to bring about a desired change.*

> **The purpose of this "Prophetic Causal Dreaming" action is to shape and change the otherwise likely future to a desired one.**

*What do we mean with the phrase "Mind Power?" Simply the *<u>focus</u>* of the subtle consciousness and energies of body, mind, and spirit "<u>under Will</u>" on bringing desired change about. In esoteric terminology we are directing the resources of the Etheric, Astral, Mental, and Causal bodies to a single purpose.

It's Not Divination, but Intentional Magick

The Prophets of the Old Abrahamic Religions did not only act as "messengers" of their god's will, but—like Moses coming down the mountain with his Ten Commandments engraved on stone tablets—they brought that envisioned future about.

Look back over some of the dream sequences in previous chapters and you will see that same enactment in several of Lou Culling's example case histories. In particular, look back in Chapter Seven at the Case examples of Emelio X and Mary V.

What we have is Dream Interpretation not as a form of Divination but as a form of Magick!

Carl Llewellyn Weschcke

THE TECHNOLOGY OF THE YI KING

Better known today as the I Ching, by whichever name it is believed to be the oldest book in the world, dating back to well before recorded history—or poetically—*into the "Mists of Time before Time."*

The Universe in ancient Taoist Philosophy, and in modern Chaos Theory

It is not our intention to write about the history of China as an ancient civilization reaching back 600,000 years (in contrast to the Bible story that the world was created just 6,000 years ago), nor to give a lesson in the basics of Chinese philosophy—except for one single point: ". . . the ancient Chinese saw the universe, including the world we live in, as governed by *perpetual change, moving in an eternal circle from potential to actual and back.* Within this overall movement at any given time, events always contained a duality: a part that was unchanged and a part that was changing. The sages called the unchanging part **YIN** and the changing part *YANG.*"*

*Quoted from *The Magical I Ching* by J. H. Brennan.

Continuing the Chinese view of the universe as an *interconnected whole*, Brennan writes: "If everything was part of a whole, then *anything that influences one part of the structure influences all others*—an insight that has recently emerged in Chaos Theory. Any question about the future . . . arises out of a desire to discover the outcome of a particular line of change. To the Chinese, the changes involved in the events that interested them travelled outwards though the entire universe."

Duality vs. Dichotomy

In other words, in this interconnected universe, there is always a duality consisting of change, represented in the Yi King by a broken line, — — (YIN), and not-change, represented in the Yi King by an unbroken line ——— (YANG). But also realize that the universe is perpetually changing, moving in an eternal circle from potential to actual and back. "Duality" is not the same as "dichotomy" where any two things always have the same qualities: in any beginning, such as a sperm and an egg, the sperm is always masculine and the egg always feminine. Yet, when they merge into a fetus, that new "thing" has qualities of both even as one or the other is predominant but not absolute.

As "qualities," we can list the fundamental parts of the duality, but must remember the fundamental characteristic of constant change from potential to actual, and back again. The following are just examples that enter into the development of a single line of the three that make up a Trigram, of which two Trigrams make up a Hexagram:

TABLE OF YIN AND YANG QUALITIES

YIN	YANG
— —	———
Tails	Heads
Changing	Not Changing
Asleep	Awake
Feminine	Masculine
Yoni	Lingam
Negative	Positive
Passive	Active
Receptive	Projective
Sustaining	Starting
Nourishing	Initiating
Following	Leading
Centrifugal Force	Centripetal Force
Introversive	Extroversive
Emotional	Intellectual
Desire	Directed Will
Soft	Hard
Weak	Strong
Night	Day
The Moon	The Sun
Cold	Hot
Winter	Summer

In a single moment, Duality manifests as a single Line of Meaning

Yin and Yang are not in an "antagonistic" dualism, but are co-equals in a continuing partnership of a constantly changing relationship. One does not exist without the other. You cannot have Negative without Positive, if there is a Follower there must be a Leader, Winter will always change into Summer, Soft only exists as relative to Hard, etc. And, we also know that these dualities exist as both "either/or" and as "one/and" the other, just as in every Man there is an element of the Feminine (Anima) and in every Woman an element of the Masculine (Animus). Another obvious point is that some dualities can change into another: Winter advances into Spring just as Summer progresses into Autumn; Night advances into Morning, and Day progresses into Evening—but others cannot: Heads do not change into Tails, and a Lingam will not become a Yoni, and while Negative cannot become Positive, Negative and Positive currents can *alternate* one with the other in a singular flow of power, and the toss of coins resulting in either Heads of Tails can produce a **Line** of meaning in a Trigram.

Magick in Quantum Theory and the Exchange between Matter and Energy

In the most fundamental (sub-atomic) level of physical existence as known in Quantum Theory, Matter manifests not only as Elementary Particles so small they have Mass, but also as Waves, which transfer Energy. What is important to us here is that the mere action of observation (Awareness) will change matter from particle to energy, and that *intention (Will) will give direction to the flow of energy as it changes back into matter.* Given "scale," you have the foundation for magickal action defined as induced change. Thus, a carefully performed magickal action will bring about desired change working through symbols corresponding to the matters of concern. *Change* begins at the smallest levels, so our magical (intentional) focus is on the small not the big—but big grows from small under the guidance of Intention and Will.

THE YI KING TRIGRAMS AND HEXAGRAMS IN THE DREAM DICTIONARY

There are 8 Trigrams in the Yi King system. Each 3-line Trigram is carefully constructed, line by line, *from bottom up* by acts of conscious focus on the question or problem at hand. Sequentially, two Trigrams are brought together to compose one of the 64 Hexagrams.

While the Yi King is itself one of the most comprehensive and distinctive divinatory systems, in **Dream ESP** we are not, for the most part, using the Yi King as a means to create a Hexagram, but are employing the basic, archetypal, meanings developed over thousands of years of practice and observation to provide a "situational" background for applying the meanings found in the Dream Dictionary. Those for the Trigrams are given in Appendix B, while those for the Hexagrams are given in Appendix C.

Using Dream Symbols to Probe for Deeper Personal Meanings

Appendix A is the *Dream Dictionary* with approximately 600 carefully composed Dream Symbols listed alphabetically for easy reference. Many of these are cross-referenced to one another to expand your thinking as to their meaning beyond that of simple definition. That's important, for in Dream Work things are rarely simple and obvious. "Thinking about" those Dream Symbols becomes the means to probe your Sub-Conscious Mind—and even the Universal Unconscious—for what they may mean to you alone.

As you continue your Dream Work over the years ahead, recording and analyzing your dreams, you should construct your own personal "Dream Dictionary" of symbols and their meanings as they apply in your life. As you do, you will see gradual changes reflecting your own growth and increased understanding and the Integration of elements of your evolving psyche.

There are some dream subjects that deserve, even require, an extended comment or analysis. In such cases, the reader will frequently be referred to a certain Yi King hexagram for an extended comment. When this is done, there will be given a referenced Hexagram Number; for example, under the word "GROUNDHOG" and also "SQUIRREL" you will see "Hexagram #45." You then turn to Appendix C, and look for Hexagram Number 45 and read what is written for clues applicable to your dream on the subject "Groundhog" or "Squirrel."

Now, each Hexagram is made up of two "Trigrams," one placed beneath (lower) the other above (upper). These superior (upper) or inferior (lower) positions themselves give distinctive meanings within the Hexagram. There are times when the long extended comment of the Hexagram is not required, and in such cases you will be referred to one of the eight Trigrams. To facilitate this process and avoid any confusion, we distinguish between Hexagrams and Trigrams by assigning one of eight letters "A" through "H" to the Trigram and one of 64 numbers to the Hexagram. For example, if the dream is about a body of clear, still water under pleasant conditions, you will be referred to "Trigram E."

Please realize that not every Dream Symbol calls for this extended reference to a Trigram or Hexagram.

Before proceeding to the Dream Dictionary in Appendix A, it is necessary to define a few words or concepts which are commonly used in the dictionary—as follows:

Understanding the Situational "Superior" and "Inferior"

It is important to remember that the same word can *change* meanings in relation to its singular application within the situation as a whole. "Superior" and "Inferior" have various meanings. If, in your dream, you are talking with your boss, basically for dream analysis, you are the "Inferior" and he is the "Superior." He is not necessarily YOUR "Superior" but he is THE "Superior" in relation to you in this particular situation.

The sum total of one's ancestors (including one's departed parents) is the "Superior" because, excluding your UNIQUE INDIVIDUALITY, you are the product of your ancestors. If this is not so, we would still be hairy beetle-browed, peanut-brained cave dwellers that had not even yet discovered how to make fire. All of our best instincts are the result of a long chain of inheritance. All of this leads to another most-important concept of "Superior."

Your true Superior is your Higher Self

This "Superior" does not have a body form, is generally unknown, and, with some people, is not even suspected. This Superior has been given many names, such as the Holy Guardian Angel, the Higher Self, the Ego, the Divine Genius, the Indwelling Spirit or God, the Great One, the Real Ruler and Director—and last but not least, "the _Daemon_." In his memoirs, Dr. Carl Jung says, "Many times I have planned and decided upon a certain course of action, but my Daemon* has forced me into another direction."

> *Once again, we feel it necessary to clarify that a _Daemon_ is <u>not</u> a _Demon_. "Daemon" is a word derived from the ancient Greek language and most closely approximates a "Guardian Angel," or "one's Holy Guardian Angel." In, other words, the Higher Self. "Demon" is a religious and mythical "evil spirit" much fictionalized and lacking reality beyond the fear-mongering programming of various religious sects and self-induced hysteria resulting from "horror" fiction and entertainment.

The "Supra-Sensual Mind"—the True Genius and source of True Wisdom

There are certain other things related to the Daemon, such as high inspiration and intuition, and also what is justifiably called the "supra-sensual mind." Therefore, when the word "superior" is used in this text, it also refers to the supra-sensual mind, which is the TRUE GENIUS and source of TRUE WISDOM. Genius and Wisdom, as used in this text, are linked with one's True Spiritual Identity, and closely related to "Intelligence" with a capital "I."

In the light of the foregoing, one can now understand the nuances of something of meaning in the ancient Chinese customs and expressions "To repair to the Ancestral Temple" and "Time to see the Great One."

Yang and Yin

Another necessary, and very fundamental, definition is that for "Yang" and "Yin." Yang is the masculine principle: the active, projecting, energetic, initiating force. Yin is the feminine principle: passive, receptive, nourishing, and developing that which has been initiated by Yang.*

> *Please remember that Feminine and Masculine, Yin and Yang, are NOT *gender-specific* but are "principles," as are Negative and Positive, Active and Passive, Giving and Receiving, etc. Each person, every man and every woman is both Yang and Yin in Body, Mind, and Soul. Archetypally, a male psyche is predominately Animus and female psyche is predominantly Anima, but each person is also Anima and Animus, and there is constant interplay of these two principles within each person. Within every relationship, and every kind of phenomenon. It takes both positive and negative to make an electric current flow; it takes both masculine and feminine to make a baby; it takes both giving and receiving for there to be a gift; it takes a beginning before there can be an ending; and it takes a starting before there can be a completion—which, in truth, is always a new starting.

THE "PROPHETIC DREAM" PROCESS, IN SUMMARY

The "Word" is the start of a story. Please remember that we do not have a *traditional* Dream Dictionary where you simply look up a word representing something spoken in a recent dream, or an image or symbol seen in that dream, and find a "canned" interpretation that is presumed to be equally meaningful for all people looking up that same word.

As constantly emphasized throughout this book, you are a unique person and your dream of a "tall blond" man or woman may or may not seem to mean the same thing to you as the next person who had a similar dream. Think about the associated details that may be involved. For one person this tall blond may just be a romantic ideal—or an *erotic* one—which may be something quite different. For another person, that same image may be associated with a very bad experience, or just the next door neighbor when you were growing up. Now, no matter what that dream image is, it is only the beginning of a "story." There will be memories of real or fantasized, or sequential events to create a complete drama.

To clarify. We are not looking up definitive words in a standard dictionary in which an Acorn is defined as "the fruit of the oak tree." For you, the "acorn" may have many associations. More likely you will think of it as a nut rather than as a fruit, and you may recall seeing squirrels hoard and bury them for over-the-winter eating. You may remember eating acorn pie, or having acorn fights with other kids, or stringing them together to make a necklace, or reading about the acorn as a particular symbol to North American Indians or to Ancient Greek philosophers.

The Dream ESP Dictionary in Appendix A
Step One: the Dream, and its Details
The Primary Dream

Remember that this is a two-step process:

First, we spontaneously experience a primary dream that makes us aware of a question or problem, and choose a Dream Word that expresses that dream, or we actively induce a primary dream by choosing a Dream Word to represent a persistent question or problem.

Second. Now that the reader has been prepared to delve into the Dream Dictionary in Appendix A, to select a Dream Word to gain a *primary* insight about what objects in his or her dreams may mean, let it be deeply impressed upon the mind that while the various interpretations are based upon broad fundamental principles, one must call into play *all of the details of the dream* for the SPECIFIC personal application. This is the foundation for what comes next to turn ordinary Dream Interpretation into one that offers Resolution to expressed questions or problems.

Step Two: the Prophetic Dream Procedure

In Dream ESP we are also using a Dream Word as a Sign to <u>induce</u> a *secondary* dream *sequence* in answer to a problem or a question. This is an ACTIVE inductive procedure, not a passive receptive interpretation. Here's the procedure:

<u>The Prophetic Dream Procedure</u>

First. We must select an appropriate Word in the Dictionary section that represents the "Sign" that we will use to initiate the "Prophetic Dream." That dream, in turn, tells a "Story" suggesting a "Symbol" that will be used in the interpretation intended to give direction to the dreamer in resolution to the initial problem or question. It is possible that this dream will lead to a third dream sequence that is "Causal" of desired Life Changes. To review, we have (A) to select a Word in the Dream Dictionary to act as a Sign, we use (B) to inspire a Prophetic Dream that tells a Story that suggests (C) a Symbol used to resolve the initial question. That Prophetic Dream leads to (D) a Causal Dream inducing a sequence of actions to bring about desired change to improve a life situation.

Second. It is important to remember that the Signs and Symbols themselves are not like words that can have specific definitions. In looking up a Word, such as "Acorn" in this Dream ESP Dictionary, you see "Growth and Development." But it is important to factor the *usual, and any unusual,* associations *you may have with the idea behind the word,* "Acorn." These are the "associated details" that must be analyzed as meaningful for you and for no one else. Your life is unique, and your dreams, properly used, can serve as powerful formulae in your true awakening, enabling you to *become more than you are* and *all you can be.*

Step Three: The Seed in the Causal Dream

First. There are both *usual* and *unusual* associations involved with any of these dictionary words, but we are starting our discussion with the acorn as a "seed" *containing a whole program* (the DNA) of growth and development, utilizing the small "kernel" of nutrient within the shell to initiate the growing of a tiny sprout up out of the ground to develop and mature into the mighty oak tree that was sacred to the Celts and Druids, sought out as constructive and decorative lumber by generations of crafts people, used in making weapons of offense and forts of defense, tools in carpentry and wands in magick, altars in religious practice and the finest and strongest furniture for rich and poor alike.

Second. In the *inductive* process, we must select from these associations those that relate most closely to our purpose—the question or the problem for which we seek resolution, a Symbol to initiated and *program* the Causal dream to induce desired Life Changes. In the subsequent *interpretive* process we must be open and receptive to any associations that "speak" to us and relate those to the expected message of the dream.

A Situation: the "Ah So" Moment

What we really have is neither a "thing," nor just a "story," but in our "fleshing out" that initial work we are describing a *situation* in which we are the main actor around which all these newly discovered associations can lead in many directions. Now, we must make choices among those potentials to create a formula to induce our desired result.

We have examined the "energies" within the parts of the situation and we have a vision of our desire. At a certain point, we see it all, and can say the Oriental expression, *Ah, So!,** and know the next step to take. Here, then, we create a new drama, and in substance, we make a "causal prophecy" presenting the desired situation as *fait accompli.*

*Actually, a common Japanese expression *"Ah so desu ka"* made famous in the old Charlie Chan movies when the detective resolved the mystery with that expression meaning "Oh, that's how it is." (Urban Dictionary)

Organized Change is a New Reality

One final note: *Every intentional act introduces organized change into the universe, thus a new reality.*

<u>Suggested Reading:</u>

Brennan, J. H. *The Magical I Ching*. St. Paul: Llewellyn, 2000.

APPENDIX A

The Dream Dictionary
And Special Introduction:

Integrating Dreams into Purposeful Living
By
Carl Llewellyn Weschcke

Dream Analysis, Dreaming True, Turning Dreams into Messages or Lessons, Making Dreams part of your Life Process, and more!

For most of us, before understanding how passive dreaming can be integrated into purposeful living, dreams are just something that happens in sleep as curious episodes or disturbing "nightmares." For most people, what happens at night during *unconscious* sleep is separate from what happens in daytime during *conscious* awake living.

Many of us think of eight hours of sleep as just a biological need like eating for energy and drinking for hydration. We may even see it as a necessary *waste of time!* A time that could be better spent in our daily work, sports, recreation, meditation, or self-improvement study and exercise.

The Great Secret: You can, and should, turn Dreaming into a meaningful part of Living. Sleep occupies a third of your life, and you can change it from "a necessary waste-of-time" into an integral part of your purposeful life. What you will discover is that *when you pay attention to your dreams, they will pay attention to you and turn into a continuing series of meaningful messages for you!* And when you respond to those messages by asking questions, the dream messages can turn into *continuing guidance for a richer and better life.*

"Sleep on it!" You've heard that expression, and perhaps you have practiced it. Simply write down, concisely, the question or problem that concerns your daytime person, study it carefully before sleep and ask your nighttime person to give you answers in your dreams.

Dreaming True. As mentioned previously, when you pay attention to your dreams, they pay attention to you. The particular nature of this system is when you do have a meaningful dream, paying attention to it and seeking to understand its meaning *and purpose,* can ignite a series of dreams that are meaningful lessons. Sometimes they are limited to the subject of the first dream, but other times they become a series of lessons about your life's purpose. *By paying attention to the Sub-Conscious Mind (and, perhaps, the Super-Conscious Mind) you integrate its wisdom and power into your daily life.*

Self-Understanding: You've often heard or read the term "Dream Analysis," and maybe you realized that *analysis* is something more than *interpretation*. Dr. Carl Jung, the founder of *Analytical Psychology*, taught the technique of using dreams in the process of *integration:* the life-long process of conscious melding elements of the Unconscious with the Conscious Mind to bring about *Wholeness of Being*. Whether working with a psycho-therapist or on your own, the *intention* is to make a life of "Conscious Living."

The Prophetic Causal Dream. *Intention* turns every action into a *purposeful action* that can <u>cause</u> change in coming events. Awareness of near-future trends and events—whether based on Intelligence, Astrological Analysis, Prophetic Dreams, Divination, or Intuition—can be represented by a Sign or Symbol and crafted into a simple vision of a changed happening to be dreamed into realization.

Intentional Action, in all you do, is the foundation for a purposeful, meaningful, magical, and spiritual life in which you become more than you are and all you can be. **Intentional Living** is the core of all growth, all self-improvement, all psychic empowerment, and spiritual attainment.

Dream Key Words, Alphabetically Listed

Dreams can be more than biological reactions to hormonal changes in the physical body, more than reactions to too much alcohol or drugs, or a bad dinner or a bad day. But the choice is the dreamer's. With intentional awareness, dreaming becomes active communication between the Conscious Mind and the Sub-Conscious, and potentially with the Collective Unconscious. Each Word in this dictionary, treated as a Sign or Symbol, becomes a KEY to open specific doors to *Depth* rather than breadth of memory, energy, subject knowledge, and collective wisdom. Treating dreams with respect, exploring the details and associated images, expands and empowers your personal consciousness.

Aboriginals: Original inhabitants continuing to live in the same land, keeping their culture and ways. Mostly a term referred to those people of Australia. To dream of aboriginals is to seek the depths of Sub-Conscious wisdom.

Abroad: Sometimes represents a wish; otherwise, going into a strange or unfamiliar territory or situation. (See **Hexagram 20.**)

Abyss: A Sign of potential danger. (See **Trigram F.**)

Acorn: Growth and development. (See **Hexagram 8.**)

Accident: Generally only a Sign of caution, merely an apprehension—stay alert to possible danger.

Accordion: A pleasant experience is coming or being contemplated—but one lacking inspiration or beauty.

Actor or **Actress:** You will, or should, play a part in something.

Agony: To suffer or see agony portends deep emotional worry about one's coming status or relationship.

Airplane: Often connotes an intuitive-led life over which you have no control.

Alchemy, and an **Alchemist:** Transformations, Development, and Spiritual Growth.

Alley: A Sign of "dark danger either feared, or real, or to come." (See **Trigram F.**)

Alligator: A Sign of potential danger. Be careful, stay alert, and protect yourself against an unexpected difficulty. Also see **Crocodile.**

Altar: A yearning for, or an actual need for consolation.

Angel: Your Divine Genius is with you in something. (See **Hexagram 24.**)

Animals: An aspect of instinct, or a primitive function of the physical body. Look for specific animal in this dictionary. (See **Hexagram 8.**)

Animals, Four-footed: Wholeness.

Anklet: An adornment of the ankle, usually having a fetish charge. Also see **Jewelry.**

Anniversary: A repetition of a happy, joyous cycle. (See **Hexagram 7.**)

Antiques: Old, established customs and patterns of living are now very significant.

Ants: A number of irritating small conditions or problems you will have, or are having, or are worried about; things which may or may not happen. Also see **specific insects**.

Apartment: Mostly of no significance. If it is a hovel or a hut, there is money concern and often unfounded. Also see **House.**

Ape: A psychological reversion to the primitive, which can be good or bad according to details. Also can represent the Shadow.

Armlet: An adornment for the upper arm, usually as a costume or fantasy item. Also see **Jewelry.**

Apple: (See **Trigram E.**) Also see **Fruit.**

Army: The dream is in reaction to something. What? Think and meditate to find out. The answer may come in a subsequent dream.

Arrest: Unless one is a crook, it may indicate a mild guilt (almost unfounded) or a real dislike for repression of one's individuality.

Arrow: The dreamer needs to get straight to the point about something. Sometimes it is something aspired to—go for it!

Atom Bomb: Might indicate the dreamer is on the verge of an explosive situation. It might be a good idea to talk with a therapist.

Atrocity: (See **Agony.**)

Auction: You are likely to have a good opportunity.

Aunt: (See **Relatives.**)

Automobile: A conveyance for personal transportation. A Sign representing "will" under conscious direction. A Four-wheel drive vehicle represents the four conscious functions of Sensation, Feeling, Intuition, and Thinking. A rear-end accident represents something coming up from the Unconscious preventing action. Also see **Travel**.

Avalanche: If the rocks or other things do not strike you or your house, you are under a special protection in something. Also see **Protection**.

Ax: A Sign of good solid progress.

Baby: Assurance of development of something pleasant.

Baggage: (See **Travel.**)

Baker or **Baking:** Happiness in the home.

Ballet: A Sign that your wants and ideas are too fancy and unrealistic.

Banana (See **Fruit.**)

Bank and **Bank Notes**: (See **Hexagram 17.**)

Baptism: (See **Hexagram 58.**)

Bar: Really a rather high-class recreational drink establishment, a Tavern. (See **Hexagram 40.**)

Barber: You make progress by being meticulous in the details.

Barn: If empty, something might be lost—or has been. Otherwise, a barn is an indicator of an important work asset that may be calling for attention.

Barrel: Develop your capacity in some certain thing.

Basement: A Sign that success and progress in something is only possible by being cautious or even secretive. In other words, there is need to keep it "below ground" and out of sight until further development is completed, and perhaps protected by patent.

Beach: The subconscious, the border between Conscious and Unconscious where things move in and out of awareness and memory, and surprises sometimes appear. Look to your intuition and respect your hunches.

Bear: Sometimes an over-protective mother (See **Hexagrams 47** and **56.**)

Bed: An empty bed reflects unrealized hopes. Otherwise, the details in the dream will provide clues to meaning. Remember that Bed is a place for sleep and dreaming—hence a door to the Subconscious. Perhaps the details will indicate the need for purposeful dreaming, or a temporary escape from daytime stress. Also, Bed is a place where sexual relations occur, and the dream details may indicate a need to pay particular attention to your relationship. It's a call for thought and meditation.

Bee: Big results from small things are possible, commonly a sign indicating a need for personal industry. Also see **Insects**, but remember that the Bee is an unusual insect and hence an unusual symbol. Recall the many variations of the Bee's nature and activities—a social structure of Queen and Workers, an insect that flies to work and brings home nutrition and manufactures Honey, lives in a hive that is also a factory and a castle for the Queen, an insect that can sting, and one that in the desert can lead towards water.

Beetles: Sometimes indicates good news. Also see **Insects.**

Beggar: Trying to teach the dreamer about humility.

Belt: Can either be a practical device to hold up one's trousers, or used as part of a woman's fashion and costume. In a Man's world, a belt can be used as a weapon, but the loss of his belt can bring a feeling of vulnerability.

Berries: (See **Fruit.**)

Bet: Will you win, or lose? It can go either way. Sometimes a warning not to be too conservative.

Birds: A flock of birds may just reflect a head filled with many thoughts. A wounded or dead bird is about some sorrow. "To fly like a bird" is either a compensation for an inferiority feeling, or it may indicate a personal superiority not recognized by others. Or, more simply, awareness of "flying" unencumbered by the body—astral projection. Also see individual birds.

Birth: A new attitude, new potentials in development.

Birthday: (See **Anniversary.**)

Blind: To see a blind person indicates that you are developing a fine spirit of compassion which will benefit you.

Blood: In itself, it represents vitality, but look to the details. It may be a good portent, but it may reflect anxiety, which is a vital loss. (See **Hexagram 3.**)

Blossoms: (See **Hexagram 27.**) Also see **Flowers.**

Blue: Spirit. (See **Colors.**)

Boat: If in good condition, indicates some easygoing pleasure and, perhaps, good luck against some annoyance or problem.

Bonfire: A convivial good time with people is surely indicated. Don't miss it.

Book: A good book is a good companion and a good resource. An indicator that you need to be more friendly and accessible.

Boss: To dream of one's boss *always* indicates good or increased relations with him or her.

Bowl: The bowl is a symbol of a container for all that is pleasant and good to man and woman. To dream of it being broken might mean nothing but anxiety or fear. If it is for bad fortune, you will surely recognize it for what it is.

Boxing: (See **Contest.**)

Bracelet: An embrace. Also see **Jewelry.** (See **Hexagram 27.**)

Bread: Sustenance, the "Bread of Life." (See **Food.**)

Breeze: A gentle movement of the element of Air. (See **Hexagram 10.**)

Bricks: The means of construction. (See **Building.**)

Bride and/or **Bridegroom:** Some joyous occasion is anticipated and likely to be happy for all.

Bridge: If not an excellently constructed bridge, see **Hexagram 34.** If it is a strong bridge, see **Hexagram 59.**

Brother: (See **Relatives.**)

Brown: (See **Colors.**)

Bucket: Prepare to carry out a service for some person.

Building: A building appears in about half of all dreams. It's the details, i.e. the type of building, that determines the relevance—such as a church, house, school, factory, etc.—(which see). Also, an act of construction.

Bull: (See **Trigram D.**)

Burglary: (See **Hexagram 47.**)

Bus: A collective form of transportation of people. There is distinction between local transportation to work, to school, or to "downtown" for entertainment, and long distance travel. (See **Travel.**)

Butter: (See **Trigram E.**)

Butterfly: (See **Hexagram 18.**)

Cabbage: Actor or beneficiary of some "simple-minded" actions.

Cactus: (See **Hexagram 42.**)

Cage: A call for deep concern about freedom of action or choice.

Cake: Eating and enjoying a cake signifies a happy relationship with one of the opposite sex.

Calf: Exuberance, playful—a wish or reality. (See **Animals.**)

Camel: (See **Hexagram** 14.) (See **Animals.**)

Camera: A Sign that the dreamer or someone within the dream should undertake some form of self-analysis.

Canary: Beauty and happiness despite restrictions (such as being caged). Also see **Birds**.

Candle: Study the *details* of this dream! Then one might see the good augury, or else the bad one which indicates that "time is running out."

Candy: (See **Hexagrams 29** and **40.**)

Cannibal: Something to do with your Sub-Conscious Mind or your primitive instincts.

Cannon: You are acting and thinking as either a hawk or a dove. Think carefully about who you are and how you are perceived.

Canoe: (See **Trigram E.**)

Capital of a nation: As the center of government and political life, it suggests the center of consciousness, the process of bringing together diverse elements into unity.

Card: Whether a Playing Card, Tarot, or other kind of Oracle, it represents "fortune-telling." Whether good or bad fortune is coming up lies in the details.

Cartoon: Reminder to tell yourself the truth.

Castle: Preservation of real value. (See **Hexagram 32.**)

Cat: This is a real augury or omen. Study the details. Also see **Animals.**

Caterpillar: Dissatisfaction will turn to satisfaction.

Cattle: Harmony among many people. Collective conditions and actions.

Cave: Mysterious "Earth" forces. Your subconscious is informing you. Look for it.

Cellar: Same as Cave. Something going on (or will be) which is very private or secretive.

Chain: Often a symbol of restraint, bondage.

Check: Either good fortune, or a warning of prolificacy. Develop a budget.

Cherry: Pleasure with the opposite sex. (See **Hexagram 35.**)

Chess: An exercise of intelligence and strategic planning. (See **Hexagram 16.**)

Chewing Gum: Restlessness or futility or waiting.

Child: A yearning for enchantment.

China: Warns to be not too confident in something.

Choir, Christmas, Church: Together, these offer spiritual assurance and consolation. Also promises a reconciliation with self or with some other person. Also see **Christmas** and **Church.**

Christmas: While a Christian religious event/holiday—one imposed over a Pagan celebration—Christmas has become primarily a celebration of giving and receiving of gifts, a time of family gathering, of bright eyes and excitement for children, and a seasonal "time-off" from school. In a dream, it is a symbol of joy and promise. For children, the dreams may be of Santa Claus bearing gifts.

Church: A place of (mostly) Christian worship. To dream of Church is often a call to take refuge from day-to-day worries and concerns. It may also be a call for meditation or prayer in response to the challenges of life.

Circle: Magick protection.

Circus: (See **Hexagram 23.**)

Coat: Often a symbol of the "Persona" that an individual presents to the world.

Cocoa, Cocktail, Coffee: Advises taking "time out" and let your mind rove. (See **Hexagram 15.**)

Coins: Generally they indicate a wish fulfillment, but sometimes a caution to watch out for good or bad signs.

College: An embrace of intellectual or professional development. Also acceptance of adult responsibility. (See **Hexagram 8.**)

Color: Color generally reflects feelings, emotion.

Colors: Some self-appointed experts have pronounced that no person sees colors in dreams; this is terrible misinformation. To dream with colors indicates both high inspiration and aspiration. Blue is associated with Spirit; Green with life and sensation; Red with warmth and benevolent feeling; White with intuition; Yellow with intelligence.

Comet: An augury of something exciting and great to happen very suddenly with the dreamer. (See **Hexagram 5.**)

Competition: You are challenged to perform at a higher level.

Concert: (See **Hexagram 3.**)

Construction, of a **Building:** A building upward from earth, hence a "heavenly" extension of the Earth Mother towards "union" with the Sky Father.

Contest of any kind: Take heed from the advice of **Hexagram 24.**

Convent: Spiritual assurance and consolation. Promises a reconciliation with self or with some other person.

Cook: (See Hexagram 13.)

Cooking: Transformation—in the alchemical sense—but think in terms of mother or grandmother cooking, canning, preserving, etc. joyfully working in the kitchen.

Corn and other grains: (See **Hexagram 40.**)

Costume: Transformation—in a fantasy sense. (See **Hexagram 27.**)

Court: (See **Hexagram 31.**)

Cousin: (See **Father** and **other relatives.**)

Cow: (See **Cattle.**)

Crab: Lice. Some guilty sense needs resolving. **Crocodile:** (See **Alligator.**)

Crook: There is something with you which is not as superior as you pretend.

Cross: Quit feeling like being a "scapegoat."

Crossword Puzzle or other puzzles and mazes: (See **Hexagram 12.**)

Crow: The crow is the "genius of the skies" and this is a wonderful Sign that your "Genius" or Supra-Conscious Mind is working with you.

Crown: (See **Hexagram 22** or **Hexagram 24.**)

Crutches: Great help with any problem in mind, but requires energy.

Cup: (See **Trigram E.**)

Curse: This is a Sign that the dreamer should undertake some self-examination.

Cut: Generally is unfounded apprehension—but do a little self-analysis as to where is the cut, how deep is it, how was it inflicted, if by yourself, if by another person, if pure accident or intentional, what was your reaction, how do you feel about it now, does it remind you of anything or recall a memory, etc.? Again, a reminder of the value of recording your dreams in a journal, and reviewing them a week later—or anytime that you feel an urge to do so. Trust your subconscious.

Cymbal: Time to consult your higher self or what is called the "Great One."

Daffodils, Dahlias, Daisies and all other flowers: (See **Flowers.**)

Dagger: (See **Hexagrams 15** and **23.**)

Dam: (See **Hexagram 52.**)

Dancers: What kind of dancing—ballroom, romantic, religious, artistic, magickal, etc? What is the circumstance—in a party, a performance, at a theatre, a celebration, a street fair, a concert, an orgy, etc.? All dance is an action expressing emotion within a structure form. Is it a spontaneous expression of joy and excitement, is it partnered with another person or in participation with a group—each adds definition to the meaning for the dancer, and hence for the dreamer. Explore the Action. Also see **Ballet**.

Dandelion: (See **Hexagram 8**.)

Darkness: Opportunity. Like a "New Land," anything and everything is possible to your deliberate action. (See **Hexagram 64**.)

Date, A: A love affair is hoped for and could happen, for there is a strange, potent magick in dreams.

Dates—to eat: (See **Hexagram 61**.)

Daughter: Transmission of your best of your dreams and genes to a new personal is the miracle birth and life. (See **Hexagram 18**.)

Death: Generally nothing to do with actual "dying," but more often a change to be followed by renewal or rebirth. Sometimes a fear of unpleasant loss, or else the removal or end of some problem.

Decorating: An act of beautification. (See **Hexagram 27**.)

Deer: Might be a love affair. Also see **Animals**. (See **Hexagram 40**.)

Dentist: Nothing is permanent, but change can ultimately be an improvement.

Desert: Freedom from all cares. It is good to be alone at times, and to consult the "Great One."

Destruction: Be not alarmed. Much clutter in one's life should be destroyed, sold, or gladly given away. Don't just hang on to "junk," instead remember that "one man's junk can be another's treasure."

Detective: May indicate a guilty feeling. A certain thing can be solved and resolved.

Devil: If you see the "Devil" with feelings of apprehension, then there is subconscious (or conscious) sense of guilt about something. If you are not fearful, then see **Hexagrams 30** and **31**.

Diamond: See both **Gem** and **Jewelry**. (See **Hexagram 24**.)

Digging: An aggressive act of *penetrating* the Earth for **Planting, Building,** or **Mining**—each with its own significance. (See **Hexagram 26**.)

Directions:

East to West: Towards the Unconscious.

West to East: Towards Consciousness.

Discovery: A wish, or something very real.

Distress: (See **Hexagram 38.**)

Dispute: (See **Contest.**)

Divorce: Necessity of parting with something.

Dog: Domesticated, instinctively helpful and protective. Also see **Animals.** (See **Hexagram 56.**)

Doll: (See **Hexagram 21.**)

Donkey: You are reminded (concerning something) of the virtues and power of Patience and Loyalty. Also see **Animals.**

Door: A means of passage. Closed, is the unknown; open, all is clear.

Dove: Spirit (the element). (See **Hexagram 33.**) Sometimes foretells a journey.

Dragon: An astral being. A symbol of Earth energies. Sometimes is **Hexagram 39.** Also can be quite marvelous as **Hexagram 18**—Great Magick.

Driving: The Driver of a vehicle is the determiner of its destination. Also see **Traveling.**

Drown, to: Submergence in the "unconscious." Advises one to consider the virtue of **Hexagram 15.**

Drum: A rhythm setting musical instrument, often used shamanically to change brain activity and alter consciousness. (See **Hexagram 31.**)

Drunkard: A reminder to be cooperative, loyal, industrious, and live with purpose.

Duck: A water and air fowl, hence movement between the elements. Also see **Birds.** (See **Hexagram 60.**)

Dungeon: An underground place of imprisonment and torture. Restraint, denial, and loss of identity. Also see **Jail.**

Dwarf: If friendly, magick is surely working for your purpose.

Dynamite: An explosive used either in Construction or Terrorism. (See **Hexagram 47**)

Eagle: "King of Air." A symbol of Freedom and Far Sight (bird's eye view). Mates for life, but lacks mercy and humility, and can be fierce and destructive. Higher Consciousness, but not always benevolent. (See **Hexagram 50.**) Also see **Birds.**

Earrings: An adornment. For women, it is often an assertion of Feminine authority. Also see **Jewelry.** (See **Hexagram 27.**)

Ears: Pay attention to your Supra-Conscious Mind, to your intuitions. Consult the "Great One."

Earth Mother (Archetypal): The source of all Life. Your inner mother.

Earthquake: (See **Hexagram 30.**) Needs to be jarred out of some fixed position.

Easter: A Christian holiday imposed over a Pagan fertility celebration. Associated with Eggs and Rabbits. (See **Anniversary.**)

Eating: Consuming food as nourishment, or as Family or Social Dining. (See **Hexagram 3.**)

Eclipse: The "occulting" of one astronomical object by another. A very good omen. Very sudden, but not long-lasting.

Eel: A surface-water being. Also see **Snake**.

Egg: A carrier of nutrition and new life. (See **Hexagram 60** and **Hexagram 63.**)

Elephant: The largest land animal, characterized by tusks and trunk. In Greek mythology, the Goddess Hera has dominion over the Earth. She had Heracles (Hercules) as the man hero of Earth. "Heracles" means "to the glory of Hera." In the animal world, the elephant is the "Glory of Hera." If, in the dream, the elephant is the only animal seen, it is a momentous augury for the dreamer. See both **Hexagrams 8** and **64**.

Elevator: A box, or cage-like, vehicle for moving people and goods vertically, i.e. rising upward of falling downward. Which movement is the critical detail? (See **Hexagram 15.**)

Embrace: Desire for affection, or is a reality.

Emerald: (See **Hexagram 40.**) Also see **Gems.**

Enemy: (See **Hexagram 47.**)

Engine: A source of power, usually in a transportation vehicle. (See **Hexagram 49.**)

Escape: Escape from what? Something feared, hated, or from a bad relation, or just boredom? Details, and associated feelings make the difference,

Eskimo: Resourcefulness of the unconscious. Valuable instincts. You should put something on a good solid basis by overcoming adverse conditions.

Excrement, human: All excrements (urine, feces, saliva, hair, nails, even scabs, dandruff, skin flakes, etc.) are primitively associated with creative power.

Explosion: (See **Dynamite.**)

Eyes: Consciousness; your way of seeing things.

Eyes, Eyebrows, Eyelashes: Possibly, an exaggerated feeling of guilt. On the other hand, it can be a blessing, and approval of your present or contemplated action by your Daemon, sometimes assurance of love.

Face: (To see only.) If it is a nice, friendly mien, then you are assured of good fortune or a happy period. If it is not of friendly mien, it is likely to give warning that your psyche is not what it should be. Think Self-Improvement.

Factory: A place where goods are produced. If active with people and machinery, other details of the dream will indicate if you are involved in too much futile activity that portends waste and stasis, or that you are assured of the benefits of some large activity.

Fairy, Gnome, etc.: You are assured of unseen or psychic help. It is a good psychological assurance of something positive.

Falcon, Chicken Hawk, etc.: Birds of prey represent swift and direct action to your benefit—if your intentions are "correct." Also see **Birds.**

Fall: The person who has not had dreams of falling is very rare. If "landing with a *thud*," it is generally associated with incomplete or interrupted Astral Projection. If an intrinsic part of a dream, then the meaning is found in the details and associated feelings. Are they of fear or joy, of loss or of release?

Family: Generally, the close and intimate group either within which you live, or see often. (Also see **Relatives**, and particularly **Father** and **Mother**.)

Farewell: A parting gesture or words. Generally, friendly loyalty is indicated.

Farm: A place where food is grown. If pleasant, see **Hexagram 40**. If not pleasant, see **Hexagram 38**. In any event, it indicates the virtue of simplicity.

Fashion: Both a means of self-expression and of self-identity. To be "in fashion" is to "be with it," an insider rather than an outsider. To ignore, or reject, fashion is an intentional statement on individuality separate from "the Crowd."

Father and Mother: To see and talk with them if they have passed on:

If it is the Father, it is definitely that all of your forces and abilities (which you have inherited at least psychically) are operating for you in something particular. It means to tell you to use all of your higher intuitive propensities and you will be blessed with good outcomes, and to *proceed actively*.

If it is the Mother, it indicates the more-feminine principle of UNDERSTANDING, and that you will receive without much active projection.

Just remember that the old Chinese custom of "repairing to the ancestral temple" is not a mere superstitious custom. Naturally, to see one's dearly loved ones who have departed may also be a wish fulfillment, but your intuition should tell you about this. All well-regarded departed relatives indicate all of the foregoing, but generally not so strongly. If they all are alive, it promises good outcome of something only they are seen in conformity with the good morals and ethics. Otherwise beware of possible ill fortune for which are a blameless. (See **Hexagrams 32** and **64.**)

Feast: Presages joy in union. (See **Hexagram 24.**)

Feeding: There is a REAL magick in people eating, sharing, and conversing together. To feed someone else advises indicates compassion.

Feet: You stand upon Earth—hence your feet represent your contact with Reality. But, feet—especially a woman's—may also reflect her feelings of "freedom" when bare, or reflect her "status" was associated with kind and style of shoes worn. Also, a foot can be a sexual fetish, opening an entirely different set of associatons.

Fence: It either fences in the good, or fences out the bad.

Festival: (See **Feast.**)

Fight: The details of the dream indicate good or bad. Sometimes it is merely apprehension.

Figs: Sometimes associated with sexual foreplay. Also see **Fruit.**

Fire: According to dream details, is either a loss or else getting one's undesirable psychology cleansed.

Fireplace: Associated with comfort and warmth of a good home. Sometimes with a romantic setting. Simple felicity and no complications.

First Dream: In Analysis, Dr. Jung assigned great importance to the first dream in the analytical process as an anticipation of the value to the dreamer. It often presents "collective images" providing perspective for the analysis as a whole.

Fish: Symbolize elements of the Unconscious. The type, and action, of the fish can be very pertinent. Calls attention to small things of the subconscious. It can also be a call to pay attention to your diet.

Flag: Depends upon the circumstance of the display. Public and official, or personal and private. Also how used—ceremonial as in a parade or military funeral, or to mark a place of encampment or residence. In a time of confirmed peace, it could merely reflect superficial patriotism.

Flea: Personal infestation. Also see **Insects.**

Flee: To flee is to escape danger.

Flood: Reminder of the impermanence of all things.

Flowers: If not faded, see **Hexagram 13.** If faded, is either a real or only a fancied fading of something.

Fly: A constant irritation of small matters. (See **Insects.**)

Flying: May have many potential meanings, calling upon your intuition for interpretation and understanding. Commonly it suggests "loss of contact with reality," but may equally reflect awareness of out-of-body-experiences. It may also reflect real or desired ascension to higher levels of consciousness. There is also the distinctions between Anima and Animus—between right-brain (feminine) creative freedom and left-brain (masculine) logic as playing out in both inner and outer life. We dream our life.

Flying in an airplane adds another dimension: Is the dreamer in control of the flight, or is he or she being flown to a significant destination against their own desire?

Sometimes it is trying to compensate for a real or imagined inferiority. However, I know of several cases where there was a real "superiority," but it was "inner" superiority unsupported by education, training, and accomplishment.

Fog: Some small recognition of the mysteries of one's subconscious. But does one see through the fog or not? This is the significant thing.

Food: Fundamental nourishment, the "Staff of Life." Also see **Bread.** (See **Hexagram 60.**)

Foreign Country: To be there, see **Hexagram 20.** Details may indicate good or bad in venturing into something that is strange to one.

Fortunetelling: What was the "fortune?" Can also indicate worry or assurance about the outcome of something. Look to the details and feelings.

Fountain: Desire or assurance of good promise.

Four-footed animals: Sure-footed Wholeness.

Fox: Assures the benefit of being clever and resourceful. Also see **Animals.**

Fright: Generally is apprehension, real or fancied problem.

Frog: An amphibian insect eater. (See **Hexagram 22.**)

Fruit of any kind: To eat, see **Hexagram 36.** If only to look at, it is a sign of unfulfilled desire, but sometimes is an unexpected invitation and sometimes is about an existing, or yet-to-come, relationship with the opposite sex, particularly figs and cherries.

Funeral: Generally is a morbid feeling about something (or of oneself)—often unfounded. Certainly advises some self-examination. Force yourself to be joyful. "Remember all ye that existence is pure joy; that all the sorrows are but as shadows; they pass and are done; but there is that which remains." (Aleister Crowley in the *Book of the Law*).

Gallery of Art: A reminder to give full appreciation to some established values of culture and ideals; to take joy in the beautiful.

Gambling and Games: Everything that we do is a gamble. If your intention or project has good merit and you are correct and sincere, you will win out; but be honest with yourself in determining the foregoing. If you gamble merely for the sake of gambling, then this is likely to be a warning to you. Games of chance presage the same. Games of skill announce some difficulty with some acquaintance—sometimes.

Gardens: Often function as *mandalas.* Think of them as unique intersections between Nature and Human. Which is the more dominant?

Gate: Something may be obscure to you. Details indicate the outcome: favorable or unfavorable.

Gems and Jewelry: A **Gem** is a precious asset. **Jewelry** is meaningful (symbolic) adornment—sometimes in Costume and in fashion, but more often with social and personal significance. **Jewelry** can combine both the precious asset and the meaningful adornment. Also see **Jewelry.** (See **Hexagrams 13** and **27.**)

Geyser: A release of subterranean (Subconscious) Force. (See **Hexagram 7.**)

Giant: (See **Hexagram 31.**)

Giraffe: Something with you (may be in the subconscious) is incongruous or impractical.

Girl: Reminder of the joys of youth, and to keep that joy.

Gnome: (See **Fairy.**)

Goat: Take care against irritation. Also see **Animals.**

Gold: High Value. May be a wish. Can be **Hexagram 24.**

Golf: A leisure game associated with wealth and class. (See **Hexagram 15.**)

Gorilla: Reminder of the great size and force of something that stems in your subconscious. (See **Hexagram 63.**)

Grand Jury, Jury or Law Court: In one of your projects, existing or intended, you are reminded of certain inexorable natural "laws" of both business and of human nature which you can neither overlook nor combat successfully.

Grandparents: (Also see **Father.**)

Grapes: Sensuousness. (See **Hexagram 40.**)

Grave: A place of remembrance, and of "re-union" between living and deceased. Also see **Funeral**.

Green: Life and Sensation. Also see **Colors**. (See **Hexagram 60**)

Guitar: Presages simple amusement; sometimes romantic.

Gun: Injustice, or a sign of unrest and even indignation.

Gypsy: A wish (or the real thing); a pleasant love affair.

Hail: A Chill in the Air. (See **Hexagram 30.**)

Hair: The Sun as Hero; thought emanations, woman's glory.

Hammer: Tool or weapon. Rebellion against restriction. You will attain to something contemplated despite obstacles. Be not passive or indecisive.

Hands: How you grasp Reality.

Heart: Seat of feeling.

Hell: A guilt complex. Details of dream indicate whether you surmount it or not.

High School: A reminder to exercise some of your early learned and acquired virtues (and **optimism**, also).

Hippopotamus: This is the full expansion and support of your natural will. (See **Hexagram 32.**)

Holiday: (See **Anniversary** and also **Trigram E.**) It is a good augury to heed the advice of alternation in your interests and to not concentrate too much in one direction.

Holy Communion: (See **Hexagram 18.**)

Honey: To eat. Sometimes one is specially favored, both in satisfaction and in love. (See **Hexagram 13.**)

Horoscope or any other Mystical Symbols: In reality, a real **Horoscope** (not the magazine Sun Sign variety) is a valuable tool of self-analysis—hence in a dream it can indicate genuine progress in self-understanding and self-improvement. To dream of **"Mystical Symbols"** portends either bad or very good fortune, which can be decided by the details of the dream. Any bad indications can be overcome by working with **Hexagram 16**.

Horse: Refers to your higher resources and help of the subconscious. Particular important in a woman's dreams. Sometimes indicates that you will not (or should not) be held down by restrictions. Also see **Animals**. (See **Hexagram 63.**)

Horse Racing: (See **Gambling.**)

Horseshoe: Is too closely associated with good luck to mean anything else; however, it may merely reflect the wish for good luck.

Hotel: It is a symbol of either luxury or a reassuring refuge, as for a clandestine love tryst. (See **Hexagram 29.**)

House or Apartment: Your own house (home) is your own psyche. The **kitchen** is a place of transformation; the **bedroom** indicates something intimate; the **basement** is the personal unconscious; a **sub-basement**—often hidden from awareness—is the Collective Unconscious; the **attic** is "thought" in a negative sense of being too abstract; the **dining room** is a place of communion and assimilation (of food, companionship, discussion, meetings, opening mail, paying bills, etc.; a **"hidden room"**—even though it may serve as a safe room or storm cellar—refers to a neglected part of the psyche. If a house is burning, collapsing or one leaves one's own house, a separation of some kind is indicated, but it can be a good separation. Building a house indicates that one is (or contemplates) starting some project, or a new relationship.

Hunchback: Good fortune in getting help, or even in speculation, unless the hunchback is aloof or unfriendly.

Hunting: One has need of pursuing something constructive.

Hurricane: A reminder that there are always forces which are beyond one's control.

Hyena: Presages more caution and discretion rather than senseless bravado. Also see **Animals.**

Hymn: A singing of religious or magical words, mostly in a slow and even monotonous style. It can be inclusive of prayer or mantra. To dream of hearing or singing a hymn is a reminder to "reach" towards the Higher Self or Holy Guardian Angel. Also of the strength and consolation of spiritual working with a group. Also see **Church.**)

Hypnosis: The experience of unity of personal consciousness. To dream of Self-hypnosis is a realization of self-empowerment.

Hypnotism: Apprehension that one's nature be divined or controlled by some other people.

Ice: Depends on the weather. If very warm, ice is a good augury. If cold, it presages discomfort.

Illness: Reminds one of the good fortune of being in good health. Also might indicate apprehension, for nothing much.

Aborigines: which see.

Indians: Animus figures (heroes) in a woman's dreams.

Infidelity: In a love affair, many times is a sign of a secret wish, but advises faithfulness to one's highest ideals.

Inheritance: Sometimes a wish. Also can be a reminder of all the good things that one has "inherited."

Ink: Sometimes presages a favorable document and sometimes is a reminder that there are things which one cannot erase, except by making amends.

Insect: All insects indicate small, petty irritating annoyances or problems, sometimes disturbances of stomach or intestines. Advises one to consider basic fundamentals.

Invention: The creation of something new and useful. Often, however, in a dream it is of a ridiculous "Rube Goldberg" contrivance. Suggests "telling myself the truth."

Island: Longing for peace and relief from responsibilities. Sometimes indicates loneliness and sadness which can be overcome.

Ivory: A reminder of the terrible slaughter of elephants (things of value) for a cheap substitute.

Ivy: A love of the real values of olden times, sometimes of higher education and knowledge, which might actually presage pleased satisfaction, in real contentment.

Jaguar: A reminder of the value of speedy activity, when the time is right. Also see **Lion**.

Jail: (See **Dungeon**.) A standstill situation, you have run into a collective value.

Jazz Music: There is good reason for the dreamer to be careful and joyous, or "to snap out of it."

Jewelry: Most often a meaningful adornment, whether in **Costume** or socially and personally of symbolic significance. Also see **Gems. Jewelry**, of real **Gems,** can also be a significant asset. Individual items of jewelry—anklets, armlets, jeweled belts, bracelets, earrings, finger rings (and rings for nose, nipples, and toes), and other bands and chains—can also have particular significance as Emblems of membership in associations or as charged with the energy of a sexual fetish or fantasy. As images in dreams, each must be understood for what it really is.

Judge and Jury: A reminder that there are both inexorable "laws of nature" and "laws of man" (community, society, and government) regulating both business and personal actions which you can neither overlook nor combat successfully. Also see **Grand Jury**.

Juice: Generally the dreamer is thirsty.

Kangaroo: Might be indicated in adventurous journey, and is a reminder to give up some of one's dogmatic standards.

Kettle: There surely is something "cooking on the back burner" if the kettle is over a fire.

Key: May indicate that you will discover something. Also see **Horoscope** and **mystic symbols**.

Keyhole: Be not shameful and mind your own business.

Kimono: Suggests a possible love affair of which may not be proud. Exercise discretion.

King: A "ruling" function. Either an inferiority state or else one has a superiority that is not recognized. If the king is sick or dying, then the ruling function is sick.

Kiss: Whether giving or receiving, dreaming of a kiss is a wish for or in regard to a love affair. The kissing of others is more often a simple social or ceremonial gesture one step up from shaking hands. Look to the details for clues.

Kitchen: Generally not much difference from other parts of the house except when associated with a party, then look to the details for other meanings. Also see **House.**

Kneeling: Sincere aspiration. Kneeling before a woman and you could make a chump of yourself; but, on the other hand, it might indicate high transcendental sex magick as in **Hexagram 18.**

Knife and Knot: The adverse symbolism of the knife is well known, but it may instead indicate an opportunity to cut through inhibiting difficulties, as untying a knot also indicates.

Knight: "Nobility" in action or association. (See **Hexagram 58.**)

Labyrinth: If difficult to penetrate, indicates difficulties and problems which must be faced and taken care of. If they are taken care of there will be no cause for regret.

Lace: Generally a "feminine" material used in fancy costume or formal fashion dress or decoration. In a man's dream, look to the feelings and associated details for meaning. (See **Hexagram 27.**)

Ladder: Indicates you are following a difficult path, but through exercise of intelligence AND hard work it is possible to climb above your difficulties.

Lake: Generally, a tranquil body of water associated with peace and relaxation, unlike the ocean. (See **Trigram E.**)

Lamb: Herd instinct; an undesirable state of innocence.

Lamp: A small, personal source of "light." Is it on or off?

Law Court: (See **Jury** and **Grand Jury**.)

Lawn: Manicured grass. Simple satisfaction and good feeling.

Leaves: Beautiful green leaves represents fulfillment of anticipation. Faded or dead leaves presage the passing of some pleasant experience.

Leg and Ankle, Woman's: If exposed, or emphasized, by her dress and shoes, it is subtly or intentionally associated with her sexual attractiveness. But, alternatively, the leg is a means to her artistic and gymnastic self-expression. Unlike a man, all her body parts have distinct meanings.

Lemon: Indicates a pleasant, satisfying event.

Leopard: (See **Lion**.)

Letter: A letter is either just a message, or it is communication. Each has a different meaning in the dream. Look to the details and associated feelings.

Liar and Lie: One may have to defend oneself, yet it may be nothing but a guilty feeling. It may advise, "I swear to tell myself the truth."

Lice: Infestation? Nuisance, or Embarrassment. Also see **Insects**.

Light: Enlightenment, Intelligence, Enabler of Seeing. Also see **Lamp**.

Lighthouse: Good fortune in an adventurous project.

Lightning: A visible explosive release and transfer of energy from Sky to Earth. Warning of Danger. Take Cover. (See **Trigram G**, or **Hexagram 55**. Also see **Thunder**.)

Lily: Calm, Peace. "The lilies of the field toil not nor do they spin."

Lingerie: The Feminine. To a man, presages adventures that anticipate sex. To a woman, it is identity, a love of finery, adornment and an expectant attraction to men.

Lion and all other Big Cats: If in freedom, means Freedom with a capital F. If in captivity, see **Hexagram 31**. A dead lion indicates that "nobility" might be defiled or hurt. A big cat hunt indicates contempt for high values. The big cats kill only for food and the collective unconscious of man knows this well and realizes that he is the most despicable predator on earth and, therefore, he has, at least, a subconscious respect for the big cats; and it is, therefore, a reminder for him to be noble, just, humane, and merciful. For this reason, the dream in which the big cats take prominence indicates the dreamer is beginning to have some hitherto suppressed high feelings and ideals. The Lion—as King of the Beasts—represent an exaggerated valuation of the Will, as in Nazi Germany (See **Hexagram 23** and **Hexagram 24**.)

Lips: Male Active or **Female Receptive? Lipstick?** Are they kissable, or thin and grim? Can well be **Hexagram 40**—or, on the other hand, see **Hexagram 45**.

Liver: Seat of Life; can also be a symbol of Self.

Lizard: Is an annoyance, and also indicates completely unfounded fears and misunderstandings and, therefore, is often an omen of unexpected good fortune.

Lobster: Presages unpleasantness sometimes. To eat, indicates something good is due to you.

Locust: A song or a pest, according to details of the dream.

Loneliness: A portent of pleasurable company.

Lottery: Less a game of mathematical or psychic skill and more just chance, a hope of good luck. Also see **Gambling**.

Love: Making love might be a wish, and yet this wish may be strong enough to bring the real thing. (See **Hexagram 21**. In rare cases, it can indicate **Hexagram 18**.)

Lunch: (See **Food**.)

Lungs: Spirit of air.

Machinery: If in good order, can be **Hexagram 7**. If it breaks down, or gives trouble, there is indicated a generally correct idea of something that is difficult to surmount, inhibiting progress.

Magician: If it is *stage* magic, one is directed to eschew trickery and be straightforward. If it is *transcendental* magick, then there are hidden forces working for one's benefit.

Mannequin: If a man dreams it, it is a pretense of some attainment, or deceit. On the other hand, it is a desire for sexual adventure which in some cases will happen. If a woman dreams it, it is likely to indicate self love and desire for show, but it might also indicate some real ideal.

Manuscript: If seen, indicates that one has a valuable or lucky idea which, if followed up, will pay off well. It can be **Hexagram 11**.

Market: A food market signifies activity and prosperity.

Marriage: "*Union of male and female*" as persons, even of respective principles in Gay Marriage. Also, "Mystical Marriage" as integration of psychological of Animus and Animus, of Yin and Yang, God and Goddess, male and female principles. To dream of any kind of marriage is to recognize the need of this "Next Step" in bringing together two halves into Wholeness. Also see **Wedding**.

Masquerade: To attend announces an exciting, pleasant experience is possible.

Matador: The Spanish word means "a killer" and, specifically, a killer of bulls. In some countries it means some heroic action, but seldom likely in other countries.

Mattress: An outlived love affair is often indicated.

Medal: Sometimes indicates a genuine honor. See **Hexagram 18**. The ideal would be **Hexagram 8**.

Merry-go-round: Happy aimless pleasure. Sometimes advises that it is entirely aimless and wasteful activity.

Meteor: Something completely unexpected is indicated—generally a good portent.

Microscope: Indicates that one is presently interested in very small things instead of something more practical and profitable. However, "smallness"—as in atoms, quantum particles, genes, and cells—is the ultimate source for intentional change, for the developmental process.

Midget: (See **Gnome**.)

Mining: The digging into Mother Earth to extract Her natural resources. When on a small scale, and with respect and restoration of the surface, it is benevolent, like the family farm. Large scale mining is often abusive, destructive of the surface and poisoning of water and soil, and polluting of the air, just like factory farms. It is ignorant and harmful.

Minuet (dancing or the music): Presages something forthcoming that is beautiful and pleasing.

Mirror: Perhaps one recognizes one's weaknesses or faults, or some person will call attention to them (or has done so). A broken mirror is the consequences of one's disregard of some person or of something.

Mob: Out of control. The lower instincts giving play, or else it is a warning about it.

Money: Most dreamers have dreamed of finding money, which is a wish fulfillment. To give money to some person, willingly, promises a good profit. Money is concretized psychic energy, libido. Sometimes, money is associated, or even mixed, with feces—something of value is being repressed or ignored or to be found where least expected. Sometimes applies to **Hexagram 25**.

Monk: (See **Church** and **Priest**.)

Monkey: Beware of deceiving imitation or trickery either to receive or to do.

Monster: (See **Hexagram 47**.)

Moon: Always a sign of change—generally for the better. You must use your intuition to the utmost to divine all possible signs of the moon. Consider very carefully all the details of the dream for clues. There is the hidden or mystery here for you to solve.

Morgue: (See **Funeral**.)

Moth: Sometimes the dream of a moth advises one to give compassion, pity or tolerance to some particular person. Also see **Insects.**

Mother: (See **Father.**)

Motorcycle: A personal conveyance of one, sometimes two, person or persons. It is suggestive of **male aggression**, **gangs**, and—to a lesser extent—**adventure**. Also see **Travel, also Automobile, Bus, Train.** Also see **Zero.**

Mountain: Stable, fixed, immovable. (See **Trigram D** and also **Hexagram 26.**)

Mountain climbing: Climbing from the Unconscious to gain a higher point-of-view, i.e. increased consciousness.

Mountain Pass: A situation of transition, leading from one attitude of mind to a new one.

Mourning: (See **Funeral.**)

Mouse: The ancient Roman said, "*Mons parturient nascitur ridiculus mus.*" The mountains are in labor; they are about to give birth to a ridiculous mouse—big deal! Too often, the dream is a subtle reminder that one is trying to kid himself (or others) that the project is mountainous in size when it is really only a tiny mouse.

Mouth: (See **Lips.**)

Mud: Generally, the only significance is difficulty of travel.

Mule: A "beast of burden." (See **Hexagram 26.**) Also, might be some of **Hexagram 7.**

Mummy: Reminder of ancient real values and their preservation.

Music: (See **Hexagram 13.**)

Nail: (See **Hexagram 31.**)

Naked: Something is to be discovered, as the "naked truth." Naked is a very common dream. Often is a reminder that one is, or should not be, putting on too much front. To see one of the opposite sex naked is either a wish or presages a special sexual experience, particularly if seductive. If people do not take notice of you nakedness, it is a sure sign of over-self-consciousness and inhibitions and that is a faulty psychology in one.

Navy: (See **Ships.**)

Necklace: (See **Gems** and **Jewelry.**)

Negro: Before contemporary Western integrated societies, for white Europeans and Americans, to dream of a Negro (African person) represented the hidden, rejected elements of consciousness, the "dark" side, raw and instinctual nature.

News: Good news may be a wish or it actually portends such.

Newspaper: (See **Trigram B** and **Theatre**.)

New Year's Eve: (See **Anniversary**.)

Nightingale: (See **Hexagram 53**.)

Nine, or any other number: (See **Astrology**.)

Nose: Intuition, feeling the "atmosphere.

Nurse: (See **Hexagram 64**.)

Nuts: (See **Hexagram 25**.)

Oak Tree: (See **Hexagram 8**.) Also, omen for Sex Magick.

Oar: Hard work, but some results.

Oath: To those who have understood this book well, and have duly practiced, there are only two oaths: *"I swear to tell myself the truth"* and *"I swear to regard every event as a particular dealing between myself and my soul."*

Occultism: You are progressing in Borderland Consciousness and will soon benefit thereby.

Ocean: A new awareness that we swim in an ocean of unknown qualities, but are being informed and helped by the Unconscious. Sometimes is **Hexagram 64**.

Oil: Details of the dream indicate whether it is a disturbing thing—on up to benediction and peace.

Old Woman: Wisdom of the eternal feminine; nature wisdom.

Olive Oil and Olives: A simple platonic love, a wonderful sexual love, or a low or forbidden love—all according to the details of the dream. Sometimes it is an assurance of getting well from some minor sickness.

One: A number. False or justified egotism.

Opera: (See **Hexagram 59**. Also see **Theatre**.)

Oranges: Health is good, or should be concerned with the health. Also see **Fruit**.
Orchestra: (See **Hexagram 11** and **Trigram E**.)

Organ: If a pipe organ, see **Orchestra**. If a reed organ, it represents nostalgia.

Organs, Body: See entries for **Eyes, Feet, Hair, Hands, Heart, Liver, Lungs, Nose**.

Otter: A fine sense of Beauty and Grace will lead to a benefit. Also see **Animals**.

Oven: A reminder of food, which see.

Owl: To see an Owl is an omen of something mysterious which will be good, or else very annoying.

Oyster: Advice to overcome one's self-consciousness. (See **Hexagram 40**.)

Package: If the contents are unknown, it indicates some small unexpected gift or assistance, or reward of something long since done.

Paint and Painter: For what reason is something being painted, and what? As always the clue is in the details.

Palace: (See **Castle** and **Hexagram 17.**) There has been full development and, therefore, no place for advance. This represents full established authority or accomplishment and, to advance, a new outlook is required—change.

Palm Tree: (See **Hexagram 35.**) There is indicated a wish to travel to some relatively distant place, but the realization of this depends on several things.

Panther: (See **Lion and all other Big Cats.**) If the panther is not unfriendly, it is a sign of some small good fortune but earned by some effort. If it be a black panther, it is an augury of some very good fortune almost as if by magick.

Paper: (For writing or printing, see **Hexagram 52.**) Do not sign any paper or document, nor write letters which have great importance, for several days.

Parchment: (See **Paper.**) You can, even unconsciously, accomplish something advantageous by magick. A fine augury for making a pact.

Parents: (See **Father** and **Mother.**) Your inner parents are the archetypal Earth Mother and Sky Father.

Parrot: To hear. You might talk too much, ambiguously.

Parsley and Parsnips: To eat is a good omen for a friendship. (See **Food and/or Vegetables.**)

Party: (See **Celebration** and **Hexagram 33.**)

Passport: Many times this indicates a desire for self-justification about something, and to make it more certain it is seen in the form of legal sanction as in some official document. It is definitely, in many cases, more than a wish and is an attempt to justify oneself in some project or undertaking which is either in present activity or is contemplated.

Path: If the path is clear and travelled without difficulty, it is a reassurance that one's project or planned intentions progress without frustration and complications. (See **Travel.**)

Peaches: To eat peaches generally indicates either the wish or a love affair to go very satisfactorily. To be offered peaches is an augury of receiving what is desired.

Peacock: Indicates great pride, show, and ostentation in something. Sometimes is over-ambitious for a recognition of success or standing by others.

Pearls: Precious tender sentiments. (See **Gems.**)

Pen or Pencil: (See **Hexagram 12.**)

Perfume: Even though the perfume bottle is empty, there is a lingering scent, and this is a simile of the reminder of some beautiful incident with a wish or a real anticipation of a beautiful and satisfying recapturing experience. It is such a strong sign of attraction that there is a good omen that the promise may be brought to realization.

Piano: (See **Music.**) If silent, it is an apprehension or feeling of something to be lost or being lost.

Pickpocket: (See **Thief.**)

Picnic: Joyous satisfaction, particularly in relationships.

Pigeon: A symbol of tender sentiments. Sometimes it presages that there is an action which will bring pleasing developments.

Pillow: Either apprehension or a real struggle for a secure position in something.

Pilot: (See **Hexagram 5.**)

Pistol: To carry, you are really preparing everything well for some intended course of action to turn out at its best, if there is no need to shoot it or threaten with it.

Plank, beam, or any high risky passageway on which you must walk with great care: (See **Hexagram 34.**)

Plant, to; and **Planting:** Participating in the continuity of life itself in fulfillment of that elementary function. (See also **Alchemy.**)

Plate Glass: To break. Do not refuse to give help to some person who will ask you for it.

Platinum: (See **Gold.**)

Plow: To be plowing. (See **Hexagram 63.**)

Polar Bear: You are seeing the symbol of a tremendous psychic force (and the intuition of the Borderland). Be prepared to recognize a wonderful opportunity, and to use your entire inspired forces, and there will then be a great result.

Police: To see or deal with. A very large percentage of people (including this writer) are reminded of limitations and restrictions which may be merely a reflection of one's own psychology, or else it can be very real in the material world and is advice of the restrictions in some project and, for that aspect, for good clues, see **Hexagrams 26, 30** and **31.** For those who see the police in the guise of father and mother protection, it is naturally a quite different significance—and obvious.

Pope: (See **Church.**)

Poppy: Red poppies, seriousness; yellow poppies, brilliant satisfaction. (See **Flowers.**)

Porcelain: (See **China**.)

Portrait: Profitable to examine oneself very honestly.

Postman: Details of dream indicate whether good or bad news or outcome of something.

Pray and Prayer: (See **Church**.)

Pregnant: To see or feel. (See **Hexagram 40**.)

Prison: Restriction, real or fancied. Can advise one to be (or actual action) in a state of genuine natural uninhibited spontaneity.

Prize and Award: Either patting yourself on the back or there may be a real award coming to you.

Protection: This writer knows of too many cases for brooking contradiction to the principle or force of protection in a person's life. It is not meant, for example, that some invisible hand deflects a bullet to prevent it from killing a soldier; but this "protection" could, on the other hand, lead the soldier into some phase of the military service where he would not be subjected to flying bullets. Often, also, the   protected one might, by a sudden intuition, stop walking as a brick wall came crashing down. In this, again, there is no miracle implied. In this sense of being protected, he may have heard something almost inaudible, such as creaking noises in the brick wall. There are many kinds of dreams which reiterate one's protection. Even the dream of falling from a great height, and yet not being hurt when hitting bottom (and knowing that it will not hurt), is very often an assurance that one is being protected in something.

Pulpit: (See **Church**.)

Pumpkin: This is a rich reminder of the fall harvest and the Halloween festival of feasting, fertility dancing, and the cycle of the year.

Puncture: (See **Travel**.)

Pyramid: To see. If it is a large structure, there will be a long period to develop something, but it will turn out to be stable and valuable.

Quarry: Definitely refers to some difficulty to accomplish something fundamental.

Quicksand: In danger of entrapment, helpless to escape or move on.

Rabbit: Too much meekness indicated in self or in some other person. Advises active doing.

Raft: A large plan, but with nothing much to substantiate it. Advancing weakly.

Railway and Railway Station: (See **Travel**.)

Rain: A "love-union between heaven and earth, for it is rain that allows the earth to become fertile. Thus, to dream of rain symbolizes a solution to the dreamer's problem, or marks the solution. Also, it symbolizes a release of tension.

Rainbow: A nearly universal symbol of realization. Also reminds one of the value of beauty.

Rape: Very rarely seen in dreaming, except by "sex fiends." It can also reflect the trauma of actual rape, or the instilled fear of it.

Rats: Not as bad as it would seem to indicate.

Rattlesnake: (See **Snake.**)

Ravine: (See **Travel.**)

Rebirth: Dreams follow the human calendar; thus rebirth dreams often follow a "death" dream—which may represent *change* in the life situation—by nine months' time.

Red Color, Red Fruit, Redhead: Warmth and benevolence. Also see **Colors.**

Relatives: Are they close or distant, living "here" or in another country, related through Mother or Father, or Siblings? Also see **Father** and other relatives.

Reunion: An intensified reminder of one's past accumulated values, and that one's Daemon and Supra-Conscious Mind is in accord with one's actions and gives a benediction.

Revenge: To see or to have; is a "cleansing" of oneself from giving vent to strong resentments and leading one from such wasted energy.

Revolving Door: Take care about getting no place. Ill-advised, futile, or wasted action.

Rhinoceros: (See **Hexagram 47.**)

Riding: (See **Travel.**)

Rifle: (See **Pistol.**)

Ring: An adornment of finger, toe, or other body part. Also a token of help, or loyalty. Sometimes felicity with one of the opposite sex or a pact or agreement with someone. If a beautiful ring set with brilliant stones, see **Gems** and **Jewelry.**

River: If it is a calm, peaceful river, then it presages that all is flowing to satisfactory culmination, but not very soon. If it is wild, rushing water, see **Trigram 46.**

Road: If to be traveled by one, see **Travel.**

Roof: You will be able to "see" more than you ordinary see about some conditions in which you are involved—or intend to be.

Room: One half of all dreams have enclosed places for a setting. What are the details or "plot"?

Rosary: A psychological surcease from some worries—or sense of guilt.

Roses: Felicity is generally indicated--or desire for it. To receive roses is being especially favored—or the desire for it.

Roulette: (See **Gambling**.)

Rowing: (See **Travel**.) Sometimes indicates harder work, but with more results or profit.

Ruby: (See **Gems**.)

Rug: If not old and worn, indicates that your going will not be very unpleasant. If it is old and worn but still useful and even lovely, it suggests comfort and stability.

Ruin: To see an old ruin reminds one to not undervalue old established values, customs and ethics.

Sailboat: If going beautifully, it portends progressing in luxurious, pleased satisfaction. If slack sails or in a storm, see **Hexagram 39**.

Salvation Army: Regulated, intelligent compassion.

Sapphire: (See **Gems**.)

Sawing: Presages cutting through obstacles or making an added value from something.

Scaffolding: (See **Hexagram 26**.)

Scales: You may come to realize that Justice is a manmade invention, but Nature is "adjustment" instead of "justice." You are "weighing" something by its real value instead of the attractive or superficial qualities.

Scarecrow: A definite reminder not to resort to anything but what is of genuineness in your project and not a cheap substitute.

School: You will utilize some old, established value to your benefit.

Scissors: To see, particularly in cutting. Dissolving the association with a woman is her move or fault. Cutting away from anything is likely to be due to the fault of the project or its aim—although not always so. Details reveal the fault.

Scorpion: Secret enmity or due to the stinging attitude or words of the dreamer is not good.

Sea: (See **Ocean**.)

Searchlight: The dreamer cannot hide his or her aims.

Seasons: The Human Calendar. The seasons symbolize exactly what they suggest:
Winter: Cold, intellectual
Spring: Youth, renewal
Summer: Warmth, fullness of life
Autumn: Maturity

Sewing Machine: (See **Hexagram 23**.)

Sex: Dreams related to sex can have many interpretations, and—if not obvious—calls for extended meditation. Sex is a fundamental factor in life—related to the reproduction of the species, the energy of growth and self-perfection (kundalini), the drive for self-expression through motherhood, or the drive for self-expression through male aggression and expansiveness. In youth, sex dream (as in "wet dreams") can simply reflect hormonal drives. In adulthood, sex dreams can reflect establishing relationships with the Unconscious. Ideas or fantasies of sex play may relate to explorations of ways to sexual pleasure, or a need to explore inner needs through role playing. See **Hexagram 21**. Dreams of sexual activity, whether or not consummated, might be a "wish" or due to one's sexual drive. However, such dreams frequently lead to a realization—if the dreamer looks for it. If the sexual play is on a particularly inspirational plane, it indicates a very propitious time and circumstances as indicated in **Hexagram 18**. Also may relate to **Hexagram 22**, which is a struggle for self-realization, psychologically.

Shaving: Be very careful in the honesty or sincerity in any relationship.

Sheep: (See **Hexagram 17**.)

Ships: In good sailing into a harbor or in a harbor, portends reaching some aim; sometimes indicates things moving for a reunion. Sailing out of a harbor presages change.

Shooting: Getting something off the chest.

Side: In a dream, the right side represents the Conscious Mind, Consciousness, Awareness; the left side represents the Unconscious, sometimes things going on beneath the surface.

Signature: Details should indicate extreme caution in committing oneself to any move or project, or whether it is initiating a good move.

Sighing: Expression of feeling.

Skeleton: Anxiety about future security in something.

Sky Father (Archetypal): You inner father.

Skyscraper: Higher aims than practical.

Snakes: Of any kind: beware of fraud or malice of one of the opposite sex. If the snake makes no overt threatening move, then certain fears or apprehensions are unfounded. Also, can be a warning of weakness or injury to spine.

Soap Bubbles: Keep your feet on the ground; be practical.

Soldiers: (See **Hexagram 57.**)

Sparrow: To be attracted or to hear it sing indicates that you will see beauty and joy in some simple things in which you had not hitherto seen nor appreciated.

Spider and Spider's Web: Unexpected inspiration will certainly embrace you. A development of your fine response to your higher imaginations and made very real in at least subjectivity.

Spotlight: (See **Searchlight.**)

Spring: A spring. Regardless of disappointment, there is an inner resource of sustainment.

Spurs: You cannot hasten your project by energetic will—only by your true Genius.

Squareness: A dream that emphasizes the "squareness" of any object indicates *completeness.*

Stagecoach: (See **Travel.**)

Stairs: To see: Peace of mind is promised if you desire to improve yourself.

Storm: (See **Trigram G.**)

Stream: (See **River.**)

Striptease: Sometimes a wish. Advises one to be correct and sincere in some particular dealing.

Suitcase: Sometimes portends a visit of a relative or close friend.

Surgeon: Sometimes indicates a desire to change occupation. Sometimes indicates the present and coming freedom from an undesirable situation.

Swallow: A bird of Promise. (See **Hexagram 16.**)

Swan: (See **Hexagram 18.**) Pleased, stable satisfaction.

Swimming: (See **Hexagram 33.**)

Sword: You are going to help in a worthy cause—or receive that help.

Tapestry: Often indicates a kind of prophecy, which advises special attention to awareness and to one's intuition.

Tattooing: (See **Hexagram 27** in respect to its lower phase.)

Taxi: A conveyance for commercial individual transportation. If riding alone, indicates help from some source. If with one of the opposite sex, is complication in the love life—or a wish.

Tea: Leisure and pleasant acquaintance.

Tears: A fortunate change in one's associations.

Telegram: (See **Letter.**) May be faster in action.

Telephone: Many times indicates an unknown (or nearly so) person with whom the relation or dealing is indirect.

Tent: A surcease from complications and reduced to simplicities. Simple "Protection," which see.

Theatre: The principle of the theatre is related to "Life Expression" which includes "Newspapers," "Speculation," and "Courtship." It will be good or unfavorable in one of these things according to the action in the dream. However, to dream of attending a play symbolizes the ending of an active roes in life's drama.

Thief: It will be very favorable for you to be led to give up or part with something.

Throat: Success in expressing the good motions.

Tiger: (See **Lion.**)

Tightrope Walking: You need better inner balance in emotions or in your bents and preoccupations. The dream may indicate that this is soon to be fulfilled.

Time of Day: The human calendar:
>   Night: Unconscious.
>   Morning: Dawn of Consciousness,
>   Noon: The Zenith of Consciousness,
>   Evening: Descent into the Unconscious.

Tongue: He who tries to prove too much proves nothing.

Torch: (See **Light.**)

Toreador: (See **Bullfight.**)

Tower: (See **Castle.**)

Traffic: Indicates complications or faultiness in plans.

Train: A conveyance to transport materials, goods and people. **Of people, t**he train is a collective way to travel—everyone is going the same direction—hence suggesting a "one-track mind." In a very large percentage of dreams, there is a difficulty in getting from one place to another. There need not be any particular destination, though this is in many dreams. In the case of such conveyances as trains, buses, and stagecoaches, the big difficulty is often the necessity of getting to the conveyance in time to go aboard. If by auto or horse and wagon, the trouble is that there either turns out to be something wrong with the engine, or in other cases, as being on foot also, the roadway or path turns out to be impassable because of such things as mud, a river, or a deep vast abyss.

The reason that this dream is so common is that the problem is so common, i.e., worry, indecision or unworked-out details of "getting to somewhere" such as working out something to a satisfactory conclusion. The worry is generally unnecessary. It actually indicates that both the Conscious Mind and the Borderland Consciousness are working out the problem and are on the way to getting somewhere. Actually, the dream is like a whip for good—it urges one on, in determined concentration. Also see **Travel.**

Travel and Traveling: The "voyage of discovery" can be almost any form of travel, especially walking tours, exploration trips, etc. It may be a symbolization of the process of "Individuation" (Jungian).

Traveling under Difficulty and Duress: Loss of freedom and independence.

Treasure: To find. This dream very often is a good stimulus to one to keep persisting in the project. The treasure is like a carrot in front of the donkey's nose, just as you will notice.

Tree: This is a reminder that stability and security are won by long-time development. If it is a dead tree, it hits one's pride and warns that "pride goeth before a fall" and then does one become filled with humility.

Trophy: (See **Prize.**)

Trousers: Is often a reminder to a man to be more masculine in principle; for a woman it is a sign of independence and self-assertion.

Trumpet: A Call to action, a Wake-up Call. Metaphorically, you will be called to do something—or, on the other hand, you may be the one who is calling or announcing.

Tunnel: Access and movement underground. The personal Unconscious. Also see **Cave.**

Typewriter: There is a reminder that something about your manner is too dated and stereotyped.

Umbrella: A reminder to keep to yourself and to your own counsel for a short period.

Undertaker: (See **Funeral.**)

Undressing: (See **Naked.**) To see the act of undressing indicates a snooping tendency in something particular, but the desired thing will not be discovered. It teaches a good lesson that the dreamer looks just as funny in long red flannel underwire as any other person.

Unicorn: An "imagined" animal representative of an instinctual response to a situation. The unicorn is a dangerous animal that can only be tamed in the lap of virgins.

Vampire: A fantasy that absorbs energy. The fear of being the victim of a vampire is a certain sign that, at least in one thing or in one phase of the psyche, there is need for psychic readjustment or therapeutics. For self-help, avoid being passive or negative at all times.

Vegetables: (See **Food**.) Indication of healthy food.

Venetian Blinds: Guard against any act which will not stand the "light of day" and all will be well.

Violets: "Violets are blue, and I love you." Subtle beauty and perfume. A reminder of young love. Also see **Flowers** and **Perfume.**

Violin: (See **Hexagram 35**.)

Voice, not of anyone present in dream: The Self has intervened in the dream. What the voice says cannot be disputed. It stands for knowledge.

Volcano: If inactive, simply means an imaginary threat. If active, a warning not to ignore announced threats of any kind. Also see **Hurricane.**

Wall: Is sometimes one of the difficulties of **Travel,** which see. In a dream it prevents a view, but it presages that things are more clear than the dreamer (or others) may imagine.

Wallet: To find is to discover someone's secret. To lose indicates: one's secrets are not well hidden and may be easily discovered. Take action.

Waltz: A slow rhythmic ballroom dance suggesting romance. (See **Hexagram 33**.)

War: An instinctual conflict between two collective attitudes. Generally stupid.

Wart: (See **Hexagram 26**.)

Wasp: A flying insect with a stinger. A warning that danger can come out of anywhere. Also see **Bee.**

Watch: Act as soon as possible on something contemplated.

Wave, of Water: At this time, do not allow the passions to go over the crest.

Wave, of the Hand: A gentle gesture of departure. A sign of a friendly ending.

Wedding: If inspiring, can refer to **Hexagram 18**. If merely formal, is **Hexagram 22.**

Weeds: Of significance only if very tall and "taking over the place." A warning that you are neglecting things "out of sight, out of mind."

Weird: Something strong in the psychic activity of the dreamer; exciting but not necessarily unfavorable.

Wheel: Change. (See **Hexagram 2.**)

Whistle: An alert.

White: Intuition. Also see **Colors.**

Wig: A disguise or a false front. Or an element of Costume.

Wolf: Your difficulties and hazards are not nearly as bad as you imagine. Use your best instincts.

Woman: For a male dreamer, all that the details of the dream may imply, though often is merely a wish or fantasy, but even this can be made real if the female dominates the scene and plot. For a female dreamer, a reminder of friends and "trust in one's own.

Words: To see, and if indistinct: Your Supra-Conscious Mind and intuition is working on something which will be a real solution for you.

Wreck: A reminder of the inevitability of blind accidents unless one has built up a strong psychic protective force—if the wreck touches you deeply.

Wrestling: (See **Competition.**)

Writing: To be writing is seldom dreamed. Look out for something important touching you and you will find it.

X: The sign or letter representing the unknown, or the actual number 10—the "perfect" number. Sometimes a sign or rejection or negation.

Yellow: Intelligence. Also see **Colors.**

Zebra: The striped horse represent the union of opposites in the Unconscious. (See **Hexagram 49.**)

Zero: A universal "unconscious" symbol of the sum total of all possibilities, but which does not manifest until activity is concentrated in some one particular point in the circle. A reminder all dream analysis must consider the specific activity that is started or is operating. (See **Hexagram 63.**) For Zero potential, see **Hexagram 64.**

Zoo: With many animals means you are operating well in your subconscious, which will be a great aid to you, and you will be able to harness and direct the psychic energy.

APPENDIX B
THE EIGHT TRIGRAMS OF THE YI KING
The Pa Kua of Fu-His

8 Pa Kua (Trigrams) of Fu-Hsi

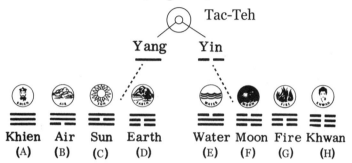

The Trigram Structure of the Yi King

The entire structure of the Yi King is based upon the eight Trigrams as given by its ancient progenitor, Fu-Hsi. Indeed, the entire Yi King philosophy and cosmology can be reconstructed from the existing keys in these eight Pa Kua.

First, note the difference in the line structures: a whole line and a broken line. This presents the idea of the duad, basic in human nature—whether it be a dualism of opposing forces or that of cooperating partners.

Second, note the three line positions, making a triad, also basic in humanity: the concept of Father-Mother-Son actively working in substance to produce a form.

For example, here's the Sun, Trigram C.

The central line is the conscious thinking and acting individual. The line is a Yin, which means that he/she is receptive and invoking. The bottom line is Yang, which means their bodily equipment is "firm and correct," including the best of instincts, emotions, and desires. All this Yang energy is projected in response to the receptivity of the central linear nurture and development. The soul powers of the upper line are projected to the receptive central line, the incarnate individual. All of this agrees with the meaning given in the classic texts: light-giving brilliance, intelligence, and realization that is the Sun. The Sun Trigram is the most auspicious in any figure.

Conversely, the Trigram of the Moon, being the opposite of the Sun Trigram, is the most inauspicious.

To illustrate this we shall study the Moon, Trigram F.

The upper and lower lines are Yin and do not project. The lower line is the desires wanting to be satisfied. There is nothing of value given to the individual or situation from his higher wisdom and direction, which is the central Yang line. The Yang individual has an instinctive drive for action, but there is nothing to support it from the other two lines. Therefore, the body, instincts, emotions, and desires give nothing much to the individual, rather they are only asking to receive and to be "filled up." The upper line offers nothing as there is no directive capacity. Compare this analysis of the lines of the Moon with the description given in the texts symbolized as "a deep, wide gorge containing a torrent of water." It is essentially restrictive, opposed to action "from above."

In comparison to the above two Trigrams, consider Khien, Trigram A. In which all the lines are Yang, signifying greatness, projective force, starting energy, and initiative. There is no Yin line of response to receive, nourish, and sustain this energy.

A Khien

Thus it is more of an abstraction, just as its opposite, Khwan, with its three Yin lines, is also an abstraction. Khien is the Great Originating Force and Khwan, the Womb of the Great Mother Earth, which receives and nourishes, supports and develops that which comes from the union with Trigram H, Khwan.

H Khwan

It is the *union*, or cooperation, of these two great principles, Yin and Yang, that brings about the various *manifestations* of the other six Trigrams.

There are four Trigrams that correspond with later concepts of the four Elements: Fire, Air, Water, and Earth.

Thus, with the introduction of the first Yin line in Khien, we have the first response in Trigram B, Air, also called Wind, "easily penetrating and penetrated," corresponding to the principle of Air. Air is characterize as Penetrating. Mental concepts, "The Planner." More male than female, the lines are Masculine, Masculine, Feminine.

B Air

On the opposite side, the first Yang line of Khwan is the first manifested activity—called Fire or Thunder, meaning sudden, exciting energy. Trigram G is described as thunder and lightning—"sudden, startling activity"—and is well symbolized as Fire. Fire is characterize as manifesting Great Energy and is called "The Arouser." More female than male, the lines are Feminine, Feminine, Masculine.

C Fire

Trigram E, Water, is described as a placid body of water of "pleased satisfaction." Water is characterized as Open. Strong desire for pleasure. The Self-indulgent. More male than female, the lines are Feminine, Masculine, Masculine.

E Water

Trigram D, Earth, is characterized as Inertia. Body, Matter, Stability, Consolidating. The Status Quo. More female than male, the lines are Masculine, Feminine, Feminine.

D Earth

It is not just coincidence that the opposite nature of Trigram E, Water and Trigram D, Earth are depicted with all lines being of opposite polarity—as are the lines of Air and Fire.

Thus we can see that even though Fu-Hsi left no written record of the eight Pa Kua, it is still possible to decipher its code and arrive at the same delineations of the eight Trigrams as stated in the two classic texts and early appendices. In Appendix C, we take these meanings and analyze each Hexagram solely upon the two Trigrams and their positions as upper or lower to produce the extended meanings of all sixty-four Hexagrams. Thus, the Hexagrams are combinations of two of the 8 Trigrams, of which there are 64 possible combinations.

The Eight Principles
The Trigrams as Polar Opposites

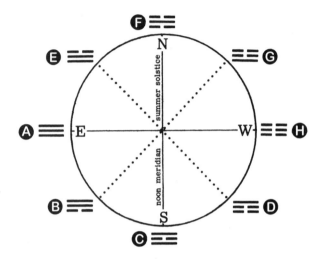

In all things there is both an "Inner" and an "Outer"

The Yi King is both a Psychology and a Cosmology—"Sciences" of the Inner World and the Outer World. The great unifier is Philosophy—the constructive analysis of both to understand our own relation to each separately and to both together. We live in a single unified world of our own perception, but one that changes as we learn to see with greater understanding and a life of purpose.

Chinese Taoism is one such unifying philosophy, the Hebrew Kabbalah is another, and Indian Tantra another. All three say essentially the same thing but with differences reflecting their historic and cultural origins.

All three should be studied by any serious student, and in doing so we should keep in mind that each was not delivered to humanity from some Divine Source (whether the Inner Divine Spark or the External Creative Source) but through the pioneering Shamans—Male and Female—who entered Altered States of Consciousness in order to comprehend the *Nature* of Inner and Outer Realities to discover how Nature itself integrates with and serves human needs in practical ways of Survival, Health, Happiness, and Knowledge.

There is no Great Mystery in their discoveries for they start from Observations experienced in both the Material World of physical substance and energies where we have our being, and the Subtle Worlds of Emotional substance and energies, of Mental substance and energies, and Spiritual substance and energies. Thus do we perceive the duality of Inner and Outer and their Unity as we learn to perceive from each higher level of consciousness.

It is these pioneers, the individual shamans, working either alone or with the help of their intimate partners that we owe the early discovery of consciousness raising practices of *induced* Ecstasy and those later of *produced* "technologies" such as Yoga, Meditation, Magick, Psychic Development, Astral Projection, and the controlled insights of Divination.

The World of Yin and Yang

"Male and Female created He them." The most fundamental observation is that of life experienced through gender: Man and Woman and Father and Mother, and then Father and Mother become parents of children who in turn grow up to become parents, and Life goes on. But, as fundamental to life as Masculine and Feminine gender is, there is more to the whole story for each is also a fundamental principle that permeates and dominates all Reality as we know it.

In an esoteric sense, "Sex" runs the Universe as the Triune Father, Mother, and Son (Child and future parent). As combinations of Two (Positive and Negative) experienced in units of Three, we realize the eight-fold interlaced Ogdoadic Star represented in the Yi King as the Eight Trigrams in two units of two combined into one of four, and then another four of the elements.

Our universe is always expanding, the earth's population is always growing, and presumably so on other planets as well. Population growth has applied to all life, not just to humanity but to animals, plants, fish, bacteria, and presumably life-forms invisible to most of us including various forms called spirits, fairies, angels, gods and goddesses, and more. Life appears as an endless spectrum.

Two and Two, and Four make Eight

The Yi King refers to Khien, The Great Male Causal Principle defined as the All Masculine Strong Creative Force, Electric Positive Energy, Projective and Penetrating, always seeking it opposite Principle, which is:

Khwan, The Great Female Receptive Principle defined as the All Feminine "Weak" Yielding Force, Magnetic Negative Energy, Receiving and Nourishing, always yearning for its opposite Principle, which is Khien.

But another fundamental observation is of Sun and Moon, the Lights in the Sky. Day and Night, Warmth and Chill, the Cycle of the Seasons and the Rhythm of Growth and Decay. Of Root and the Fruit that becomes the Seed of the Renewal.

On it goes, duplicated in the Stars and Planets in the Heaven above and Earth and Oceans below.

The Sun is The Day source of Light, Giving Brilliance and Cycles of Awakening nascent Life, defined as More Masculine than Feminine.

The Moon is The Night Source of Light, Giving Coolness and Rhythms of Rest to Life, defined as More Feminine than Masculine.

Khien and Khwan, Sun and Moon function "hand in hand" as one foursome to manifest and regulate physical Life.

And then there are the four Elements from which everything else is manifested and experienced. Here, too is another duality, but one also experienced within a Quadruplicity. The opposites of Fire and Air and of Earth and Water which exist for each other and through all of which all material existence manifests.

The Great Secret of Interpretation

There is one Great Key to the correct interpretation of each of the 64 Hexagrams in relation to any question or to any consultation. This Key is the right comprehension of the meaning of each of the eight trigrams, plus the special implications of the trigram's position in the hexagram: Superior (upper), or Inferior (lower). This principle is so important, so functional, that many teachers kept it as the final secret revealed to the disciple as the final instruction. With it, the worker in the Yi should be able to deduce the meanings of the hexagrams as applied to the many hundreds of questions asked by clients simply by considering the nature of each trigram, and the special meanings of its position in the hexagram.

With this understanding, you should not, then, have to depend entirely on the detailed dictionary of meanings provided in Appendix A. It is of the greatest value, therefore, and can be realized by simply memorizing the following short exposition of the natures of the eight trigrams, or *Pa Kua*, as they are called in Chinese.

The Basic Meanings of the 8 Trigrams
Trigram A KHIEN

Khien—Strong. The Great Male Causal Principle. The Creative Force. All male, no female—Masculine, Masculine, Masculine.

All three lines are YANG, fully projecting the Positive Male, strong and aggressive, always leading, never following. It is the Originating and Penetrating force active at the beginning of anything that then must be nourished and developed by some Yin female response before it can correctly manifest. The Higher Will: Creative, Fertilizing, Initiating. Good Fortune. It is infinite space for all creation.

Nature Image: the Sky; **Direction:** Northwest; **Body Part:** the Head; **Family:** The Father.

If in the upper position in a Hexagram, it means "The Great One," if in the lower position it does not give response easily. Also called "the Sky above."

Trigram B, Air

Air—Penetrating. Rules over mental concepts, and is very good at planning. The Planner. More male than female—Masculine, Masculine, Feminine.

Easily penetrating and easily penetrated, easy movement, and easy success in small things, with emotional satisfaction—but not solidly substantial or long-lasting. Ease of operating,

Nature Image: Wind; **Direction:** Southeast; **Body Part:** Thigh; **Family:** Eldest Daughter.

If in lower trigram, like air, it has no solid substance and it therefore, at times, becomes,

Trigram C, SUN:

Sun—Light-Giving Brilliance, Realization, Capability, The Practical Mind. More male than female—Masculine, Feminine, Masculine.

In a general way it is the best trigram: intelligence, down-to-earth common sense, and practicality of how to employ the energetic drive. Realized position. Receptive to good and rejective to bad, but fair, amiable and noble. Depicts excellence and accomplishment. Union, Self-integrated.

Nature Image: Flame; **Direction:** South; **Body Part:** Eye; **Family:** Middle Daughter.

The center position is YIN, highly receptive to the upper line (super-sensual mind) and also to the lower line (the best physical equipment).

Trigram D, EARTH:

Earth—Inertia. Body, Matter, Stability, Consolidating. The Status Quo. More female than male—Masculine, Feminine, Feminine.
A firm solid basis of things or people. Fixed and not easily moved nor penetrated. Good for consolidated affairs rather than progressing forward. Stable, holding a good position, but can be stubborn. Resting. Bound.

Nature Image: Mountain; **Direction:** Northeast; **Body Part:** Hand; **Family:** The youngest son.

If in lower trigram is too fixed and immovable, too materialistic, too stubborn.

Trigram E, WATER:

Water—Open. Strong desire for pleasure. The Self-indulgent. More male than female—Feminine, Masculine, Masculine.
If in lower trigram it is self-indulgent, lacking ambition, and too easy-going.

Nature Image: Lake; **Direction:** West; **Body Part:** Mouth; **Family:** The Youngest Daughter.

If in upper trigram, there are no great demands upon consultant.

Trigram F, MOON:

MOON—Danger, Peril. Symbol: deep gorge with rushing water. The Reckless Adventurer. More female than male—Feminine, Masculine, Feminine.
The central line is YANG (strong) but the other two are YIN (weak)—not an easy situation or condition. Indicates more ambition than good judgment, ability or fa-

vorable conditions. At best, a struggle for growth; at worst unrestrained recklessness. There is the Great Energy, authority and strength of Yang, but the Water of pleasure, satisfaction, and innocent complacency limits it.

Nature Image: Water; **Direction:** North; **Body Part:** Ear; **Family:** The middle son.

Also, the Moon trigram describes an adventurous or contentious person (or conditions). The warnings are:

1. Do not perpetuate contention.

2. Retire from contention.

3. Do not advance or retreat, but be firm and correct.

4. Beware lest being unequal to the contention.

5. One may fully contend if one has invoked the wisdom, strength and blessing of the Divine Genius, and this hexagram does indicate "advantageous to see the Great Man"—literally or metaphorically.

Trigram G, FIRE:

**Fire—Great Energy. Manifesting. The Arouser.
More female than male—Feminine, Feminine, Masculine.**

The bottom line is Yang, the driving energy of the physical body, with the emotions, and the instincts. It spells thunder and lightning, sudden great fire energy. When this is coupled with Khien, great initiating energy and force. Favorable if guided by purpose and intelligence—otherwise, regret.

Nature Image: Thunder; **Direction:** East; **Body Part:** Foot; **Family:** The Eldest Son.

Lower trigram position aspect is undirected IMPULSIVENESS. Upper trigram is more fortunate.

Trigram H, KHWAN:

**Khwan—Yielding, Negative. The Great Female Receptive Principle.
The Receptive. All female, no male—Feminine, Feminine, Feminine.**

All three lines are YIN, totally feminine (no Yang line), Pure Matter, and dependent on outside initiative and strength. Great capacity and containment. Infinite desire. Feminine.

The "Great Womb" of Nature in which all things are nourished and developed (of what has been started). Infinite response. Infinite desire, yearning to be satisfied—filled up. Solidness, stability, too much fixedness and even stubbornness—in some cases. The good side of Earth is stability and consolidation; the unfavorable, immobility, constriction and restriction. Also called "the Earth below."

Nature Image: Earth; **Direction:** Southwest; **Body Part:** Belly; **Family:** The Mother.

Lower trigram aspect—TOO DESIROUS, ruled by emotions. If for a woman questioner, it is best that the upper trigram is strong enough to "fill" her.

Whether you memorize the above basic meanings or not, there is one point that must be constantly in mind, the position a trigram holds: the upper position which is called "superior" or the lower position which is called "inferior."

The Superior and Inferior Trigram Positions

The nature of a trigram is always the same, whether holding the superior or the inferior position, but the applications and implications are different, sometimes even opposite. This fact must be constantly considered, else we have hardly even half of a coherent system. Let the diviner, for instance, refer to what is said about Hexagram 8 and Hexagram 57, where the two trigrams which make up the hexagram are the same, but with their positions reversed. Indeed, the prime purpose of this section is to lay stress upon the significance of position: *inferior or superior.*

Let us now give a condensed but adequate analysis of the correspondence of the two positions.

A boss, king, president, executive, teacher, or director holds the *superior position* to those over whom he has charge: *the inferiors.* The one in the superior position may be a weakling or an incompetent, but still holds the superior position. Of course, all of this applies only when *position* is involved rather than *ability.* On the other hand, if ability is the significant point, then status or position would be of small significance and the person of superior ability in the subject under question would properly hold the superior trigram position. Decisions about position pose no difficult problem—they are a matter of common sense.

But the question of the diviner may be more individual and personal, and not directly involved with another person or persons—a personal project, activity, procedure, or attitude. Then we have a different kind of superior and inferior. In this case, the project or procedure could actually correspond to the superior position if (and it is a big "if") beyond the natural ability or experience of the person. If one asks, "Will I find gold on this prospecting endeavor?" then, most certainly, good fortune or luck is something that the person cannot direct or control, and the project would hold the superior position. On the other hand, in many questions, the diviner is better described by the superior position—again, largely a matter of common sense.

The Diviner's *Daemon*

We have now arrived at a point that is difficult to understand for many people, mostly because they refuse to acknowledge the principle. Here it is a good idea to quote Dr. Carl Jung, a most-competent observer and evaluator, as well as a psychiatrist of highest standing. Jung writes:

"The Daemon means one's true spiritual identity (also called the soul, the guardian angel, the real director of the person, the supra-intelligence, the source of inspiration, the wisdom of the 'higher self,' and the 'intelligence' of the higher instincts and intuitions)."

In any personal question, the upper trigram position *always* represents the Daemon and those qualities previously mentioned in connection with the Daemon. In such questions, very often, the deduced answer is inadequate when not considering the relationship of the Daemon. Does the Daemon give strength or support, inspiration or wisdom, or is the Daemon indifferent or uncooperative? It will be seen that this has been given much consideration in the analysis of the 64 figures of the hexagrams in Appendix C.

(Note: Lest it be thought that the subject of the Daemon is a modern interpolation into the Yi, be it noted that in the Yi Classic of King Wan, twelfth century BCE, it is often stated: "Advantageous to 'see' the 'Great One' and also 'Time to repair to the Ancestral Temple'"—a popular formalized religious practice of the same thing, in essence.)

The Intuitive Method

Let us have an understanding of this thing called "Intuition" and its relationship with both Awareness and with the Borderland Consciousness.

In ordinary intellectual reasoning, one begins from some supposed known facts (hypotheses) from which he or she comes to conclusions (deductions) by simple basic rules of intellectual logic. But in the process of intuition there are also the necessary "facts" (hypotheses) with the resultant deduction. *What then is the difference between intellectual deduction and intuition?*

In the process of intuition, observations (hypotheses) are typically stored up in a quasi-subconscious manner (the borderland). From this stored-up content can come the end conclusion by the intuitive method.

(Note: Dictionary definition of intuition: *Immediate cognition. The power of obtaining knowledge (deductions) without recourse to conscious logical reasoning.*)

There is no place in this book for a long thesis on intuition. The main point has been to call attention to the close relationship between the following five states of "Mind":

1. Awareness

2. Dreams

3. The Borderland Consciousness

4. Intuition

5. The Subconscious

And, in closing, may I add: The Supraconscious.

APPENDIX C
THE 64 HEXAGRAMS OF THE YI KING

See the instructions in Chapter Thirteen and follow the guidance in Appendices A and B. Remember, this is not a book devoted to the Yi King as a system of Divination but to Dream Work—the practice of Dream Interpretation and Problem Solving, and Prophetic Causal Dreaming to guide the individual's immediate future development.

While not a book on divination, a short treatment of the subject is given in the final section titled "The Next Step—the New Yi King Oracle to Probe the Unknown."

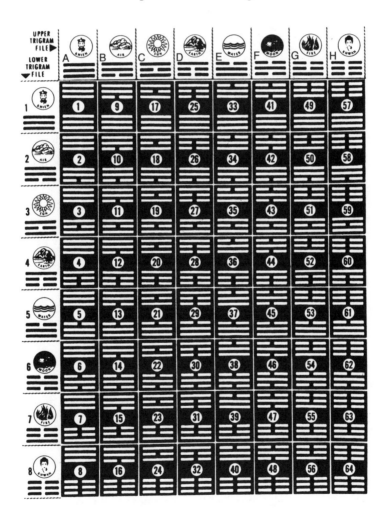

Instructions for Determining a Hexagram Number

Use the master file chart on the previous page to determine your hexagram number. Locate your upper trigram and lower trigram in the two master files. The point of focus at which they meet is your hexagram's losation and number. For example, upper trigram file #C and lower trigram file #1 point of focus yields hexagram #17.

HEXAGRAM 1—KHIEN

Name of Hexagram	Description
KHIEN OF KHIEN —A of A	
☰	Khien
☰	Khien

"The Great Transformer." Great and originating. Both upper and lower trigrams are Yang—all lines are masculine, projecting penetrating energy and force at its greatest—originating activity. Note there is not one line that is Yin, the receptive, nourishing, and developing feminine principle. Without some Yin response to the originating and starting Yang energy, there is no immediate development promised, and this development must depend on future response and support. It may be a general rule that, when initiated with firmness and correctness, there must be a result; but this hexagram, per se, does not guarantee great responsive result.

However, if the projected energy and force has good merit, it will eventually attract the feminine responsive support. This does not arise spontaneously and immediately. (For further understanding of such singular force, refer to the opposite hexagram, Hexagram 64, Khwan of Khwan.)

There is some valuable advice in this Hexagram 1. "It is to not exceed the proper limits of activity. It warns against blind, excessive, uncontrolled or misdirected activity and energy." *Do not blow off steam for the mere sake of activity.*

This is a well-advised time to "meet with 'the Great Man'" (to resort to one's higher intuition, vision, and high counsel). Counsel: to exercise aspiration and presages benefit therefrom.

For the Man-Woman relationship: Obviously not at all good with not one single Yin line in Hexagram 1. But it is good for mutual aspiration rather than active doing.

HEXAGRAM 2—KAU

Name of Hexagram	Description
AIR OF KHIEN —B of A	
☰	Khien
☴	Air

The old Wan texts state, as a metaphorical description, "Suddenly meeting a bold woman, but associate with her for not a long time—do not wed her." This means to not allow "low people" (nor one's low impulses and ideas) to have much ascendency in one's affairs, nor in one's psychology. It advises to keep one's flighty desires and emotions within reasonable constraint. But all of this is advice rather than the meaning of the hexagram.

The emotions, desires, and active instincts of line 1 (Yin) of the lower trigram invokes and receives the active energy and strength of the upper five Yang line positions. There is some urge to self-transcendence in line 1, and this should not be undervalued. (Always remember that each Trigram is built from bottom up, and hence we count lines upward from 1, to 2, to 3, and then to 4, 5, and 6.)

The Air trigrams mean "easily penetrating" and also "easily penetrated."

"Air" is the "idea" or "mental concept" and, in this hexagram condition, it easily starts something; however, it will not have great stability and long-lasting potential. However, there can be a great substantial thing even in the mental concept if it be in accordance with the possible potential, and not be too fantastic and impractical.

This hexagram is an excellent auspice for the superior person (thing or idea) to uplift the inferior. However, on the other side of the coin, it there is the possibility of the opposite—that the inferior adversely influencing the superior, knowingly or unknowingly.

For the Man-Woman relationship: from the foregoing, it obviously has a high potential for mutually influencing for "good," but if it is not idealistic, it contains the opposite potential.

HEXAGRAM 3—ZAN

Name of Hexagram	Description
SUN OF KHIEN —C of A	
☰	Khien
☷	Sun

"Sun" represents brilliance and also self-realization, and when this is coupled with the "Great Khien" we have the cooperative and respectful "Union of Mean"—union of the lower and the higher trigrams. The thinking (but receptive) person is in union with the Superior of true wisdom. Note: this also advises that it is auspicious to aspire to the union with one's "Divine Genius."

The Wan texts rightly state, "It will be advantageous to cross the Great Stream, and also advantageous to maintain and support the firm correctness of the Superior man"—or whatever is Superior in the particular situation.

This hexagram well describes the two sides of the Leo sign: (1) The truly kingly or queenly person; or (2) the insufferable self-assertive person who demands subservience rather than due respect and loyalty. An excellent augury for invoking the help, wisdom, and guidance of one's "Superior Genius" (or of a great person); good for asking favors from those in a superior position. Promises the potential of brilliant self-realization.

The ideals of this Hexagram are very high. If these ideals are recognized and lived up to in sincerity, then this hexagram is a wonderful augury. There is an inner pride; and there is also the ostentatious pride which can bring regrets and disillusionments to others. It can even spell the downfall of a project—but not very likely with this hexagram.

For the Man-Woman relationship: if there is a real loyalty and aspiration in the woman, then it is excellent. If the woman is too proud and self-assertive, watch out!

HEXAGRAM 4—THUN

Name of Hexagram	Description
EARTH OF KHIEN —D of A	
☰	Khien
☷	Earth

The lower trigram is Earth, and it spells solidness and stability, but in some cases there may be too much fixedness and even stubbornness. It is for this reason that the Wan texts state, "There is a growth of small men before which the superior must retire." "Small men increase in power" means a stubborn fixedness against imitativeness and superior direction. As in all trigrams and hexagrams, we have favorable and unfavorable sides. The good side of Earth is stability and consolidation; the unfavorable side is immobility, constriction, and restriction.

On the bad side, we have restriction of the Great Khien projecting energy; on the good side is the stability and consolidation of the Great Khien initiating force, which, by the way, is excellent of concentration, making plans and decisions, and for deciding when it is advisable for a temporary retirement from activity or advancing.

Earth represents Form. On the one side, we can have the hampering or restriction in form. On the other hand, when there is too much activity it reaches the stage where it must be consolidated and made stable in form. The Initiate in the Yi King should have no trouble in determining which is applicable.

For the Man-Woman relationship: the woman will be either too materialistic, or too fixed to a point of bullheadedness. The man is not likely to receive any docility nor willing cooperation; strictly materialistic, self-seeking, before which, can the man assert anything? Yet, this is still an excellent hexagram for the man and woman to put things on a solid, stable, practical basis—if that be the objective.

HEXAGRAM 5—LU

Name of Hexagram	Description
WATER OF KHIEN —E of A	
☰	Khien
☵	Water

This hexagram means "Treading" as in "treading on the tiger's tail, yet it does not bite." This means a person is innocently protected even from danger or stress. The text continues: "Those who tread the accustomed path and those who tread the level, easy path; those who have due caution and those who are resolute; and those who examine the path beforehand—all of these will not be harmed. The only one who will be harmed is the one who is a "low" man but through bravado treads defiantly a dangerous path, bad fortune for him."

Let us get to the meat of this. Trigram E, Water, means "pleased satisfaction, complacence." Yes, there is the Great Energy, strength and authority of Trigram A, Khien, but here it is conditioned by the Water of pleasure, satisfaction and innocent complacence. The Superior trigram, Khien, whether representing superior people, superior conditions or strength, or "The Great One" (one's Divine Genius and Real Ruler)—whether any of these, the person is under a conditional temporary benediction which grants "pleased satisfaction," but not the phony bravo!

For the Man-Woman relationship: Most excellent for the woman, though the man could wear himself out in fulfilling all her desires.

HEXAGRAM 6—SUNG

Name of Hexagram	Description
MOON OF KHIEN —F of A	
☰	Khien
☷	Moon

The name of this hexagram is "Contention." Here, contention refers more to strong, active striving, which, in combination with Trigram F Moon, is likely to bring contention unless there is self-restraint, good judgment, and sincerity (self-honesty).

To explain the two trigrams: The lower, Moon (Trigram F), is well described as "more ambition than good judgment" or the project in question may be too big, and even incompatible with present opportunities. The Moon trigram describes an adventurous or contentious person (or conditions). The warnings are: It is better not to perpetuate contention but to be firm and correct. Do not advance or retreat, but stand firm. Be careful that you are not unequal to the contention. One may fully contend if one has invoked the wisdom, strength, and blessing of the Divine Genius. This Hexagram does indicate it to be "advantageous to see the Great Man"—whether literally or metaphorically.

Remember, also, that this trigram means "Spirit."

Although this hexagram advises "Restraint and Caution," it can be a favorable hexagram if one invokes the strength, wisdom, and support of the Superior tri or person rather than to evoke one's own restricted or limited resources.

For the Man-Woman relationships: Can be very good only if the woman remains near completely invoking and quells the tendency to be active instead of passive in the relationship.

HEXAGRAM 7—WU WANG

Name of Hexagram	Description
FIRE OF KHIEN —G of A	
☰	Khien
☳	Fire

The texts assert that this hexagram means "Freedom from Insincerity." It means nothing of the sort. It is just good advice as an antidote against the great energy of this hexagram.

The trigram Fire with its Yang on the bottom is the first move out of Khwan and it spells thunder and lightning, sudden great fire energy. When this is coupled with Khien (Trigram A), great initiating energy and force, it is like setting off a charge of dynamite. If done under intelligent, purposeful direction, its force is great and correct; but without intelligent direction and rectitude, then this dynamite can have the same destructive effect as symbolized by thunder and lightning.

If—we say IF—one is free from insincerity, "There will be progress and success," so sayeth the text. By this word "sincerity," we are forced to conclude that it means "sincere self-honesty and with good purpose" and rectitude. Summed up, it is a hexagram of good auspice of great moving energy and force if the subject is truly sincere.

Due to the domination of Khien (Trigram A), there is no small assurance that all will go well just as a matter of assured "good fortune."

For the Man-Woman relationship: it emphasizes two extremes: either very favorable or very unfavorable.

HEXAGRAM 8—PHI

Name of Hexagram	Description
KHWAN OF KHIEN —H of A	
≡	Khien
≡≡	Khwan

This hexagram and its opposite, Hexagram 57, are distinctly unique (please see number 57). If one has a question which involves another person or persons, it is extremely important to make a coherent decision as to which trigram (upper or lower) fits the questioner and which fits the other person; also, if it be a project, does it belong in the upper or lower trigram?

In some cases, it is naturally easy to decide. For example, between man and woman, the lower trigram is the woman. If the project is completely materialistic, then the lower trigram is the project. There are other projects which would be better attributed to the upper trigram. This is an excellent hexagram for invoking the Great One or invoking help and wisdom.

Generally, the lower trigram (Khwan 8) is completely receptive and cooperative with Khien (Trigram A), but we also have the involving strong emotions in Khwan (Trigram H), which can be very demanding.

For the Man-Woman relationships: Thus, for instance, in this hexagram is a fine relationship between man and woman, but only under the conditions that the woman's emotions and desires are not too demanding. The lower trigram is very good for those things which have been initiated to be nourished and developed.

HEXAGRAM 9—CHU

Name of Hexagram	Description
KHIEN OF AIR —A of B	
☴	Air
☰	Khien

The text calls this Hexagram "Small restraint." This is because Air (Trigram B) is in the upper position, meaning "easily penetrating" and energetic Khien (Trigram A) is in the lower position, brooks no restraint. We, therefore, have strength and energy coupled with flexibility. It is clear that there is no strong obstruction to pursuing one's objective. Air B is the mental image of Khien A, the will, and obviously this applies largely to the first stages of a material project which will be easily carried out without serious obstruction.

The auspice is "progress, success, and good fortune," but it generally applies to first stages rather than to full development. Preliminary action can be very important, and this conditions there will be progress and success.

The upper trigram represents the "Superior One," which, in this case, puts small restraint upon the person or things belonging to the lower trigram. This could even describe getting the best of one's superior, but note: this is no guarantee that it is essentially "good." We can say that self-honesty is in order, lest one be badly influenced by attaining success in small, menial things.

This is an excellent hexagram for teaching others; also, is converting others to better aspirations. It is also good for receiving inspiration.

For the Man-Woman relationship: Generally mute on the subject of sex, the text chastely states, "If the wife exercises restraint, no matter how correct, she is in a position of the man prosecuting his measures." The hexagram indicates that she would be too aggressive, anyway.

HEXAGRAM 10—SUN

Name of Hexagram	Description
AIR OF AIR —B of B	
☴	Air
☴	Air

The text: "Under the conditions which it denotes, there will be some little attainment and progress." True, in materialistic projects, nothing big is indicated, but, for writing or for influencing other people this is a fine augury.

We have the key words: flexibility (allied to docility); penetrating easy movement without restraint, allowing for some little attainment, or moderate achievement. Don't overlook that this hexagram is the very picture of the unstable. It is an instability that advises vigilance and correctness. Also, let the subject be well aware of the fact that while he or she can make "easy penetration," he or she is also vulnerable to being penetrated. Both trigrams are identical in this hexagram!

Beware also, this is the flexibility of the mind itself and also is the "line of least resistance" urge! What is most advantageous is that the mind be firm and correct. The important place occupied by the mind is seen. That the mental image must be firm and correct is the first thing necessary to its regulation.

The text well describes the rattle-brain mind: "He hides his head and employs diviners and exorcists in a way bordering on confusion". With considerably more sense, the text states, "If the man has lost the axe with which he executed his decisions, no matter how firm he be, there will be evil."

For the Man-Woman relationship: It is required that they mutually make "good decisions" and that they do not lose their axes.

HEXAGRAM 11—MA ZHAN

Name of Hexagram	Description
SUN OF AIR —C of B	
䷁	Air
䷁	Sun

The text: This hexagram means a household or family, and the proper regulation of the household is the implied symbolism. All this is a *Deux ex machina* symbolism.

Looking to the two trigrams for meaning, we have number 3, Brilliant Realization of number 2 the mental concept. This denotes ideas and ideals brought to manifestation.

Note that the lower trigram, Sun, describes one of a well-integrated personality (brilliant realization); now this person has free course of the upper trigram being Air. The Daemon, Genius, Id, Great One does not assume the part of Jehovah in "warrior mood" and be despotic, but rather is agreeable and tolerant with him or her.

The same applies to the conditions of the project in question, if any. If the person be the negative aspect of the Sun (the big-shot megalomaniac), "stern severity" would be futile anyway!

The text does not so state, but it is good advice for the subject to look to the Great One, and also to invoke wisdom instead of falling in love with one's intelligence and reasoning mind.

For the Man-Woman relationship: Sun describes a woman who is inclined to be too dominant, forceful and masculine, on the one hand, yet on the other hand, Sun describes a fully integrated woman with a capital "W" but with great understanding and capabilities. Fortunate indeed would be the man described in the upper Trigram.

HEXAGRAM 12—KIEN

Name of Hexagram	Description
EARTH OF AIR —D of B	
⚏	Air
⚏	Earth

The text: This hexagram means "gradually advancing." The hexagram, per se, does not mean gradually advancing except in the sense that everything in the universe is evolving This quotation is from my book "The Pristine Yi King" (Llewellyn, 1989):

"Lower trigram, Earth, the body or the set physical pattern regulates or binds Air, the mind or mental image, good for maintaining anything in a stable way in conformity with certain fixed patterns or conditions."

The foregoing means making something solid, stable, and consolidated out of something that has the intangibility or insubstantiality of air—on whatever plane it may manifest—and bringing one's ideas down to earth. On the negative side, there can be too much fixedness and constriction. Sometimes, and under some conditions, the text admonition can be well taken, i.e., to bring about this consolidation "by gradual successive steps".

This is an excellent hexagram for concentration. The hexagram spells fixed laws and customs which do not bend according to the circumstances—unbending, unyielding, and dogmatic. The solidity of Earth is at the crossroads—useful versus constrictive.

For the Man-Woman relationship: Very good when coupled with fixed ideals versus restrictive chores.

HEXAGRAM 13—KUNG FU

Name of Hexagram	Description
WATER OF AIR —E of B	
☴	Air
☵	Water

The text: Name of this hexagram is "Inmost Sincerity." This is good advice, but it is not the meaning of the hexagram. The text rightly states: "We have the attributes of pleased satisfaction (Water) and flexible penetration (Air) . . . ." and then continues with "Sincerity is thus symbolized." Actually, "sincerity" (self-honesty) is a requirement to get the best from whichever hexagram is involved.

The upper trigram, Air, represents "superiors" (or high conditions) which can both easily penetrate and be penetrated, and is, therefore, condescending and easygoing to those of the lower trigram, Water. There is no contention or dissatisfaction between the upper and the lower trigrams. Rather, there is much mutual response leading to satisfaction.

This hexagram describes the easy and happy union of the mind with the exalted imagination. It well describes fiction, poetry, music, and drama of a pleasant imaginative type—also this type of person. The vulnerable side is the outsized or overemphasized pleasure and imagination—could even border on the psychopathic. It is well to notice that there is the possibility of the lack of stability in this combination of Air and Water. Hence, the injunction of the text to be of "Inmost Sincerity." It is good auspice for "Crossing the Great Stream."

For the Man-Woman relationship: One of the very best hexagrams; particularly is sincerely desiring inspiration.

HEXAGRAM 14—HWAN

Name of Hexagram	Description
Moon OF AIR —F of B	
☴	Air
☷	Moon

The text names this hexagram "Dissipation or Dispersion". This is a good description: it corresponds with Moon in the lower Trigram, and it has full course under Air in the upper Trigram. "There is a scattering of what should be scattered, and what should not be scattered may be collected." All very well, but not very realistic, nor practical. It is practical only for the truly Great One to play both Tao and Jehovah.

To make anything good out of this hexagram, the text enjoins the diviner to do the following, all with what is right, firm and correct: Retire to the Ancestral Temple (for aid of the spirits); Enlist the help of other good, capable people; Muster all of his or her contrivances (for security); Discard any regard to his or her own person; Cross the Great Stream (venture beyond the scope of this hexagram).

Every hexagram has some good augury. For this hexagram it is: For whatever needs to be dissipated, dispersed, scattered, and alienated because of its own bad qualities, this is the hexagram for it. This hexagram can be used for good, but it is more likely to spell immaturity or incapability by being over-ambitious or else scattering its forces by untamed emotions and strivings.

In summary: A bad augury concerning the average run of people. Of good use only to the superior individuals.

For the Man-Woman relationships: The advice in the above summary also applies.

HEXAGRAM 15—YI

Name of Hexagram	Description
FIRE OF AIR —G of B	
☵	Air
☲	Fire

The text says that this hexagram means "Adding or Increasing." This name is arrived at by a quaint contrivance that says, "The upper trigram is diminished and the lower trigram is added to."

The lower trigram is Fire (great energy) which is given free course by Air in the upper position. This also means energy and the force of the mind—and the mental concept. A better name for this hexagram would be "Unrestricted Energy of Fire." Good, yes, but it also can be bad when this fiery energy and drive is not under intelligent control and direction.

All three lines of the upper trigram are of opposite polarity to the corresponding three lines of the lower trigram. This means complete response between the two trigrams on all three planes. This is a most-powerful hexagram. The lower trigram is a great driving energy of the body, the emotions, and the instincts; it is given full response from the upper trigram. There is nothing saying "no" from above, unless it be one's own inherent superiority and wisdom.

The text states, "There will be advantage in every movement which shall be undertaken, even to crossing the Great Stream." Let one not get into the habit of being "restricted" when the hexagram is not of such "advantageous" augury.

For the Man-Woman relationship: From the foregoing, one can see the very good and the very bad aspects—in the long run—regardless of the temporary situation.

HEXAGRAM 16—KWAN

Name of Hexagram	Description
KHWAN OF AIR —H of B	
☲ Air	Air
☷ Khwan	Khwan

The text names this hexagram "Showing, Manifesting," and also "Contemplating, Looking, at." The reasoning is: "Shows how the upper (Air) manifests to the lower (Khwan) and the lower contemplates the higher." This hits the mark to some extent, even though it is Khwan that "manifests" instead of Air. Also, Khwan invokes the upper rather than "contemplating" it. Let us examine the meaning of the figure by its component Trigrams: Nourishment, reception, expansion, and development (Khwan) of the mental concept or mind (Air).

We may also correctly say Khwan (lower trigram) invokes and manifests the higher. One wonders why the text does not advise, "It is well to see the Great One." Khwan, being the lower trigram, is Woman (at least from the Chinese view). Should not the woman look up to her husband (upper trigram)?

Exemplar: Khwan, the woman, supports the initiatory activity. She nourishes and develops it into manifestation—the child. This is a good illustration of this hexagram. The upper trigram, Air, is the initial force of the mental concept, the plan, easily penetrating, easily penetrated. Thus, this hexagram represents the development of something that has not yet been fully developed. It is the feminine nourishment and development to a larger manifestation, or one that is more concrete. The vulnerable side of the hexagram is in giving full course to the desires and emotions, which may be excessive without restraint.

For the Man-Woman relationship: Just as all of the foregoing implies, it is particularly good for the woman.

HEXAGRAM 17—TA YU

Name of Hexagram	Description
KHIEN OF SUN —A of C	
▤	Sun
☰	Khien

The text names this hexagram "Great Havings" meaning an abundance of the "good." "There will be great progress and success. The threatening danger is the pride which it is likely to engender."

Trigrams: Khien, the great creative energy acting upon the Sun, bring Realization and the realized Self. Line 5 is the Superior One. There is a reciprocal sincerity between this and all other line positions. He or she is tolerant (even the Daemon), but there is an inherent proper majesty.

This Hexagram means the brilliant realization of the creative impulse: Trigram Khien to Trigram Sun. It indicates a current condition of "great havings" but no auspice for further acquisition—just brilliance in the present state of "having." This hexagram spells "brilliant intelligence" even to a point of initiated wisdom.

Here is a good observation from the text: "It shows the 'feudal prince' presenting his offering to the Son of Heaven. A small man would be unequal to this." This implies that a superior person should keep the use of his or her great resources under restraint, not to be the "high and mighty" nor to give himself or herself airs. Heaven will give its approval.

While no further greater accumulation is promised in this hexagram, it is a most auspicious time to put everything in good order—to consolidate one's "havings" which, in the end may assure greater "accumulation in the future."

For the Man-Woman relationship: Both trigrams are essentially masculine. It would be a rare and great woman to fit this empowerment.

HEXAGRAM 18—TING

Name of Hexagram	Description
AIR OF SUN —B of C	
![hexagram lines]	Sun
![trigram lines]	Air

The text calls this hexagram *Ting*, meaning "The Cauldron." The text mostly treats the "Cauldron" as a symbol of nourishment, whether it is for cooking food as nourishment or "nourishment of talent and virtue." "There is no changer of the character equal to the furnace and cauldron."

This hexagram (Ting) is the Great Transformer. King Wan's son sees the person much distressed because of the "transformation upon the person," but this is for the person's own good (his or her self-created necessity). The Yi writer seems to be well aware of this because he says, "The cauldron has rings of jade—great good fortune—all action in every way is advantageous." True, it would have been better said that the subject is brought to a realization of his (or her) brilliant higher self.

For this Ting hexagram, I go further than calling it the "great transformer". Ting is the Hexagram of Transmutation. This is the Great Transmutation in the High Magick of the Eucharist. This is the transmutation accomplished in high Sex Magick.

Under the auspice of this hexagram there comes the transformation aspired to, in end result. But let not the subject suppose that his or her unworthiness will pass without challenge. His attendant faults or insincerity will also meet with transformation—to the subject's discomfort.

For the Man-Woman relationship: There is none better for Sex Magick.

HEXAGRAM 19—LI

Name of Hexagram	Description
SUN OF SUN —C of C	
	Sun
	Sun

The name of this hexagram is "Brilliant, Intelligence." It is a double Sun C. The text also correctly states, "Inhering to or adhering to." The two Yin lines picture the "Ruler" (both the ordinary man or woman and the superior man or woman being fully receptive (and cooperative) to the strength of the lower line, and also to the wisdom of the upper line. In its best sense, this understanding is due to the reception of wisdom which implies "Intelligence" and "Realization."

The vulnerable side of this hexagram is that the subject acts "coarsely and vehemently and with inordinate pride." But the stronger indication of the hexagram is adherence to the right, and, in reverence to, self-realization. All of this is the distinction between the "low" person and one of sincerity, and an "adherence" to the correct! Be it remembered that in every hexagram there is the unregenerate man or woman and the worthy man or woman.

Since there are no responding lines in this figure, the two Trigrams being identical in quality, there is a demand that the subject adhere to the best in the figure. The same principle applies to the subject's affairs; then there will be free course and brilliant success.

The advice is to "invoke" the good strength of the lower line and the unseen higher strength and wisdom of the upper line.

For the Man-Woman relationship: The good force of this hexagram is entirely of the "invoking" and none of the "evoking."

HEXAGRAM 20—LU

Name of Hexagram	Description
EARTH OF SUN —D of C	
▬▬▬▬▬▬ ▬▬▬▬▬▬ ▬▬▬▬▬▬ ▬▬ ▬ ▬▬ ▬▬ ▬ ▬▬ ▬▬▬▬▬▬	Sun
▬▬ ▬▬	Earth

The name of this hexagram is "Strangers; Traveling Abroad". This is justifiable only in the sense that the lower trigram (Earth) applies to low people among high people, (Sun), the entrenched inhabitants.

By the trigrams, the fixed Earth is the restricted image (or condition) of Sun, the realized self or conditions. The better side is "consolidation" of what is "realized"; this is based upon the assumption that nothing is completed to its ultimate nor is forever stable; hence, to take advantage of the "consolidation" principle of the hexagram.

Advancement is not promised except in a small way, but consolidation prepares for future advance.

On the one side is a stubbornness and unjustifiable pride (Sun); on the other side is a firm, stable condition which contains neither need nor ambition to advance (Earth). Materialistic, fixed stability versus constricted ideals. Low men and good drives are restricted, and the upper Trigram (supposedly superiors) is in the same position, although of better status.

Probably the best advice is to quiet down the fixed idea of being self-sufficient and to seek help and support. This is not good rivalry nor contention.

For the Man-Woman relationship: Not auspicious unless the woman seeks to give solid support to the highest qualities of the man and can give up her materialistic desires—then very good.

HEXAGRAM 21—KUEI

Name of Hexagram	Description
WATER OF SUN —E of C	
 	Sun
 	Water

"Disunion. Division."

"There is diversity even though in general agreement." After opening with these gloomy notions, proceeds blithely and inconsistently to assert good auspice for all six line positions. It is sophistically explained that the "fire of Sun goes upwards and the water of the lake flows downward," hence "division, disunion, and alienation".

Water (E), the pleased satisfaction of Sun (C), the realized self or other realization. Here we may see so much self-satisfaction that one has no yen for real friendship nor deigning to ask for help or cooperation; but this, per se, does not spell disunion and mutual alienation; this would be merely the result from the "low" side of the hexagram.

On the other side of the hexagram is the humble pleased satisfaction in attaining to some realization or "brilliance." Naturally, low people fall into the stage of egotistical self-satisfaction. The hexagram indicates "resting on the oars" and the result will be as the text states: success in small matters.

There is very good response between lines 2 and 3 to lines 5 and 6. If the aim is sincerely high, it is auspicious to both invoke and evoke the "genial rain of Heaven".

For the Man-Woman relationship: "The happy union of the Yang and Yin" in Nature and, therefore, excellent Man-Woman relationships.

HEXAGRAM 22—WEI CHI

Name of Hexagram	Description
MOON OF SUN —F of C	
☲	Sun
☵	Moon

This hexagram means the "Struggle for Completion" which, in the philosophy of the Yi, with ever-changing polarity and position, is never accomplished, i.e., there is no perfect and abiding state.

The metaphor used in the text is "A young fox gets its tail wet in trying to cross the stream." This aptly describes the immature (or without due ability) with the attendant condition of more ambition than good judgment—aims, plans or drives beyond its presently existing ability or present scope of development. It is a good metaphor.

This hexagram has both good and bad auspice—very strong. The auspice of the three top lines (three grades of superiors) is good, but only under the following restrictive conditions:

1. That the person or project be not over-ambitious and adventuresome.

2. That there be intelligent restraint and cognizance of the involved difficulties.

3. Invading the Demon region after due preparation.

4. If having the bright intelligence, moral force, and sincerity of a Superior person.

5. At the proper times, to remain quiet in the confidence of his or her own power and not trying to prove himself or herself by contending with peril.

Seems contradictory? Yes. It is a perilous hexagram and there is a thin line between success and failure.

For the Man-Woman relationship: Like all of the foregoing.

HEXAGRAM 23—SHH HO

Name of Hexagram	Description
FIRE OF SUN —G of C	
䷔	Sun
☲	Fire

This hexagram means "Union by gnawing." This is a handy phrase, but not relevant.

Fire (G) is exciting action and energy of a willful nature and is in conjunction with Sun (C) intelligence and realization. There is only small agreement between these two trigrams.

There is excessive energy which is not intelligently directed, with small, diligent continuous action and not well-planned and with small discipline.

Then what can be done to achieve successful progress?

1. Start nothing that is not intelligently planned.
2. Diligent continuous action under self-discipline is demanded.
3. Instinctive and emotional action must be avoided.
4. Strong force and energy are advised for removing obstacles.

The entire problem of this hexagram is that obstacles must be removed or bested before there can be good cooperation.

The problem then is for the person to decide whether he or she, or his or her project, is capable of overcoming any blind, sudden, great emotional drive for forceful action, because from the fire and energy of the lower trigram emanates the emotional and almost-automatic drive for action—without capable and intelligent direction. Generally, the result of the activity must await a future time for its material support and full development.

For the Man-Woman relationship: Not auspicious, except if it be under good direction in the great exciting energy and drive for self-realization.

HEXAGRAM 24—CHIN

Name of Hexagram	Description
KHWAN OF SUN —H of C	
☷☲	Sun
☷	Khwan

The name of this hexagram is "To advance." All good people (and things) "advance unless close to termination," so this is not a very specific name. "Great development and increase (Khwan in lower position) of brilliant realization (Sun in upper position)" better describes this hexagram.

The lower trigram symbolizes the materialistic and its desires wanting to be filled up; this indicates some preliminary difficulties, but not persisting long.

The lower trigram is "invoking" and the upper trigram is "evoking." Therefore, the superior is successful in evoking the good support and cooperation of the inferior. The sole adverse phase of this hexagram is if the upper becomes enchanted with the drive of the lower to be filled up, and the brilliance of the upper abandons itself—but this would be only temporary and the "advance and increase" is assured, ultimately. "Great Increase" describes this hexagram better than "Advancing"—increase in realization and brilliant manifestation.

Let the superior not be hard on the strong desires or rebelliousness of the lower. Rather, let the intelligence support the lower, as if by magick.

For the Man-Woman relationship: None better. Great for the woman and, by reflex response, equally great for the man.

HEXAGRAM 25—TA CHU

Name of Hexagram	Description
KHIEN OF EARTH —A of D	
☷	Earth
☰	Khien

This hexagram means "The Great Accumulation." This is an excellent name. The text also well states, "Advantageous to cross the Great Stream."

Khien (A) is great energy and strength; however, it is under the dominion of the upper Earth (D) which is "fixed" and, therefore, works a restraint upon the exercise of forceful energy, so that what is repressed results in an accumulated strength and volume, especially of "Virtue." Certainly this is so if done with intelligence and purpose. However, psychologists know the "negative" side of this thing called "repression." Is there much of this condition of repression? Only with low inferiors who lack "virtue" and intelligent willed self-direction.

Although there are some unfavorable indications, we should note that the urge to accumulate by the exercise of restraint comes from the upper trigram position, not the lower, and is, therefore, of good result, mostly. Compare this hexagram with Hexagram 4 where the trigrams are the same, but in reversed position. This hexagram is excellent for intelligently consolidating one's strength for good planned future.

For the Man-Woman relationship: Indicates the woman to be acting in a very assertive manner, which could be good only if the man is in a state of great receptivity.

HEXAGRAM 26—KU

Name of Hexagram	Description
AIR OF EARTH —B of D	
☷	Earth
☴	Air

The text names this hexagram "Painful Service to Perform." Great progress and success to one who deals properly with the condition represented by this hexagram. But we may ask, who would "deal properly," i.e., perform due painful services both efficiently and willingly, without complaining? Obviously, a person of high virtue with a sense of responsibility.

What do the two trigrams really spell? Air (B), the mind, under Earth (D), binding restriction: At best, the enforced solution of material things. The nature of the trigram Air is "easy penetration or easily penetrated," but here the "penetration" seems to be limited to some demand or compulsion to be concerned only with small materialistic affairs, but with some due credit and reward.

This hexagram is good for concentration and for any mental work which requires single-pointedness, but again, this is generally considered to be akin to "Painful" by lazy, indifferent people.

The text states that there will be advantage in trying to cross the Great Stream. This is trying to advance beyond the sphere of rather-fixed limitations. Even though not completely successful, it is advantageous.

The highest indicated augury of this hexagram is to be busied in serving only one's higher self—the real superior.

For the Man-Woman relationship: To limit the relation to bring about a restoration of soundness and vigor.

HEXAGRAM 27—PI

Name of Hexagram	Description
SUN OF EARTH —C of D	
☷	Earth
☲	Sun

The text names this hexagram "Ornament and Adorning" and continues with "There should be free course (only in what the hexagram denotes) and only small advantage for advancing."

Sun (C), brilliance and intelligence, is limited in scope by being in the lower position. Yet, there is "free course in Sun to take advantage of what it inherently has, and to express the "brilliance" of Sun by "ornament and adorning," thus making the best of the limitation. The superior one, however, resorts to personal adornment only by dressing in a "white robe" and is satisfied to see beautiful "ornament" in Nature and the personal envieronment.

Due to the limitation of this hexagram, the best-advised procedure is the plans and activity of preparation. In this limited advancing condition, it is well to note that "proper" ornament leads to transformation; this is a psychological principle well known in ritualistic Magick. Occultly considered, Sun is the "realization" of Earth, the physical body. But Earth is the upper trigram and, hence, the urge to idealize it in some manner—by following the simple urge for beautiful customs and ethics—ameliorating ornament and "brilliance."

The hexagram, therefore, rather than indicating advancing activity, indicates a time for preparing by "adornment" or beautiful plans and preparations. The beautiful marriage ceremony is an expression of this hexagram.

For the Man-Woman relationship: As indicated in the foregoing.

HEXAGRAM 28—KEN

Name of Hexagram	Description
EARTH OF EARTH —D of D	
☷	Earth
☷	Earth

The text very well names this hexagram "Resting and Arresting" and, also, well observes that any attempt to advance will be in "error." Only the superior person has "good fortune" if he or she "rests in principle" and is not motivated into action by selfish thoughts and external objects or people.

This is one of the eight hexagrams in which the upper and lower trigrams are identical, making them almost abstract in nature. It is the fixed, constricted immobility of Earth operating to the "nth degree"—exclusively within its own sphere. The immobility of the mountain is immobile to something else.

Let us be content to say that, for all practical purposes and considerations, "Resting and Arresting" is existing strongly enough that it is almost futile to combat or circumvent the condition. Everything on all planes is fixed and stable and, therefore, no forward movement of any kind is auspicious. There is small chance of cooperation between people, and, at best, all they can do is to say "yes" to each other. The opportunity (and advice) is to consolidate all of one's affairs—and one's self. This hexagram is good for absolute body rest, when at its best.

For the Man-Woman relationship: As the foregoing indicates.

HEXAGRAM 29 —KIEH

Name of Hexagram	Description
WATER OF EARTH —E of D	
☷	Earth
☵	Water

This hexagram means "Diminishing or Diminution" of what is unduly excessive. This is not very well named. Earth (D) is a limitation or fixing of any Water (E), or excessive desire for pleasure or satisfaction; the key word "diminishing" tends to lead one astray.

Water, being in the lower trigram position, could indicate a very strong desire for pleasure and satisfaction among lesser cultured people, but the influence of the upper trigram (whether in reference to superior people or superior conditions) causes some restraining influence. However, there is some conflict between the desires of the lower and the austerity of the upper, which should not be completely ignored.

The text states that there will be "good fortune," "freedom from error," and "advantage in every movement" but only if one be unselfish, generous, and restraining his or her wrath and desires. This may seem to be an excessive "if," but the nature of this hexagram is in conformity with the "if." The hexagram spells stable, pleased satisfaction—steady flowing and not excessive.

Note that the polarity (Yang and Yin) of the corresponding lines of both trigrams are mutually different. This spells strong and good mutual response between the two trigrams and indicates very small conflict.

In the Man-Woman relationship: Good for "Sex Magick," especially as indicated by line 6—increase not subject to diminution. Fixation of pleasurable desires in matter or the body.

HEXAGRAM 30—MENG

Name of Hexagram	Description
MOON OF EARTH —F of D	
☷	Earth
☵	Moon

The text describes the hexagram as "Youthful Inexperience." It continues, "In the case which it presupposes, there will be progress and success." What this process may be is not stated, nor can I define it. The upper (superior) trigram is Earth (solid, fixed, consolidating) and in its best implication, "practicality". If one of "inability" (referring to the Moon in the lower position) is forced to become practical and tackles only what is consistent with the ability or opportunity, then there could be progress and success.

Example: A certain well-known orchestra leader had first tried to be an accordion player, but he did not have the ability, nor did he have the ability to write good orchestral arrangements. He hired an arranger to make catchy arrangements, and he hired an outstanding accordion player, and since became a very successful orchestra leader.

The foregoing shows that one can (and should) recognize an inadequate condition and yet, by resourceful practicality, still attain "progress and success." The text stresses sincerity, and implies the values of self-appraisal and self-honesty iun considering any course of action.

Advice: Do not have more ambition than good judgment. Neither envision nor tackle projects which, in being sincere, honest and practical, you should suspect are beyond your known ability. This does not mean that one should forego the idea of the project in its essential nature—there are ways and means: be goodly, therefore.

In the Man-Woman relationship: At best, only good for the woman.

HEXAGRAM 31—

Name of Hexagram	Description
FIRE OF EARTH —G of D	
☷	Earth
☲	Fire

The text names this hexagram "Upper Jaw: nourishing and cherishing." It continues, "There will be good fortune in what is denoted in the hexagram (nourishing and cherishing) if with firm correctness."

Let us see what the two component trigrams indicate by "nourishing and cherishing." We have Fire (G), strong, exciting energy operating under the conditions of Earth (D), the stable and fixed. The text sees the upper jaw as the solid, fixed, and the lower jaw as active energy (as in eating). There is a third factor, which is not contained in the symbolism, i.e., that which is being chewed. It would have to be something which "nourishes or contributes" to the objective. It has to be something that contributes to the nature of the upper trigram, i.e., stability and solidness, which, from a practical standpoint, is consolidation of the position or project.

In other words, the best hexagram is to resort to strong, sudden energy, but only to bring about some sort of consolidation of the effort.

The subject is not generally equal to the requirements, in the initial stages. It is only in the long run that the objective is achieved. Ask your stolid boss (the superior) for a favor or increased salary and, if granted, it will not be immediately. Things progress by temperate regulation—slowly. The superior environment is not easily changed or moved.

In the Man-Woman relationship: Not propitious.

HEXAGRAM 32—PO

Name of Hexagram	Description
KHWAN OF EARTH —H of D	
☷	Earth
☷	Khwan

The text names this hexagram "Falling—Overthrowing."

The lower trigram position of a hexagram indicates people of lesser culture and education, i.e. the "masses." Khwan being in this position indicates many, and strong, desires yearning to be satisfied—filled up. The upper trigram, being Earth, does not indicate much that is satisfying to the desires. However, we may say that it is good that inordinate desires do not meet with other than solidity and immobility—or proper restraint.

In the other side of the picture, solidity and stability being in the upper position represents something very good under the conditions of this hexagram, and the lower trigram, in its better phase, nourishes and supports the stability of superior people and also of projects. In other words, on the one hand is the inordinate demands of inferiors and of desires, while, on the other hand, the lower gives nourishment and support to the stability of anything. There is a great support and development of what is inherently stable—great and good stability.

No actual movement in any direction is of much value—even difficult. This is better described as preparation for advance or movement, rather than movement in itself. It is only in the long run that anything or person acquires fresh vigor for later advance. Usually the top line does not refer to a person; it refers to the invisible "ruler," one's Daemon, of the invisible results of one's past actions.

In the Man-Woman relationship: Not very propitious.

HEXAGRAM 33—KWAI

Name of Hexagram	Description
KHIEN OF WATER —A of E	
☵	Water
☰	Khien

The text calls this hexagram "Displacing or Removing." It is good advice to be prepared to displace or remove some possibly challenging people or things, but this does not make it the meaning of the hexagram.

The Superior is the upper trigram of water, which is self-complacency, and, in some cases, indulgence in pleased satisfaction, while the Inferior trigram is great strength, energy, and demanding drive. This is very good for the Inferior dealing with a Superior if the inferior is sincere, correct, and does not go too far in challenging the superior.

The upper trigram represents one's Daemon, the hidden director, the higher phases of the subconscious; in this case, because the trigram is water, there is a "complacency and pleased satisfaction" which allows one to fully proceed according to one's own conscious force, energy, and initiative. But, if one is not sincere and "correct" in manner and action, the whole thing can degenerate into something offensive to one's own superior self—which will certainly boomerang back.

This can be a very good hexagram for energetically starting something in confidence of good fortune, but the good fortune itself should be regarded as something loaned to one and to be gratefully received, and well used. The text says, "Do not tempt the gods!" If one is not sincere and correct, it becomes an excessive offense.

In the Man-Woman relationship: Not to be recommended. This hexagram's feminine aggressiveness versus an easygoing, complacent man will surely run its course into "displacing."

HEXAGRAM 34—TA KWO

Name of Hexagram	Description
AIR OF WATER —B of E	
☵	Water
☴	Air

The text name for this hexagram is "A Weak Beam." This is a fair name under the concept of being a bridge which can carry success only in small proportions. In fact, there is indicated easy attainment of success in a small way, not on a grand scale.

The hexagram, being the trigrams of air and water, indicates that there is an easygoing superficial satisfaction, but lacking in the solidly substantial. The text symbolizes this as an old man with a young wife, and an old woman with a young husband, an easy attainment of pleased satisfaction or of the desires!

Air (B) is the mental concept of Water (E), pleased satisfaction, which is easily attained, but not of long-term substantiality. Water, as the "Superior," indicates pleased satisfaction and complacency. Air, as the "Inferior," indicates a mercurial cleverness and exigent adaptability. If the Inferior is sincere, there is a good relationship with the Superior.

There are little or no demands upon the questioner. And there is free course for diversions, amusements, vacations, and also mental occupations that are not too weighty—a good augury for dealing in a pleasant way with people.

Line 5, the "King," may not carry out the requirements of the times, even though able to do so.

For the Man-Woman relationship: Good superficially, but also see the above indications.

HEXAGRAM 35—KO

Name of Hexagram	Description
SUN OF WATER —C of E	
☵	Water
☶	Sun

The text name for this hexagram is "Changing." The text states, "Advantage comes from being firm and correct, and then is great progress and success." It also states that the change is believed in only after it has been accomplished.

The text preaches that "Change" is received by the multitude with dislike, and only fairly received when proven necessary. The Sun is in the "inferior" lower trigram position, but the Sun (C) is a superior trigram. It is the intelligence and brilliance of the inferior that would be initiating the change. Heed the poetic advice of the text:

Proceed not hastily; time's a friend to thee.

Haste may wreck all; discuss thy plans untried.

First, gain man's confidence, then saddle and ride

Swift as a tiger, with the Yi for guide,

Confirm thy change with firm sincerity.

Sun, Realization of Water, pleasure brings about a realization of the imperfection of images and a reconciliation to transforming change.

This is a good augury for both dealing with "common" people (if correctly) and also with the superior! It is good for projects that are not too ambitious or on too large a scale.

For the Man-Woman relationship: Good for higher transformation if under due preparation and not carried out too hastily—good in final end result.

HEXAGRAM 36—HSIEN

Name of Hexagram	Description
EARTH OF WATER —D of E	
☵	Water
☷	Earth

The text names this hexagram "Mutually influencing, all together, jointly." This meaning is evidently arrived at by the fact that the corresponding lines of the two trigrams are of opposite polarity. But there are sixteen such hexagrams! Fact is, in all 64 hexagrams, there is always one trigram that "influences: the other trigram."

Here we have the materialistic Earth (D) operating under the complacent Water (E). The text states that "there will be free course and success" (upon the fulfillment of the conditions implied in the hexagram). Here are the conditions: Aim for stability and consolidation of one's affairs or of oneself under sincerity and correctness, this being the good side of Earth (4); but do not succumb to the other side of Earth, which is senseless fixedness, stubbornness, or the grossly materialistic. The Water trigram, holding the superior position, is complacently in accord.

This is a very good augury for consolidating one's efforts and affairs if not inordinately ambitious. There is "free course," but this does not mean advantage in pushing forward. It promises good consolidating security, resting in pleased satisfaction while doing so. Correct aims are surely effective in bringing about transformation.

For the Man-Woman relationship: Best to merely bring things to a firm foundation; advance later. Ideally, this in itself can bring about a transformation.

HEXAGRAM 37—TUI

Name of Hexagram	Description
WATER OF WATER —E of E	
☵	Water
☵	Water

Both trigrams are Water (E) and, therefore, the meaning of the hexagram is "Pleased Satisfaction, Pleasure, and Complacency." It promises: "Under the conditions of this Hexagram there will be progress and attainment." The main necessary conditions are firmness, correctness and sincerity, and not to be submerged in sensuous pleasure, per se, nor to be lazy. The text says:

Appease thyself; harmonious in thy sphere.

Single thy will, most utterly sincere.

Turn not aside when siren pleasures woo;

Search well thyself to make thy purpose clear.

Too trustful customers may buy too dear.

Still waters may run deep and free,

But mistake not slackness for philosophy.

Even the superior one encourages conversation with all and the stimulus thus derived. Both of these trigrams are of Yin nature and are capable of invoking and evoking attraction. This is the **Hexagram of Attraction.** Let there be no great attraction for wasteful sensuous pleasure. Yet there is good course in seeking and following the path of pleasure when sparked with constructive purpose or ideals. For any project, this hexagram gives the necessary preliminary attractive quality, rather than sustaining development.

For the Man-Woman relationship: Very good if carried out under the implied conditions contained in the above poetry.

HEXAGRAM 38—KHWAN

Name of Hexagram	Description
MOON OF WATER —F of E	
☵	Water
☷	Moon

In this hexagram, the text has pictured the symbolism of a tree (among larger trees) which does not have sufficient room to spread its branches; hence, the hexagram's name "Straightened or Distressed" is, indeed, an unfavorable augury.

We may see some good in the worst hexagrams, such as this one. The text says, "Even though the augury is very distressing, there still may be some progress and success for the really great man, if he be firm, correct, and persists in development."

One could emulate what this great one would do under the "straightened" circumstances; the superior man would not be discouraged by the feeling of being "distressed", but would maintain an unruffled feeling and persistently continue despite the difficulties, as did that tree.

It is good advice that one not enter into any project which is under this bad augury. Wait! Wait! Growth and development can take place even with the straightened tree.

Take note that the Straightened and Distressed comes from the lower trigram— not the upper—meaning it is a good time to seek the guidance and wisdom of the Great One.

For the Man-Woman relationship: No!

HEXAGRAM 39—SUI

Name of Hexagram	Description
FIRE OF WATER —G of E	
☵	Water
☲	Fire

The text name of this hexagram is "Adherents; Following after; Seeking; Obeisance."

This is the ideal to be strived for, rather than direct implications of the hexagram. Ideally, there is cooperation and reconciliation between the upper trigram of Water (easy complacency) and the lower trigram of Fire (strong, exciting energy).Thus, the superior man welcomes adherents who loyally strive for harmony and satisfaction.

Naturally, there is the other side, where uncontrolled fiery energy challenges the status of pleased satis-faction. But being forewarned, the person of sincerity and in-tegrity can forestall this. Then the drive for a harmonious pleased satisfaction takes the ascendancy.

Heed this poem from the text:

Wit of age employ,

Make sure thy way is straight.

Follow excellence with eager gain.

The King may sacrifice with joy.

Ideally, the fiery will cooperating with pleasure. The ordinary person (lower Tri-gram) is driven by energetic will and is not hampered or denied by the superior Tri-gram of the agreeable Water. This is a free course to energetic activity and progress, and success is indicated. But not in great things—not a great project—though it is a good augury for satisfaction.

For the Man-Woman relationship: For good results, the position of the two tri-grams should be reversed, unless it be a masculine woman and a feminine man. However, the man might gain an adherent even in a highly energetic woman if he is a superior man.

HEXAGRAM 40—ZHUI

Name of Hexagram	Description
KHWAN OF WATER —H of E	
☵	Water
☷	Khwan

The text name of this hexagram is "Collected together; Things collected; Union." It is well named, although it also implies full development.

Khwan is great capacity and nourishment, and development of a state of satisfaction (Water). There is no dispersion or separation for ill, hence, "collecting" instead of disunion. There is union between the high and the low. The desires of the "inferiors" are in accord with the acquiescence of the superior, be it one's own desires or of others.

The augury is development and completion to a state of high satisfaction. It is even pleasing to the "Great One" and, therefore, well to "repair to the ancestral temple and meet the Great Man." This is the full expansion of satisfaction—or pleasure. The averse side of this hexagram is uncontrolled, avid desires for pleasure. Excellent hexagram though this be, it is well to remember that there is an "averse" to every hexagram: too much pleasure.

For the Man-Woman relationship: In that operation known as high Sex Magick, this is one of the best hexagrams; but note well, all of the above conditions—as one must do with all hexagrams.

HEXAGRAM 41—HSU

Name of Hexagram	Description
KHIEN OF MOON —A of F	
☷	Moon
☰	Khien

The text name of this hexagram is "Waiting." This is merely advice, rather than the real implications of the hexagram—nor is it good advice in all cases. In fact, the inferiors on all planes are very strong (even correct) and, instead of waiting, it is good to challenge the incapacity of the superior position. A weak ruler and henchmen are vulnerable to the challenging strength and activity of the lower trigram, Khien.

The text states that this is "Strength confronted by Peril," but fails to note that also it is peril and ineptness confronted by strength.

The superior is in a restricted and vulnerable position; he or she cannot expect to have good followers, because Khien does not "follow." Rather than having docile followers, he or she must have followers who take strong, responsible positions, as denoted by the lower Trigram. Let the superior person call upon available material resources and the activity of his or her physical vehicles (followers), even though they may be devoid of inspiration, wisdom, and intuition but are correct in strength and activity. It is not the time for progress and advancement, therefore the advice of waiting. Sincerity, firmness, and correctness are very essential; otherwise there will be peril and restriction.

For the Man-Woman relationship: Unfavorable. There is no inspiration, no aspiration, and no idealism in this hexagram. Moreover, it tends to be combative.

HEXAGRAM 42—ZING

Name of Hexagram	Description
AIR OF MOON —B of F	
☵	Moon
☴	Air

The text names this hexagram "The Well." Saying that even though the town goes to pot, the pure water of the central community well remains as a source of supply is mere optimistic preaching.

This is the mental concept of Air (B) and of the restricted "universe of self" (i.e., the Moon). The best thing that the superior can do is to resort to the rational and logical intellect to understand the deficiencies in any project, and in one's self. This should lead to self-cultivation, and thereby one may stimulate mutual helpfulness between himself or herself and others. This also applies to inferiors. Here, then, can be the "common well" or fountain of supply and increase, i.e., the inferiors or multitudes.

We may say that the only good augury of this hexagram is the ability to use the rational intellect and, thereby, come to an understanding of internal and external deficiencies, restrictions and difficulties—all of which can lead to self-cultivation and improvement. This can lead to mutual helpfulness with others, and with one's own many and various propensities and forces.

There is nothing to indicate much progress and advancement in any materialistic project; all indications point toward correcting faults and arriving at an under-standing of the difficulties and restrictions.

For the Man-Woman relationship: Superficial.

HEXAGRAM 43—ICI YI

Name of Hexagram	Description
SUN OF MOON —C of F	
☷	Moon
☳	Sun

The text names this hexagram "Past or Completed; Helping; Completing." Nothing of the sort is true. King Wan used this hexagram to picture the final overthrow of the Tyrant King and establishment of his own rulership.

This is the realization (Sun) of the usual restriction (Moon) of all people. It promises help to be attained, and also success, but only in small things (restrictive Moon). The Moon is incapable and perilous, but Sun ameliorates the condition enough to indicate some realization, but advises not to attempt anything new on a large scale.

The ideal polarity of the lines is that the bottom line should be Yang and then the polarity alternated in each succeeding line. This is the only hexagram that fills this condition, and, to be consistent, should be the best of all other hexagrams. No hexagram is of such good augury which has Moon for the upper trigram. In this hexagram, the superior is "Dim" and inferior is "Brilliant," making it good for inferiors to outshine the superiors. The physical vehicles and the intellectual mind is superior to what little exists in the superior Trigram.

For the Man-Woman relationship: Not very good.

HEXAGRAM 44—MEN

Name of Hexagram	Description
EARTH OF MOON —D of F	
☷	Moon
☷	Earth

The text very well names this hexagram "Incompetence in the Feet," meaning "inability to advance under the conditions of Earth (D), which is fixedness." Moon is ineptness and inability, and also peril, faced with the solidity and immobility of Earth.

As usual, let us search for something favorable in this unfavorable hexagram. The superior subject is distressed and in a state of peril. What can be done in conformity with the nature of this hexagram? The answer is to work to consolidate and arrange all affairs of Earth (D) so that the peril and restriction of Moon (F) can be weathered and balanced. It is possible to secure some help (by arranging it) from solid down-to-earth people. One must attain stability, rather than having ideas of advancement. Let it be discreet and of small movement. The poem in the text states:

Adamant! Friends come to prosecute thy plan.

Advance not! Wait for aid from the Great Man!

Esoterically, this hexagram is the Formulation in Matter of Restriction, meaning "Incarnation and Sacrifice."

Under this hexagram it is well, and auspicious, for self-examination. The fifth line represents the King and is very well-aspected; this favors both the exercise of aspiration and receiving inspiration.

For the Man-Woman relationship: Solely under the conditions as outlived above—no bright promise. Sacrifice to attain stability.

HEXAGRAM 45—SUN

Name of Hexagram	Description
WATER OF MOON —E of F	
☷	Moon
☵	Water

The text names this hexagram "Joints of Bamboo," meaning literally "Regular Divisions" such as the four divisions of the day and of the year. This implies the idea of regulating and restraining, and it is only this regulation that will bring good results from the conditions of this hexagram.

Let us first examine the unfavorable aspects of this hexagram. There can be an "unregulated" drive or desire for pleasure and satisfaction (Water) under the cycle or condition of Moon, which is peril, undevelopment, lack of competence, or even restriction. For example, "Nero fiddled while Rome burned" is an illustration of the meaning of this Hexagram.

Now to the favorable side of this hexagram. What can be done, and what must be done, to get any success or satisfaction under this hexagram? The central line of a trigram is the intelligent, thinking man or woman, and it implies intelligent will under direction and regulation, particularly regulation in this case. The central lines of both Trigrams are Yang-strong—and the lower line of the lower Trigram-physical equipment—is also strong. In summation, let there be the desire for pleasure and satisfaction, but let it be confined and regulated by the intellect under will. Only under these conditions can there be the "progress and attainment" as promised in the text. This progress depends solely upon one's intelligent self-regulation. It is also indicated that recourse to one's instincts and intuition help greatly under the conditions of this Hexagram.

For the Man-Woman relationship: Can be unfavorable or excellent, all according to the above conditions.

HEXAGRAM 46—KHAN

Name of Hexagram	Description
MOON OF MOON —F of F	
☵	Moon
☵	Moon

The text names this hexagram "A perilous Defile or Gorge." In the text we see that it is well-recognized that a hexagram is the combination of two trigrams, one conditioning the other; here, where both trigrams are the same, the obvious recourse is to name the hexagram the same as the trigram, and thus "perilous defile or gorge."

The advice in the text is to maintain one's own territory and not to advance. Also, that "experience in meeting difficulty makes character." It continues, "It shows the possession of integrity through which the mind is penetrating: do this and it is of high value."

Let us examine this indication of a "penetrating mind." The central line of a Trigram represents the thinking, intelligent man. In the single Trigram of Moon, the man is in a perilous position because both the upper and lower lines are Yin, which is weakness. The physical body, the lower line, and the higher wisdom or direction, are also weak due to the upper line being a Yin.

But there is one saving grace in this Hexagram. The central line of the upper Trigram (the fifth line) represents the King, or higher intelligence. Thus we have the promise that the exercise and application of the intellect, at its highest, leads one to stand fast amidst the hazardous conditions with a minimum of discomfort or unfavorable influence. Avoid ambitions beyond one's assured abilities.

For the Man-Woman relationship: Must be under intelligent will and direction— without emotions and strong desires.

HEXAGRAM 47—CHUN

Name of Hexagram	Description
FIRE OF MOON —G of F	
⚏	Moon
⚎	Fire

This hexagram is pictorial in the text. It metaphorically illustrates struggle as the first stage of growth of a plant, from seed, struggling to arise from the surface of the earth. This correctly implies initial energy and movement amidst hazards, obstacles, and difficulties.

The lower trigram is Fire (G), sudden, exciting energy and action, but it is in the face of the Moon (F), unfavorable or difficult when in the lower position. At its best, this is in the Will breaking up restriction, if under the correct conditions. Because of the daring and impetuousness of Fire, any movement in advancing should not be undertaken lightly. It should be well noted that there is no static security indicated, and that, therefore, no great things should be attempted.

One may well call for aid from his or her own higher propensities, and the better instincts and intuition.

For the Man-Woman relationship: The lower trigram always represents the woman; its being Fire (exciting energy) suggests an aggressive woman. It may be this is why Aleister Crowley suggests in his private notes that this hexagram indicates "failure of the phallus." In any event, it is not a favorable hexagram between man and woman because it means struggle for expression, struggle for growth, and struggle for experience.

HEXAGRAM 48—PI

Name of Hexagram	Description
KHWAN OF MOON —H of F	
☷	Moon
☷	Khwan

The text names this hexagram "Union." Its implication is that the superior person may secure the compliance, help, and harmony from all other classes of people. It is not actually the meaning of the hexagram.

The lower trigram is infinite desire and expansion in the difficult, restriction universe. We, therefore, have contradiction: expansion and development versus restriction and difficulty.

Now, to the favorable side. The lower trigram, Khwan, yearns to be filled up, to nourish, support, and develop that which has been initiated by the Yang principle in the central line of the superior trigram which not only indicates the superior person, it also indicates willed intelligent direction, the requirement to get anything favorable from this hexagram.

The person must evoke all of his or her sincerity, force, and integrity to bring support of that which is indicated by the lower or inferior; and they are willing supporters—cooperation and union with others—or with one's physical equipment and forces.

Follow the advice of the text, which says, "Let the principled party make sure that his virtue be great, non-intermitting, and firm; and, let this not be done too late—before the way is exhausted." There are difficulties!

For the Man-Woman relationship: Excellent if the man lives up to the requirements.

HEXAGRAM 49—KWANG

Name of Hexagram	Description
KHIEN OF FIRE —A of G	
☲	Fire
☰	Khien

The text names this hexagram "Abundance of Strength and Vigor." Clearly, the lower trigram is great, originating strength, and the upper trigram is just plain willful, exciting activity. Common sense tells us that, under these conditions, there can be a drive to unregulated or unrestrained and undirected strength and energy.

Obviously one is warned about violent action and contention. Strong action should be held in subordination to intelligence, what is right, and exerted only in harmony with it. Ideally, this is Khien (1), the creative force, stimulating and informing the material will, Fire (G).

Let the superior man or woman use the activity and strength of the inferiors to look for permission or acquiescence of the superior to exercise this strong activity, but always under the direction of down-to-earth common sense and utility.

For the Man-Woman relationship: The lower trigram position, which indicates the female, is in this case completely masculine. Not favorable between normal man and woman.

Success of any kind under this hexagram demands natural, firm correctness and restraint. At best, promises neither good fortune nor consolidated progress.

HEXAGRAM 50—HENG

Name of Hexagram	Description
AIR OF FIRE —B of G	
☲	Fire
☴	Air

In the text, the subject of this hexagram is "perseverance in well doing, or in continuously acting out the law of one's being."

This "perseverance in well-doing" is merely an ideal, because of the simple fact that the figure almost indicates the contrary! This is one of the 16 Hexagrams where the corresponding lines of each Trigram are of mutual opposite polarity. Therefore, there is a strong rapport between the superior and the inferior that does not promise "long continuance." On the other hand, it indicates easy penetration (Air) by or into sudden, exciting energy, Fire.

This is Air (B), the mind, informing and assisting Fire (G), the will, the mental concept of physical strength and energy. On the purely physical plane, the upper trigram is strong and active, and the lower trigram is passive. Movement and easy penetration in any direction is advantageous. This poem from the text says:

Lust of result mars will in every way.

Passive love sins, where active loses fray,

And violent efforts end in swift decay.

This is the mind assisting one's energetic will, and one should not impetuously change methods.

For the Man-Woman relationship: Favorable for some conditions according to the foregoing, which also indicates that which is unfavorable.

HEXAGRAM 51—FENG

Name of Hexagram	Description
SUN OF FIRE —C of G	
⚏	Fire
⚍	Sun

The text well names this "Large and Abundant—Prosperity." This is the Sun, the full realization of Fire, energetic will. It is best to receive, maintain, and manifest the realization of the "large and abundant" (and brilliance) rather than to be over-concerned with accumulating more and for further advancement. The superior should employ the talents of the inferiors. (Note: actually the lower [inferior] trigram, in this case, has much of the superiority over the superior, and the inferior must dampen the impetuousness superior.)

This poem from the text says:

First meet thy mate, then multiply thy force.

Let not its accidents disturb thy course.

United with sincerity, 'tis fortune's source.

Then, call the clansmen of ability!

Remember, pride and insolence slay majesty.

Strangely, although the inferior trigram position is occupied by a trigram (Sun) that is far superior to the upper trigram, nevertheless there is no conflict between them. This hexagram means inherent brilliance of the exciting, energetic, forceful will. If the will is wrong or selfish, this augury can be awkward.

There is certainly no indication of high intelligence in the upper Trigram. The lower trigram is intelligent, down-to-earth common sense, and practicality of how to employ the energetic drive.

For the Man-Woman relationship: A certain secret Order has stated "Excellent for Sex Magick."

HEXAGRAM 52—HSIAO KWO

Name of Hexagram	Description
EARTH OF FIRE —D of G	
⚏	Fire
⚏	Earth

The text is named "Small Excesses." It means "exceeding in what is small." True, this hexagram indicates a restriction of excessive activity, but this hardly describes the essential nature and value the hexagram. Philosophically, and quasi-psychologically, the upper trigram is the subtle behind-the-scenes director which Jung calls the Daemon. The upper Trigram is the brooding rulership of the eight sub-Trigrams. In this case it is Fire.

Fire (G) is "exciting energy," a drive to activity, and, combined with Earth (D), symbolized as a mountain, is stable, fixed, and not movable. Therefore, this is the energy and activity of Fire partly restricted by the fixation of Earth. Here is the great value and condition that the text fails to note. It indicates the conditions where it is both favorable and advisable to fix and consolidate one's affairs rather than to continue an active drive to advance. This is the great value of the figure, and the text rightfully states that aggressive activity can only promise "exceeding in small things." One should even beware of great things or great advancement.

For those who seek Magickal implications, this is the ideal hexagram for forming and establishing the "Magickal Link" (fixation on the will and consolidating energy).

For the Man-Woman relationship: A time for practical and stable preparation, rather than active advancement in any Magick. A time for harnessing emotional drives.

HEXAGRAM 53—KWEI MEI

Name of Hexagram	Description
WATER OF FIRE —E of G	
▬▬	Fire
▬▬	Water

The text name "Disparity of Conditions or Things" intimates the youngest daughter initiating (improperly) her marriage. It continues, "Under these conditions (of the hexagram), action will be evil and in no wise advantageous."

In plain English, the foregoing describes "a disparity of conditions or things" between Water (E) (pleased satisfaction) and Fire (G) (compelling energetic action). Taking stirring, energetic action without due thought to correctness, in order to attain pleased satisfaction, can, in the long run, result in dissatisfaction or difficulty. But this is only one side of the picture.

If the desires are not inordinate, an energetic drive for pleased satisfaction could be of value; under some circumstances, exciting energy might even be necessary for good results. However, note well, there is an "if" that requires some intelligent restraint and correctness, which might not be duly exercised.

Here is a condition where, as a general rule, superiors cannot stir inferiors out of pleased satisfaction. Nor can inferiors reconcile to the stirring energy and activity of the superior. But what is so wrong about an energetic drive to attain pleased satisfaction, if the desires are not excessively inordinate?

For the Man-Woman relationship: Mostly favorable. Great drive for pleased satisfaction.

HEXAGRAM 54—KIEH

Name of Hexagram	Description
MOON OF FIRE —F of G	
☲	Fire
☷	Moon

The text name is "Untying a Knot or Unraveling a Complication, and Peril demanding Quick, Energetic Action." For good outcome, this is a necessity, but it is not the meaning of this hexagram. Actually, this hexagram is of much worse augury than the preceding hexagram.

Moon (F), by itself, spells more ambition than ability, and, when coupled with stirring energy of Fire (G), the condition is aggravated. Instead of untying knots and untangling obstructions and complications, the exciting energy of Fire makes things worse than ever. However, in some cases, the Daemon might demand energetic action to overcome incompetence or the unworthy.

Neither Moon nor Fire is conducive to binding oneself to intelligent regulations, and yet this is the only practical method of avoiding the "peril" of Moon, unless one be greatly superior. The superior man or woman may find circumstances where sudden quick, energetic action is necessary to conquer or circumvent the obstruction, the restriction, or the danger. The text states: "If some operations be called for, there will be good fortune in the early conducting of them." "Early"?—almost immediately!

Considering the nature of this hexagram, it may be even difficult for the native to make up his mind not to try any advancement whatsoever, and to be content in amusing himself or herself in unraveling knots.

For the Man-Woman relationship: Not good. In all matters it is advisable to restrict action as much as possible.

HEXAGRAM 55—KAN

Name of Hexagram	Description
FIRE OF FIRE —G of G	
☲	Fire
☲	Fire

This hexagram is the doubled trigram of Fire; therefore, the only recourse for the text is to name it the same as the trigram, "Sudden Moving, Exciting Energy." The poem from the text advises:

Take lofty ground; the tide will ebb and flow.

Distraught? May danger teach thee low to go.

Fight fire with fire, or sink in mud supine.

Troubles mean profits for men who know.

Caution! Foresee the action of the foe.

Fire! Beware, but smile with mien divine!

Let nothing scare thee; spill no wine!

In the foregoing poetry are the various courses that one may try to take to meet this moving, exciting energy drive. One should be apprehensive about this moving power and energy, and also should cultivate his or her virtue and examine his or her faults. But the big question remains: Just how successfully can one do all of this while being beset with the drive for energetic action?

Let us examine the Hexagram for the best course. The bottom line of both Trigrams is Yang, which is the strength of the physical body and also the strength of the multitudes. Let this be used as an aid. The lines of intelligence and wisdom are Yin, which is a good augury for invoking inspiration. This is the best I can see in this Hexagram.

For the Man-Woman relationship: Not good. Sudden moving, exciting energy.

HEXAGRAM 56—YU

Name of Hexagram	Description
KHWAN OF FIRE —H of G	
☲	Fire
☷	Khwan

The text names this hexagram "Harmony and Contentment." It is a fact that the ruler of the upper trigram (Fire) can get the willing and harmonious support of the subject or subjects of the lower trigram (Khwan).

The ruler of the upper trigram can put all of his or her physical force and energy in action to evoke the sustaining and supporting subjects of Khwan, the lower trigram. Thus, there is harmony between the upper and the lower, between one's higher forces and more materialistic forces.

The Yang line of the upper trigram symbolizes the "feudal princes" and King Wan rightfully states, "He may set up and appoint feudal princes to put the 'hosts' (Khwan) in cooperative motion—with advantage."

In a nutshell, the implication of this hexagram is that Khwan gives full nourishment, cooperation, support and development to the energetic action of Fire: great capacity for the awakening force and energy. We should also note the capaciousness of Khwan—expansion—as stated in these lines of poetry from the text:

Harmony spreads through all thy coasts.

Appoint thy princes and send forth thine hosts.

For the Man-Woman relationship: Excellent, even for Magick. Great stimulus to great support.

HEXAGRAM 57—THAI

Name of Hexagram	Description
KHIEN OF KHWAN —A of H	
▆▆ ▆▆	Khwan
▆▆▆	Khien

"Small things gone and great things come." Here is the great initiating Will of Khien (A) combined with the great nourishing and sustaining quality of the upper Trigram of Khwan (H).

This figure suggests that Heaven is submissive to Earth, which in this particular instance is allowed the dominant force and energy. Yang is always stronger, regardless of its being the upper or lower Trigram of the whole figure.

The upper trigram always signifies the superior, be it a person, a condition, or one's unseen identity—the supra-sensual self. In this case, it is Khwan (three Yin lines) and, no matter what this superior is, it is acquiescent and supporting to the will and energy of the man or woman on the physical or material plan. Khwan is in agreement that anything initiated by Khien shall have nourishment, support, and development.

Anything that one starts or originates is in accordance with, and assent of, one's own Daemon or spiritual identity and, therefore, progress and success are indicated.

Mankind's ingrained egotism prevents the acknowledgment of a true spiritual identity, a self-going Genius, of which humans consciously know little or nothing, but the concept is important in this hexagram.

For the Man-Woman relationship: This hexagram spells an active, extroverted, mannish woman, and a soft, acquiescent, feminine man. Make of it what you can. Full welcome to great initiating energy.

HEXAGRAM 58—SHENG

Name of Hexagram	Description
AIR OF KHWAN —B of H	
☷	Khwan
☴	Air

The text names this hexagram "Advancing Upward (in status or attainment)," and adds "Ascend the stairs and meet the Great One. Great progress and success."

The easy penetration of Air to the acquiescent support of Khwan assures progress. This poetry in the text says:

Make thyself welcome with the great; aim high!

Small gifts are sweetened by sincere good will.

But empty voids, art thou bold to fill?

The Superior rewards thy true sincerity;

Ascend the stairs with proper dignity.

This is the mental image, Air (B), of Khwan (H), the infinite desire, or mental concept of the universe. The superior pays careful attention to his or her virtue, and accumulates and nourishes development.

The rulership of the upper trigram—the central line—indicates a welcoming of the advance of the lower trigram; there are favorable opportunities to advance. Everything in high position (even the Daemon) welcomes and sustains, and develops the projection and aspiration of the lower trigram.

The very ease of advancement of the lower contains the seed of a warning: It definitely is not well to have and maintain an inordinate desire for more and more advancement. One must realize when, and how, enough is enough.

Man-Woman relationship: Not generally good. The higher sustains and welcomes development.

HEXAGRAM 59—MING I

Name of Hexagram	Description
SUN OF KHWAN —C of H	
⚏⚏	Khwan
⚎	Sun

The text names this hexagram "Intelligence—Wounded or Repressed." The text gives this advice: "Advantageous to realize the difficulty of the position." Viewed from the concept of the upper trigram representing a superior person (symbolized as "king"), contains three Yin lines from which there is no projective force—weak or only receptive—no directive stimulus.

However, there is another important facet of interpretation. The upper trigram represents one's own personal spiritual "director"—the Daemon—one's own guiding "Genius." In this case, the director is not directing, or demanding and giving, full compliance to the upper trigram; being all Yin, it gives free consent to the full course of the subject of the lower trigram—intelligent man and woman of Earth. In the exercise of, and expressing of, one's brilliance, he or she has free reign. One, however, does not get any inspiration from his or her higher self, so, therefore, the scope of one's achievements is limited. It is advantageous, therefore, to realize the limitations of the position. This means it is not well to be over-ambitious to achieve great things, but to be content with a modicum of success.

For the Man-Woman relationship: Ideally, not good. It would be excellent if the position of the trigrams be reversed.

HEXAGRAM 60—CHIEN

Name of Hexagram	Description
EARTH OF KHWAN —D of H	
☷	Khwan
☳	Earth

The text names this hexagram "Humility (but requiring Honor)." Occultly, this is the fixation or restriction in matter (also materialism) of indefinite desire.

This is materialism carried to a point of fixation. Only through extreme effort or ingenuity can there be any appreciable mobility. Hence, it is said that excesses are diminished and restrictive fixation is increased.

The only Yang line in the hexagram is the upper line of the lower trigram, which indicates that one should resort to the forces evoked from the religious attitude. Hence, humility. The subject is full of desires, and he or she may as well be reconciled to using self-discipline, for the desires will not avail themselves to him or her very satisfactorily. Aspiration may well be active but accomplishments are not much—for the time being.

The text states that "the Great Stream may be crossed," but this does not apply in a materialistic sense. Rather, it applies to aspiration.

This is the hexagram of the Fertility of Mother Earth, but, as yet, there is no life-giving force of the sun to initiate it into development.

For the Man-Woman relationship: Not very favorable, unless it be preparing the consolidation of Fertility and Nourishing Support of the Mother Earth.

HEXAGRAM 61—LIN

Name of Hexagram	Description
WATER OF KHWAN —E of H	
☷	Khwan
☵	Water

The text gives this a name which means, "The approach of real authority" which is "to inspect, or to comfort, or to rule."

The upper trigram (Khwan) is nourishment and development of pleased satisfaction (Water). Water symbolizes a mirror-like reflection, and here we have a reflection of the formulation of Desire—realization of Desire insomuch as the upper trigram welcomes expansion of pleased satisfaction. Higher Authority submits to a state of contentment.

The two lower lines of the lower Trigram being Yang indicates that the better desires, under the direction of the intellect, will bring progress and success to attaining a state of pleased satisfaction. This success in material affairs is not on a grand scale, but it is sufficient to give pleased satisfaction and contentment. The bad side of this is desire runs rampant.

For the Man-Woman relationship: Satisfactory if confined to the conditions of the above. Good for that process known as the formulation of the "Magick Link" which brings material realization at a later time of development. Full higher support to attaining pleasure.

HEXAGRAM 62—SZE

Name of Hexagram	Description
MOON OF KHWAN —F of H	
⚏⚏	Khwan
⚎⚎	Moon

In the text, the intimation of the meaning of the name of this hexagram is "The Hosts or Multitudes." There is only one Yang line which, by its position, would be a general close to his "host" or soldiers. Here is the poem from the text:

Mark well the rules of martial strategy.

To a chief of the host, the king confers the post.

Divided counsel—inefficiency!

Retreat is not an error if need be.

Seek and destroy bad faith and mutiny!

But find good men for posts of dignity.

Despite all the advice of what one should do, the augury of this hexagram is largely unfavorable and, if possible, one should pass it up. In any event, the superior should not attempt to handle things; he should appoint a competent inferior—one of age and experience. Take heed: this is the infinite expansion of restriction and inability. The only promising good is: one may give trust to practical, capable people; not good for trying to direct the project by oneself.

For the Man-Woman relationship: Nothing much to recommend it. Intelligence is the only protection. No risk must be taken.

HEXAGRAM 63—FU

Name of Hexagram	Description
FIRE OF KHWAN —G of H	
☷	Khwan
☲	Fire

The text name for this hexagram is "Returning; Coming Back; Over Again." If we accept the idea that King Wan was a true initiate in the Yi, then we are forced to assume that his very illogical, constricted sequence of this hexagram was a secret code to his followers. This hexagram is most certainly not the hexagram of "returning and coming back." On the contrary, the trigram of Fire, with the bottom line being Yang (and no other Yangs), indicates the first stirring energy and force that brings energetic action in the existing passiveness.

This hexagram is strong, exciting action and energy (Fire), having full, free course with Khwan. There is no deterring obstacle except that which is within itself, i.e., blind, indirect or misdirected active energy.

There is no guarantee that this energetic drive for activity will be intelligently directed; if it is, there will be advantage in the movement. Misdirected energy (sudden drives) remains a constant warning. This is an augury that can be good for starting, if handled correctly and intelligently, but it is not for finishing things.

For the Man-Woman relationship: Sudden energetic drive out of the passive condition—or into it.

HEXAGRAM 64—KHWAN

Name of Hexagram	Description
KHWAN OF KHWAN —H of H	
☷	Khwan
☷	Khwan

Since this is Khwan doubled, the implication of the hexagram is simply as intensification of the trigram.

There is great receptivity, nourishment, development, great capacity of wide comprehension, but of this is a mere potentiality until the action of Yang unites with Yin. But there is not a single Yang line in this hexagram. The Yin egg is nothing without the union with Yang. The fertility and development of Earth is nothing without the action of the Yang sun.

What then can we expect from this hexagram? Any project must rest in the great womb of time until a Yang force initiates the action.

If there is any promise at all in this hexagram, it is that it rests safely in the womb, awaiting the initiatory force which stimulates development—safely and securely. However, one may also receive, but the text correctly states that "If he takes the initiative in any movement, he will go astray." On the other hand, "If he follows, he will find his proper direction."

For the Man-Woman relationship: This hexagram indicates a propitious time to receive and to collect resources and sustaining power for future action based on what is resting in the womb of potentiality.

THE NEXT STEP
THE YI KING ORACLE TO PROBE THE UNKNOWN
The Complete Method of Constructing the <u>NEW</u> Yi King Hexagram for Divination

After making an extensive analysis of the 64 Hexagrams in Appendix C, it would be an unforgivable omission not to provide a good method for obtaining the relevant Hexagram in a traditional Yi King Divination.

There are many presently prevailing methods in use, but most of them are faulty in that those methods depend upon blind chance in determining the hexagram. The original method did not use such systems of blind chance, but, unfortunately, over the past four thousand years or so, methods of divination have been sadly changed and degenerated into forms of entertainment. Instead of a serious procedure to tap into levels of the Unconscious Mind, divination became an amusing game of "fortune telling" of no real value.

The resultant "chance methods" do not involve the "Director General" (i.e., the Deeper Self) in constructing the pertinent hexagram in response of a properly presented problem or question.

Here is the procedure to be used as an <u>**Extension**</u> of the *Dream ESP* system of the previous chapters. It is, in fact, **The Next Step**, or a **Step Beyond**—allowing the user to more deeply **Probe the Unknown**. Remember, the purpose of all these techniques is to *link one state of consciousness with another for the **greater empowerment of your total being**.*

The New Yi King Hexagram Oracle
Establish the Question

The first thing that one must do before "casting" the hexagram is to establish the question that one propounds to the oracle. The question must be completely coherent in one's mind and mentally asked very articulately, i.e., concise and specific. Surely one can see that if the question is not definite and clear in one's mind, then the answer will be of the same kind—not definite and not clear. In fact, the answer to an ill-defined question can be very misleading.

We are setting up the Yi King Hexagram Oracle as an optional <u>Next Step</u> to what you have learned or resolved with the preceding Dream ESP operation. Note the distinction: Dream ESP is a dual method of (1) Programming your Dream to tell you

"What's wrong" in regard to something, or things, in your life; and (2) Program a new dream to project the event factors into the immediate future with the means to causally change the future as a fix to what was wrong or hurtful to your life and desires. Now, (3) by constructing a New Hexagram (unrelated to the preceding process) we enter a new phase.

The method goes from "Dream ESP" where you see the problem to the "Prophetic Causal Dream" when you fix the problem by bringing about change. Taking the *Next Step* with the Yi King Hexagram Oracle extends or continues the development from the Causal Dream Change, or alternatively, goes *a Step Beyond* to ask the next question from a "Higher Level." This is the level of "What's the *purpose* of it all so that you can better align your life to one of greater meaning and spiritual growth."

"Dream Work" is like other techniques of 'self-knowledge': it is progressive and expansive, and brings different levels of consciousness into an integrated "whole." It may be helpful to compare these three actions to the traditional education process of (1) graduation from High School, (2) graduation from College, and (3) graduation from post-college advanced degree program.

Question: the Next Step? Or the Step Beyond?

That's your challenge. Only you can ask the question, and only you can determine which of these two steps is right for you, now! You may have to frame several questions, and then through meditation carefully select "the ONE" to ask for now. Never confuse matters by having more than one question in mind. This is not an amusing matter of "Fortune Telling," for true divination is to <u>tell your fortune</u>, and make it happen.

Cast those Dice!

Preparation: Have Pen and Paper ready to record your Lines—always from the bottom up. Procure two dice.

Step One: Place the dice in front of you as follows: On the right hand, set the die with the number "1" on top and the number "3" facing you. On the left hand die, have the number "6" on top and the number "4" facing you.

Step Two: Review the Question, and keep it alive in your awareness. This is vital, so that in step four, the "feeling" to stop is directly responsive to the question even though it is an unconscious level.

Step Three: Close your eyes, and let yourself go into a "semi-conscious" state. Feel yourself open to the Dream World, but do not fall asleep. You are in the Borderland.

Step Four: Now, with the right hand fingers (always touching the die) turn the die over in different directions until you have a "feeling" to stop. Look at the number facing up. If it is an odd number (1, 3, or 5) it is a Yang (_____). If it is an even number (2, 4, or 6) it is a Yin (____ ____). Record the Line.

You erect the Hexagram from the bottom upwards (like a house) and the result of step four is the bottom line position.

Step Five: Repeat the operation, but with left hand fingers for the next line position, and record.

Step Six: and onward and upward. Now reset the dice in the original position and, by the same method, you get the next two lines of the lower trigram.

Step Seven: One more complete cycle and you get the three line positions (from bottom up) of the upper trigram—the second trigram above the first—and the hexagram is now complete. Now, look at it, and remember that it is actually two trigrams, one on top of the other.

Finally, refer to the table of the 64 figures in Appendix C to determine the number of your hexagram and look up the "meaning."

Questioning the Oracle

On the subject of the "question," one must not insult the oracle by asking the same question twice, but one may ask many different questions in relation to the subject. Example: Restaurant Man.

A man asked: "If I get a woman partner to go into the restaurant business, will it be a success?" The answer indicated "progress and success" if he selected the right partner. He then asked this very concise question: "What would be the requirements of a good partner for this in relation to me?" Answer as indicated by the lower trigram (the woman) was that she must be in complete cooperation and "nourish and sustain" what he initiated. Again he asked a different question: "What must I be and do to get this result?" The answer was in Hexagram 8 which indicates that he must always take the initiative, but that, in this, he must be the "Superior" in the wisdom of his directing, so that it would evoke full support from her. He followed the advice and the restaurant and partnership was a fine success.

Now, when one examines this case well, one comes to the conclusion that the man most likely knew all of this in advance because he knew his own nature. Yes, in a dim way he did know it, but the Oracle was the thing that made it very coherently and strongly known to him, and he was cautioned to choose the right partner under the terms mentioned. Again, one can see that one is not limited to the number of questions—but never ask the same question more than once.

Interpreting Dreams with the Yi King Hexagrams

As a reader interested in dreams, are you surprised to learn that it will help you to interpret a dream by casting a hexagram for that purpose? Perhaps not, if you have digested the contents of this book. Perhaps a number of readers have already divined the fact that practice with the Yi King puts one closer to the "Knowledge and Conversation" of the Borderland Consciousness and, thereby, enhances one's ability to have better and better informative and valuable dreams.

It works both ways: the better the dream practice, the better one can work well with the Yi King Oracle. This is no fanciful theory. Indeed, many have already seen that it is possible to contact the Borderland to the extent of acute and significant awareness, so that one can get much without taking recourse to either the dream technique or the Yi King Oracle. Actually, this is what the "Restaurant Man" in our exemplar did. He finally developed the ability to see and recognize his intuition without any need of having his intuition told to him through the Yi King Oracle.

Many of our readers will want to have a working knowledge of the Yi King, which is more than merely reading the meanings of the 64 Hexagrams in this text. Therefore, in this section you will learn the full rationale of deducing the many ramifications of the application of each hexagram by learning how to synthesize the implications of the two trigrams which go to make up the hexagram. This is very valuable and the author knows of no works except his own which have given any clues in this that are worthwhile or adequate.

How the Yi can Influence Dreams

Before outlining the Trigram Method, there is one more thing that is well to mention about the Yi King in connection with dreams. The author knows of a number of people who have chosen some particular hexagram's nature to function to set the pattern he or she would like for the dreams to conform. The Dream Technique is:

1. Select a hexagram, meanings of which to use to influence your dreams.
2. Upon retiring for sleep, go over meanings of the hexagram until fully drowsy.
3. Drift into a sleepy state beyond your ability to meditate.

Generally, it will require several nights of practice before you will experience results of dreaming in conformity with this method. In other words, you are *training* the Sub-Conscious Mind to respond to this technique. "Training" is always the road to advanced development of any skill.

The Trigram Method of Deduction

The beginner may have some strange notions about any and all systems of divination. A common idea is that any good method should give a specific answer to a specific question.

On this subject, let us examine the possibilities of the 64 Hexagrams of the Yi King. First, the number of common questions. There are certainly no less than 100 different common questions or subjects of inquiry for each. When these are to be answered by one of the 64 Hexagrams, we have 6,400 different "answers," of many words—too many words—and too complicated and involved for practical use.

There is a way to get around this problem. It is by the method of Trigram Analysis.

There is some necessary deduction and induction practice in order to arrive at specific answers, but it is all very simple when one follows the rules outlined here. Above all, you may be assured that you do not have to develop special psychic abilities for divination to arrive at a good interpretation of the oracle—just some common sense deduction, coupled with a modicum of facile deduction, which should ultimately be memorized.

In short, you do not need to have the "fortune-telling" talent that is so necessary when using the King Wan system of hexagram interpretation.

When one considers the fact that there is no such thing as a "hexagram," as such, but that the 64 hexagrams are made up of a combination of any two of the eight trigrams, the following procedure of interpreting each hexagram is seen to be a coherent and efficient method for wide application.

The Eight Trigrams (Pa Kua)

There is one Great Key and only one (almost secret) to the interpretation of each of the 64 Hexagrams in relation to any question or to any consultant. This Key is the right comprehension of the meaning of each of the eight trigrams, plus the special implications of the trigram's position in the hexagram, upper or lower. The worker in the Yi should be able to deduce the meanings of the hexagrams as applied to the hundreds of questions that may be asked, simply by considering the nature of each trigram, and the special meanings of its position in the hexagram. He or she would not, then, have to depend entirely on the list of meanings, which will presently be given.

Try to memorize the following short exposition of the natures of the eight trigrams, or Pa Kua, as they are called in Chinese.

#A Khien.	The Great or higher will. Starting or initiating … projecting: Masculine. It directs and leads and never follows. The great manor great force. If the upper trigram means "The Great One." If in lower trigram, does not give response easily.
#B Air.	Easily penerating and easily penetrated. The mind or mental concept, Particularly 'ideas.' If in lower trigram, like air, it has no solid substance and is therefore, at times, unsubstantial; small things; short lasting.
#C Sun.	Brilliance: Realization: Capability: Union. Self-integrated. Intelligence. In a general way it is the best trigram. Realized position. receptive to good and rejective to bad, but fair, amiable and noble.
#D Earth.	Body: Matter: Stable: Good for consolidation of things. If in lower trigram is too fixed and immovable—too materialistic—too stubborn.
#E Water.	Placid still water which is pleasure, pleased satisfaction, or complacency. If in lower trigram it is self-indulgent, lacking ambition and too easy going. If in upper trigram, there are no great demands upon consultant.
#F Moon.	"A deep gorge of rushing water," hence danger or peril. Restriction; incapable; immature. Sometimes more ambitious than good judgment. though an unfavorable oracle generally, it bodes well if one restricts ambitions to the sphere of capabilities—or to the conditions.
#G Fire.	Like #A Khien, this is also will but not the "high" will of Khien. Motion; exciting energy; active will. Often sudden. Lower trigram position aspect is undirected IMPULSIVENESS. Upper trigram is more fortunate.
#H Khwan.	The "Great Womb" of Nature in which all things are nourished and developed (of what has been started). Great capacity and containment. Infinite desire. Feminine. Lower trigram aspect—TOO DESIROUS, ruled by emotions. If for a woman questioner, it is best that the upper trigram is strong enough to "fill" her.

The first thing that is required of the Yi operator is to have a good working knowledge of each of the eight trigrams; however, after one has worked with this system for a relatively short time, and has referred to the following exemplar and technique of interpreting the answers, then one almost automatically gets a working knowledge of the meanings of the eight trigrams without any contrived effort at memorizing.

Refer back to the instructions in Chapter 13, and Appendices A and B in particular—and then *just do it!* Dream Work increases your Life by a full third, and integrates Conscious with the Unconscious to be more than you are, and all you can be.

GLOSSARY

A glossary is not a dictionary but a list and description of words, phrases, concepts, and techniques as used within the particular book.

The descriptions used, however, are not arbitrary. Though they are "standard," they do directly relate their meaning and particular application to their usage as expounded in this particular area of practical application. In this glossary I have tried to do so in particular regard to Dream Work and to techniques drawn from ceremonial magick, archetypal psychology, symbol science, and the ancient Yi King (aka the I Ching).

Ceremonial magick and the "secret" orders that developed particular methodologies should no longer be perceived as isolated and elitist but as simple variations on a common theme—that of integrating the disparate elements of the human psyche and to provide a roadmap to the development of the as yet unrealized potentials of the Whole Person. Their graded curriculums are like those structured for any serious study and our eclectic study of them provides an expanded understanding coincident with our broader knowledge and understanding of both inner and outer worlds. See, in particular, for further understanding, our book *The Complete Magick Curriculum of the Secret Order G∴B∴G∴*.

The goal of all programs of self-development whether set in a framework of ceremonial (or "high") magick, self-help, psychological therapies, the various yoga's, the martial arts, Qabalistic path-working, shamanic practices, or any of the many spiritual paths, is summed up in my favorite phrase: *To Become More Than You Are and All you can be.* In other words, to grow, to develop your innate powers into skills, and to fulfill the biblical promise (shared by most traditions) that we are all created in the image conceived by the Creator Source of our being, and hence must have all the attributes of deity albeit we are in the process of making that image reality. As has been said through the ages, "We are Gods (and Goddesses) in the Making."

The premise is that we can and should accelerate the natural evolutionary process that brought us where we are today by taking individual responsibility for what the esoteric traditions name the "Great Work" and which I also call the "Great Adventure."

But it does mean work—work on Self through a serious and structured developmental program whether that of a magickal order or that found in books and online courses, or as self-developed to fit your own particular needs and circumstance. Your opportunities are no longer geographically limited to the lodge system or to membership in organizations that may have particular agendas beyond facilitating the Great Work.

The Great Adventure is a journey we must all travel. The more you know about the territory ahead, the better can you map out your own road from your particular starting point and adjusting to circumstantial detours and short-cuts, taking opportunities for side trips to visit subjects of interest, but always looking ahead to the goal of *Becoming More Than You Are.*

Carl Llewellyn Weschcke
June 21, 2014

Abramelin the Mage: Supposedly (because we have no historic verification) an Egyptian magician who taught a unique system of Magick to a German also bearing the name Abramelin (1362–1458). Recorded in a near diary form (a "Grimoire"), it was translated by Samuel Liddell MacGregor Mathers into English with the title *The Book of the Sacred Magic of Abramelin the Mage* in the late nineteenth century to become an important text to the Hermetic Order of the Golden Dawn and then to Aleister Crowley's Magickal Cult of Thelema.

Adepthood: An adept is "master" of particular skills. Within esoteric groups and magickal orders, the achievement of adepthood is often accompanied by ritual *initiation* into one or more particular "grades." In some, this means no more than the completion of a study curriculum as distinct from the *mastery* of that same curriculum. In Crowley's restructuring of the Golden Dawn grade system for his group, we have:

> Student
> Probationer—The Order of the Golden Dawn
> Neophyte
> Zelator
> Practicus
> Philosophus
> Dominus Liminis—The order of the RC (Rose Cross)
> Adeptus Minor
> Adeptus Major
> Adeptus Exemptus
> Babe of the Abyss—The Order of the S. S. (Silver Star)
> Magister Templi
> Magus
> Ipsissimus

In other systems, "adepthood" is not as high an achievement as a "Master" who has accomplished true psychological integration and advanced psychic skills so as to control his own destiny free of new karma. In Theosophical and other esoteric literature, the "Master" is a human being who has attained such a high spiritual level as to no longer need physical incarnation and who then serves to help advance all of Humanity.

Adonai: One of the many names for God in Hebrew. In magickal practice based on the Kabbalah, different names are ritually associated with the psychic centers.

See Israel Regardie's *The Middle Pillar*, 2002, Llewellyn

Aeon of Horus: Following the channeling of *Liber Legis—(which see)*—The Book of the Law—in 1904, Crowley believed he was to lead a new age, the *Aeon of Horus* replacing the older matriarchal *Aeon of Isis* and the patriarchal *Aeon of Osiris*. The *Aeon of Horus* is based on the magical union of male and female polarities, and replaces all repressive religious traditions. According to Kenneth Grant, the *Aeon of Horus* will be followed by that of *Ma'at*, the Egyptian goddess of truth and justice.

Age of Aquarius: The zodiacal age of approximately 2,150 years length following the Piscean Age. The *spirit* of these Ages is expressed in the symbolism and general astrological characteristics of the zodiacal sign. As the Piscean Age is identified as the age of Christianity (and its authoritarian offshoots), the Aquarian Age is associated with the "New Age" which Carl Jung believed to have begun in 1940. The general association ascribed to Aquarius is that this will be the Age of Man, of Intellect rather than Emotion, and of self-responsibility rather than the *shepherd's crook* of patriarchal (and patronizing) religion.

While the ending of on age and the beginning of another is theoretically well determined by the astronomical position of the Sun at the Spring Equinox, even that is debated as occurring in a range from 2012 to 2374. As a practical matter, like "morning" or "evening," the transition between zodiacal ages is indefinite and extends over several hundreds of years and the "old age" gradually diminishes and the "new age" gradually becomes dominant. Much of the transition is marked by conflict and controversy not only in human affairs but in extremes of weather and earth movements. It's as if everything is "stressed."

The Aquarian Age demands that Knowledge be applied to Man's Spiritual Needs, and that schools as "places of knowledge," become the temples (not that temples become schools!).

There is no real secrecy in the Age of Aquarius—no magical secrets that only the initiate can attain. Esoteric Knowledge is coming out into the open to provide the opportunity to everyone who can to "walk with the Gods." The World of the Mind is the new dimension for exploration—it is Inner Space through which we travel now. Our scientific and technological thrust must direct itself to saving the planet and opening the inner doors of consciousness as well.

There are today opportunities for people to come together in learning Esoteric Knowledge, in research and the sharing of discovery, in participation in the reviving Nature Religion, and in learning how it is that Man and Woman can liberate each other.

The new *Aeon of Horus*, the demands of world crisis, requires us to make of our spiritual knowledge a living and growing knowledge, not a static faith. That is why we make our celebrations renewals and conventions of discovery and teaching as well as festivals. We take joy in the responsibility that the Age thrusts upon us, for with it is the opportunity for a tremendous leap forward in spiritual evolution.

Man is balanced upon a precipice—but he has the opportunity to ascend to the Gods if he chooses not to fall. He must, like Icarus, make his own wings if he is to fly—but he must turn to the guidance of proven Knowledge and Technique if, unlike Icarus, his wings are to carry him through to his victory.

Suggested Reading:

Slate, Joe H., and Carl L. Weschcke. *Communicating with Spirit*. Woodbury: Llewellyn 2015.

Alchemy: The alchemy of the occultist and of sex magick is the transformation of the 'baser' self into the 'gold' of the higher self. The procedures, tools, and materials of the *physical* alchemist become symbols for the psychological and magickal operations of the occult alchemist.

All-knower: The Higher Self, and the object of magickal and spiritual growth practices and of psychological integration.

Alphaism: *Alphaism* **means first or beginning because** *alpha* **is the first letter of the Greek alphabet. Alphaism was the beginning of the G∴B∴G∴ Instruction Sex Magick. Alphaism simply means no sexual intercourse. Erotic thoughts of imaginations should not even be entertained in the mind during the one or two months that the practice was required.**

Instead of sex, the Alphaist member was to begin with the first verse of the first chapter of The Book of the Law, and take one sentence every day, in sequence, and meditate/concentrate on that sentence for at least an uninterrupted fifteen minutes one or more times daily. "Beware against making an intellectual study of this book. This is a very cryptic book, and is beyond intellectual rationalization. Get what you are capable of getting by inspired meditation."

Concentration is defined as: "Close mental application or exclusive attention." The mental activity is confined to a definite point. When one visualizes tracing a pentagram in green light, one must really concentrate in order to make it subjectively real.

Ancestors: (Yi King/I Ching) In many of the Hexagrams there is reference to "going to the Ancestral Temple." In occidental thought, this means to try to get inspiration from the Collective Unconscious and perhaps from the subconscious. It implies that intellectual analysis is not enough.

Anima: The unconscious feminine archetype that a man possesses (or, sometimes, that seems to possess or dominate him). It focuses in emotion, expresses through relationships, and manifests in creativity. It is structured to contain not only the Eternal Feminine but the Male Self's experience of the feminine throughout all his lives. In his current life, this sensitive feminine inner self is sometimes repressed to manifest in aggressive male behavior or in psychological and physical abuse of women and in the repression of women in particular cultures where aggressive male behavior is culturally dominant.

Carl Jung believed that anima development goes through four stages:

1. The focus on the external feminine as an object of desire. This often includes attraction to various fetishes and fantasized behavior.
2. The focus is on women as persons of intelligence and personal power capable of self-reliance and personal success.
3. The focus is on women's spiritual qualities and his respect for her as a mother and the progenitor of the future humanity.
4. The focus is on the woman as an individual, and as one who both expresses and projects a particular feminine wisdom.

Animus: The unconscious masculine archetype that a woman possesses as unconscious masculine attributes and potentials. Jung viewed the animus as being more complex than the anima, and that women have a host of animus images while the male anima consists only of one dominant image that is early on projected as the "object of desire."

The Animus development also goes through four stages:

1. The focus is on the male as the personification of pure physical power, i.e., the athlete, the warrior, the hunter, the defender, the leader.
2. The focus is on the male as the initiator of planned action and of romance including the arts of seduction and love. At its best, he intuitively knows what "turns her on."
3. The focus is on the man as teacher, interpreter, discoverer, adventurer, pioneer, inventor, innovator, the "King."

4. The focus is on the man as the incarnation of meaning and mediator of spiritual truth. He is the "messenger of the gods" and the helpful guide to her spiritual growth.

Anima and Animus: In a positive and dynamic relationship between a Man and a Woman, the respective archetypal functions are to *initiate* the progressive development of these phases in the other. In a "bad" relationship, the negative aspects often manifest in male aggression and female "bitchiness"—each to the detriment of the other. Sometimes, there is progression into a healthy relationship, but just as often, each hurts the other and themselves as well. Jung himself warned that every personification of the Anima and Animus have both a light and dark aspect. They can bring life-giving development and creativity to the personality, or they can cause petrification and psychotically "death."

In Magickal Working and as expressed through Dream Work, Male and Female/Anima and Animus, are the empowering forces that energize and guide spiritual growth. In Magick each "incarnates" god or goddess; in Dream Work each appears in the archetypal role most meaningful to the situation.

Aquarian Age: See Age of Aquarius.

Archetypes: Archetypes are "forms" carrying the inherited experience of each person through many lives and shared with those of other people and (I speculate) those of other life forms and perhaps even of the evolutionary "program" from the *Beginning. ("In the Beginning was the Word," and the Word was the evolutionary Program guiding all development and manifestation down through Time.)* Thus there are universal experiences of *Mother, Child, Defender,* and *Provider,* as well as a particular Soul's cumulative experience of *Mother* as modified by the individual's personal experience of *Mother.* But even before the first *Mother* there was the idea of *Mother* serving as the prototype of all *Mothers* in whatever form *Motherhood* has taken.

As innate, universal prototypes that we experience both spontaneously or through conscious invocation, each archetype serves as a Symbol for ideas and may be used to interpret observations in both objective and subjective perception. A group of memories and interpretations associated with an archetype is a "complex," such as a "mother complex" associated with the mother archetype.

Carl Jung treated the archetypes as *psychological organs,* analogous to physical ones in that both are morphological constructs that arose through evolution. Archetypes are the basic forms made concrete by recurring images, symbols, or patterns embodying common human "drives" and "actions" such as the Quest, the Community, the Creative Source; or recognizable character types such as the

Hero, the King, and the Magician; symbols such as the Apple or Snake, the Lion and the Horse, and other images that have all been laden with meaning through human history. These Forms are true objects of study that can provide us with real knowledge pertinent to our needs.

Augoeides: *Augoeides* is an obscure term meaning "luminous body" in reference to the planets and also to the Daemon of the ancient Greeks. Aleister Crowley used the term in reference to the Holy Guardian Angel of Abramelin (see above) and the Atman of Hinduism. In modern Esotericism, the Atman is the highest body of consciousness.

Babalon: Mother Earth. Also called the *"Scarlet Woman"* by Aleister Crowley as the ruling spirit of Earth. Crowley said Babalon was the goddess of the New Aeon as found in Thelema, the cult he founded in 1904. She represents the female sexual impulse and the most fertile Great Mother, the womb of all life and the mother of each of us. She can be invoked into a living woman as priestess in working Sex Magick to manifest the energies of the *Aeon of Horus*. She is the Liberated Woman in real life and the archetypal *Anima* within the *Persona* of every man and woman.

It is Babalon who gives birth to Life and Beauty, and who transforms men into Masters of the Universe for she frees them of fears and inhibitions. In Sex Magick she becomes the "Scarlet Woman" and the mixture of semen with menstrual blood is called the "menstruum of the lunar current."

Her number is 777, and her symbol and sigil is the seven-pointed star drawn and visualized in one continuous line. This is the same Star seen in the 17th Tarot Trump bearing the same name where she is commonly represented as a naked woman kneeling at the edge of a body of water pouring water from two vessels, sometimes one onto the ground but other times both into the water. The card shows the Hebrew letter, *Tzaddi* with the divinatory meaning of spiritual guidance, hope, help; the 28th path on the Tree of Life connecting Yesod to Netzach.

Barbarous Words: (Quoted from the Llewellyn Encyclopedia) "These are really 'words of power,' whether intelligible or not. Originally, the name comes from the languages spoken by the 'barbarians,' those who did not speak Greek when the Greeks thought they had invented civilization."

"In ritual, barbarous words and names don't have to make sense or be understood by the ritualist. Many are derived from Hebrew, ancient Egyptian and Persian; some are based on the Enochian language provided to us by Dr. John Dee. Rather than rational sense, they make emotional sense with the drama.

"There is some evidence—see Patrick Dunn's book, *Magic, Power, Language, Symbol: A Magician's Exploration of Linguistics*—that experienced magicians created certain barbarous words without regard to proper language but entirely to have a magical effect. Or, rather, the magician spontaneously speaks these words without plan as if derived from or through the Sub-Conscious Mind. It is, perhaps, related to 'speaking in tongues' where a person speaks with no awareness of what she is saying."

Esotericist Dion Fortune writes: "Upon the subtler planes are many different types of force, each with its own vibration-rhythm; if the rate of that rhythm can be discovered, and either its root or prime factors be ascertained, and sounds be formulated which have the vibration-rate of the several factors, and these be enunciated in sequence, they will evoke the complementary vibration in the subtle body which corresponds to the plane it was intended to evoke, just as musical tone causes the color to which it bears a ratio to rise in consciousness. This is the rationale of the use of Sacred Names and Words of Power." *(The Esoteric Orders and Their Works)*

Barbarous words have been used in shamanic chants, religious and magickal ritual, in spell work, and in Wiccan practices. An example for opening the Circle:

Facing East, chant *Ecko, Ecko Azarak*   (EH-koh,Eh-koh AH-zah-rahk)
Facing South, chant Eko, Eko, Zomelak   (EH-ko, EH-ko ZOH-meh-lahk)
Facing West, chant Eko, Eko, Cerunnos   (EH-ko, EH-ko kehr-NOO-nohs)
Facing North, chant Eko, Eko, Aradia   (EH-ko, EK-ko ah-RAH-dee-ah)

Suggested Reading:

Dunn, Patrick: *Magic, Power, Language, Symbol: A Magician's Exploration of Linguistics*, 2008, Llewellyn

Borderland Consciousness: I will quote Louis T. Culling for emphasis: "the dream state is the Borderland Consciousness state. *The importance of the ability to function in a quasi borderland-state may well be more than half of the technic of Magick.* It is involved in making the IMAGINATION to be SUBJECTIVELY REAL. Without this, a large part of Magick is a futile thing."

He describes the Borderland Consciousness as approximately 15% awake and 85% asleep. Regardless of the actual percentage, these states are also called the hypnagogic and hypnopompic states of being awake and falling asleep and being asleep and waking up. It is also called the *Borderland State*. It is during this state of consciousness when we are most receptive to images, symbols, impressions, sounds, ideas, and feelings. It is also a state very receptive to Intuition.

Borderland State: An alternative state of consciousness in which the demarcation between ordinary reality and subjective reality disappears, and that which is built in the imagination becomes magickally and psychologically real. The woman partner in Sex Magick becomes the Goddess incarnate.

The aim of the *G∴B∴G∴* practice of Dianism is to continue sexual union until trance occurs. This not the trance of hypnosis, or of spiritual or shamanic practices, but rather a state characterized by poise and non-movement. The sexual stimulation is felt, but controlled and the focus is on consciousness and not the body. Louis Culling wrote: "A hallucinatory meditation may be achieved, in which one is submerged in spiritual inspiration and aspiration."

It requires two hours or more "to build up the energized enthusiasm of the Magickal Imagination which gives one's thoughts subjective reality." It should be felt as a *force field* about the couple. Some may even see it as a glowing aura.

Calypso borealis: A variety of orchid also known as Fairyslipper and Calypso bulbosa.

The sepals and petals are poetically described as fairy wings, while its large sac, striped and mottled with deep rose color and variegated with yellow spots and fine white hairs give the blossom the appearance of a beautiful butterfly poised on the stem. As a medicinal herb, the bulbs are chewed or the flowers sucked to treat mild epilepsy.

The bulbs have also been eaten raw by young Native American Indian women to increase the size of their bust. Otherwise, they are usually boiled before being eaten.

There have been unverified claims that the combination of appearance and perfume have mild consciousness altering effects.

Calypso Moon Language: I am rather at a loss to give definition to this. There is some indication that it closely resembles Modern Greek, while Culling calls it a quasi-Enochian Language. Researching, I find that Calypso is a West Indian musical style influenced by jazz; it's also a small species of orchid (*Calypso borealis*), having a flower variegated with purple, pink, and yellow that grows in cold, boglike localities in the northern part of the United States. It is also the name of a tiny moon of the planet Saturn, discovered in 1980, and in 1983 named for the goddess Calypso who detained Odysseus for seven years in Homer's *Odyssey*. And, finally, it is a fashion in which women tie a knot in their shirt to bare her waist.

Causal Self: Basic to esoteric (occult) science it the recognition that each person <u>is</u> (not just has) many bodies or "envelopes" or levels of consciousness, substance, and energy variously working together as a composite. As physically incarnate beings, we are primary focused in the physical/etheric body but we are also simultaneously functioning in the astral (emotional), mental, and causal bodies. Of far less concern for us at this stage of our being is a second composite of still higher bodies functioning independently of the first composite.

As the alternate name indicates, the astral is the *vehicle* for our emotionality. And just as the name suggests, the mental is the vehicle for our mentality, while the causal is the vehicle for what we commonly think of as our spirituality.

It can be said that the basic lessons of esoteric science and magickal practice are how to focus, experience, and operate in and with these bodies, and thus turning into vehicles of purposeful activity at (not <u>on</u>) each level or *plane* of our whole being as contained in this first composite.

We can't explore all the details of this in a single entry in this glossary. Most readers are somewhat familiar with the "out-of-body" experience otherwise known as *Astral Projection* in which the focus of consciousness is centered within the astral vehicle which can then "travel" (but not in the same manner as the physical body moves about) to experience and act in this non-physical dimension. But, remember, in our emotionality, we already experience, act, and react through our astral "self." Likewise, through our mentality, we do function in and through our mental self.

But "feeling" and "thinking" are not the whole story for these bodies any more than "walking about" is the whole story for the physical body, and—by now—it should be clear all function together but in different degrees of awareness and <u>willful</u> intention. Will is the primary function of the Causal Self, and integration of the physical/energy, emotional and mental bodies, and spiritual will is the goal of incarnation and hence of all esoteric, magickal, and "spiritual" practice.

I placed that word, spiritual in quotes because it is one of the most misunderstood and misused terms. We are Spirit—<u>not</u> a spirit—but SPIRIT. Spirit, like Consciousness, extends everywhere even as we function as individual conscious and spiritual entities. Spirit and Consciousness function in all our bodies and through Spirit and Consciousness we potentially can function at all levels and depths of the Cosmos.

But our concern is with Spirit expressed through WILL in the Causal Self. Will means purpose, and to function as the Causal Self means we have to a Vision of our purpose in each and all the lives we live. To gain that vision requires the integration, under Will, of all the lower selves, and with that consciousness becomes centered in the Causal Self. The Causal Self carries the essence of all previous lives and thus is the summation of all we've been and are.

The Causal Self is NOT the Soul. The Ultimate Individuality that we mean by the word *Soul* is part of a yet higher composite—but we can refer to the Causal Self as the "Son" of the Soul.

One great difficulty arises because spirituality is thought to be the province of religion, and the institutions of religion limit themselves and their adherents to rigid theological interpretations of scriptures written down long ago within specific cultural environments vastly different than today. The truth is that spirituality is not religion but involves study of the higher levels of the psyche and an understanding of their role in the growth of the Whole Person and their beneficial applications to personal life and cosmic relationship.

CONSCIOUSNESS MODEL Based on Theosophy:

Logos	*Adi*	Father, Son, and Holy Ghost
	Anupadaka	Son and Holy Ghost
	Atma	Holy Ghost
Monad	Lower *Adi*	
	Anupadaka	
	Higher Atma	
Spirit	*Atma*	

Ego, Incarnating Individuality, the Higher Self—Atma, the Spirit, or the Will

Buddhi, the Intuition, or Wisdom

Manas, the Abstract Mind, or Activity

Soul's Vehicles:

Causal Body (Higher Mental)—	To evolve with—Ideals and Abstract Thought	
Mental Body (Lower Mental)—	To think with—Ideas and Concrete Thoughts	
Astral Body (Upper and Lower)—	To feel with—Emotions and Desires	
Physical Body (incl. Etheric Body)—	To act with—Sensorial Reactions and Actions	
Personality, the Lower Self—	Lower Manas, Concrete Mind	Mental Body
	Astral, Desire Nature	Astral Body
	Physical, Functioning Body	
	Physical/Etheric Body	
Body Consciousness—	Autonomic nervous system	

Partial Source and Suggested Reading:

Jinarajadasa. *First Principles of Theosophy*. 1861.

Channel: (Psychic Empowerment) 1) An alternate name for a medium, and 2) a specific connection similar to a television channel for astral and mental plane communications.

Suggested Reading:

Denning, Melita, and Osborne Phillips. *Foundations of High Magick*. St. Paul: Llewellyn, 1991.

Slate, Joe H., and Carl L. Weschcke. *Communicating with Spirit*. Woodbury: Llewellyn 2015.

Collective Unconscious: A kind of group mind inherited from all our ancestors and including all the memories and knowledge acquired by humans. It is believed to exist on the higher astral and lower mental planes and to be accessible by the super consciousness through the personal Sub-Conscious Mind in deep trance states induced through hypnosis, self-hypnosis, meditation, and guided meditation. **The ability to call up infinite information and integrate it into your present life needs is of enormous benefit—similar to but beyond the capacity of any present-day Internet Search Engine.**

It is the function of the Personal Consciousness to bridge to the collective tribal, racial, cultural, national, mythic, even planetary memories and the world of archetypes of the Universal Consciousness, making them available to the Psyche mainly through the Sub-Conscious Mind.

The memories of all of humanity, perhaps of more than human, and inclusive of the archetypes. The contents of the collective unconscious seem to progress from individual memories to universal memories as the person grows in his or her spiritual development and integration of the whole being. There is some suggestion that this progression also moves from individual memories through various groups or small collectives—family, tribe, race, and nation—so the character of each level is reflected in consciousness until the individual progresses to join in group consciousness with all humanity. This would seem to account for some of the variations of the universal archetypes each person encounters in life.

The contents of the collective unconscious progress from individual memories to universal memories as the person grows in spiritual development and integration of the whole being. There is some suggestion that this progression also moves from individual memories through various groups or small collectives—family, tribe, race, and nation—so the character of each level up to union with consciousness with all humanity. This would seem to account for some of the variations of the universal archetypes each person encounters in life. Also see *Akashic Records*

Suggested Reading:

Dale, Cyndi. *The Subtle Body: An Encyclopedia of Your Energetic Anatomy.* Boulder, CO: Sounds True, 2009.

Communicating with your Higher Self: *I swear to tell myself the truth. I swear to regard every event (or condition) as a particular dealing between myself and the Holy Guardian Angel.* These were the two primary oaths in the work of the G.∴B.∴G.∴ (which see).

What we're doing, of course, is building more lines of communication between the middle (everyday) consciousness and the super consciousness, or between the personality and the Holy Guardian Angel. And, we are doing one more important thing: in promising to tell the truth we are building trust between the selves that often act as if separate entities. Therein lies a mystery and an important recognition.

On this basis of trust, the Higher Self knows that its messages will be respected and attended to.

But, there remains a problem to our communications, and that is that—in part—the Higher Self doesn't speak directly in the common language. Your Holy Guardian Angel doesn't just shout: "Hey, down there, listen up! I want you to stick with the G.∴B.∴G.∴ for six more months."

Instead, through the use of clues and symbols, you have to put effort into understanding the message, making communication a two-way street and a learning situation with direct application to your needs of the moment. In other words, despite the cautions against a pathological belief that everything is a message just for you, almost anything can be used to bridge the gap between meaningless and meaningful. A crystal ball is just a polished rock, but it can open your vision to another world. With intention, anything can become a key to unlock the doors of the Unconscious.

Before Integration there must be Communication. Divination and Meditation on the divinatory results and your dreams provide the basis for communication.

Communication: Real "Communication" is a two-way transaction, i.e., an exchange of information and knowledge and a response thereto. It is not just the "one-way street" as presumed in the "Communications Industry" and by politicians and religionists.

Conditions: (Yi King/I Ching) In describing the auspice of a Hexagram, the text may make a reference such as: "Fortunate under the conditions which this Hexagram denotes, or presupposes." For instance, if the Hexagram denotes the condition of "waiting," then the good fortune is limited to planning or consolidating one's project or position.

Congrex: Here's another of Lou Culling's fancy words he was so fond of using. It just means *intercourse, having sex, sleeping together.* But the use of an unfamiliar word, even when the meaning is obvious, does have a certain value of "stop, look, listen, pay attention."

Having Sex is more than a physical act. In the G∴B∴G∴'s Alphaism you were instructed to avoid any sexual thoughts, feelings, and fantasies for an entire month. It was not so much denial as it was to emphasize their importance and the role they do play in whole and healthy sex whether within the context of Sex Magick or not. When you do have sex, all of these are present because sex is a *complex* of physical, emotional, energy, mental, and spiritual exchange between two people.

Even fantasy is part of real sex whether recognized as such or not. *Is your lover a 'big, strong, heroic man?' Is she 'beautiful, soft and loving?'* No matter the outer reality, the answer through emotional fantasy is 'yes' and that brings you into contact with the archetypal levels of the Sub-Conscious and Collective Unconscious important to the program of Wholeness.

Openness with regard to emotion-level fantasies is important to release associated repression and fear and childish dependencies so the powerful fantasy *Imago* can become more inclusive of the 'real' lover, making the exchange between two people deeper and stronger, building a partnership at all levels.

In Dianism and Sex Magick, the fantasized *Imago* is <u>not</u> the personal fantasy but rather that of a god or goddess. The technique is similar and the imagined god or goddess can eventually impose and transform the personal fantasy.

Even if others tell you that your lover is nothing but a beer-drinking no-good lay-about, this transformative power of the *Imago* is one of the greatest things that we can give and receive within our intimate relationship with our partner. With the added empowerment of Sex Magick, the old reality can become a new reality.

Conversation: Yes, it is possible to converse with your Higher Self. First you have to honestly believe in the Higher Self, and that the person you think of as your self is not it. At the same time, don't let the name "Holy Guardian Angel" deceive you into thinking of a separate being that is so *holy* as to be beyond your ability to deserve the attention of the HGA.

True, the HGA is normally distant from the personality that is the everyday 'you,' but the function of the Great Work is to build a relationship between the personality and the Higher Self leading towards *Integration*—when the two become as one.

"I swear to regard every event (or condition) as a particular dealing between myself and the HGA." Culling had done a beautiful job in explaining the practical issues around this magickal oath, and his examples demonstrate its value and effectiveness.

This practicality is rather unique among magickal oaths! Many are too grand for realization within a single lifetime. While their intention is to stimulate spiritual growth and attainment, it is usually not some grand event or rare or expensive artifact but very ordinary things that call to us for our deeper awareness. Their symbolism may be obscure—normally—but suddenly they glow with meaning or practically yell at you for attention. Or, it may seem like nothing, but still your attention has been re-directed to the event as if it has a special meaning for you, *and it does!*

But, note further: this oath directs your attention to everyday events of all kinds so that your awareness is alerted to the greater meaning and potential that each may represent. Magick and meaning may be found in the most mundane of events when there is that possibility of relationship between the inner you and the inner side of the event. The effect is to activate connections to your Higher Self, and that is the goal.

"I swear to tell myself the truth." This, of course, is very challenging. *What is truth?* Can we ever really know it? Again, Culling has given us a good but simple example. It is perhaps too simple. The real requirement is to be *honest* with yourself; to test your answers for their truth and honesty. This is more than "knowing yourself" for it is also a test of your truth and honesty in relation to others and to the world you live. We too easily deceive ourselves and once again the entire purpose of the oath is to prepare yourself to communicate with your Higher Self, the HGA.

Even though your communication with the HGA isn't always in *plain English*, it is not a game! The Great Work is serious business.

Crossing the Stream: (Yi King/I Ching) This means to enlarge or to go beyond the natural sphere intended, to venture or advance confidently.

Crowley, Aleister: (1875–1947) was one of the most controversial figures in recent Western occultism. He inherited a considerable fortune, and died a pauper. He had great intellectual genius and wasted a lot on shocking the world as he knew it with occasional bizarre antics and lifestyle. He was trained in the Hermetic Order of the Golden Dawn and later formed his own Order of the Silver Star and then took over the O.T.O (Ordo Templi Orientis). He was a prolific and capable writer of magic technology and is best known for his transcription of the *Book of the Law* received from a spirit named *Aiwass* proclaiming Crowley as the Beast 666 in the Book of Revelations and announcing a *New Aeon* of terror and advancement for the world. His magical books and his Thoth Tarot Deck are worth study.

Louis T. Culling: A memory, by Wanda Sue Parrott
LOUIS T. CULLING
Mystic, Mentor, Man of Mystery

Describing Lou Culling isn't easy. If I knew more about him, it might be simple to sum up our friendship that started in October 1960.

Lou was 66 and I was 25 when we met at a birthday party in the hills northeast of Hollywood, California. On surface level, transportation drew us together. Lou said he needed a ride home; I had a car, so I drove him to Coldwater Canyon and Ventura boulevards. There, we shared our first of many bowls of soup. Lou spoke of his belief in one's Holy Guardian Angel, or HGA.

Sex, I later discovered, was the true reason we got together. Lou rescued me from being forced to participate in birthday party games involving Aleister Crowley-style Rosicrucian "sex magick" just as they were set to begin.

In retrospect, Lou realized I was so inexperienced that being made an unwitting Vestal Virgin could cause irreparable damage to my psyche and life. Instead of saying he had been a high-ranking officer in the OTO group, to which he and his friends at the party belonged, Lou said he was once an organist in movie theaters for silent films, and he now belonged to "Thinking Unlimited."

In 1961, I drove him to an invitation-only meeting of Thinking Unlimited in Highland Park. I was the youngest of six or eight elder men and women, who were pleasant, bright, and anything but sexy as they shared true psychic experiences with a wiry white-haired pooch who wrote philosophical letters to the editor of the *Los Angeles Herald-Examiner* and signed them with a paw print. I was admitted since I had begun doing automatic writing.

Also in 1961, Lou made a hypnosis pinwheel that he tried out on me. It did not work to hypnotize me, but Lou claimed I hypnotized him! For that first-ever feat, he gave me a Doctor of Philosophy certificate from a long-dissolved corporation he once ran in the San Diego area, Colegium Orthogenesis Nuit. The diploma was inscribed "Wanda Sue Childress, Ph.D." My specialty? Sex Magick! I kept it out of fondness for my friend who always wore a rumpled suit and soup-stained necktie and was such a gentleman that I don't think we ever touched each other even to hug!

In 1962, Lou gently nudged me to leave Hollywood. By then, he was inventing scented oils to stimulate female libidos, and I was "scent sniffer." When an envelope from Lou arrived, I could smell it about 30 feet before I reached the mailbox. He addressed me as "La Encantadora." Some enchantress! I critiqued his oils as scented bug sprays!

By April 1963 I was married and a neophyte member of the conservative Rosicrucian Order (AMORC) in San Jose, California. Lou's letters stopped when I entered its portals, as if to say I was now where I belonged. I have been a practicing Rosicrucian ever since.

I never again heard from, or about, Louis T. Culling, until 1973. Then, I read of his death in *FATE Magazine*. Shocked? Indeed! I had no idea the man I called Lou was not only famous as a writer who specialized in Sex Magick, but was also a Crowley-style Rosicrucian.

Lou was a mystic, mentor, man of mystery and—I suspect—my Holy Guardian Angel.

Wanda Sue Parrott, June 25, 2014

Daemon: Not a "demon," but a mythical being, part-human and part-god serving as an intermediary between God and humanity—an inspiring intelligence similar to if not identical to the Holy Guardian Angel.

Note the role of "an intermediary between God and humanity." Once attainment of the Knowledge and Conversation of the Holy Guardian Angel is achieved, the Great Work takes on added dimension. The role of a Co-Creator expands in service to all humanity, and to all life and consciousness of our planet as a whole.

The path to glory is endless to our still limited vision just as Love knows no bounds.

Dee, Dr. John: Dee, Sir John. (1527–1608) With Edward Kelley as clairvoyant, the source for the Enochian language and the eighteen Enochian Calls.

Dianism: The Second Degree of Sex Magick in the *G∴B∴G∴*, Dianism is sexual union without climax. It's further training, but unlike Alphaism with its emphasis on avoidance here the partners should be warm and ardent, but controlled. It's like a surfer riding the crest of the wave forever. There should be no feelings of frustration for it is without "lust for result." Rather than allowing oneself to be submerged in the full flow of pleasurable sensation, one should allow the ecstasy to feed the fires of aspiration and inspiration.

Dianism is not an end in itself but rather is the means to a greater end than orgasm, which is fleeting. One *comes*, and then it's gone. Here, Dianism uses the energy of sexual ecstasy to feed the fire of concentration—which we will learn to project in the attainment of our magickal goal.

Both concentration and meditation disciplines are involved in the practice of Dianism. The role of the male is the more challenging, and he should withhold from consciousness any awareness of a known earthly personality. Each partner regards the other as a god or goddess. While it is natural at first for the known personality to intrude, it should be as persistently suppressed, so that the partner is regarded, finally, *as a visible manifestation of one's own Holy Guardian Angel.*

The aim of Dianism and its highest magick lies in continuing the union until such time as one goes into the "Borderland" state. A hallucinatory meditation may be achieved, in which one is submerged in spiritual inspiration and aspiration.

All things require time, regularity and persistence for results. Many experiments indicate that one or two hours, or even more, are required to attain to the Borderland state. And it takes time to build up the energized enthusiasm of the Magickal Imagination which gives one's thoughts subjective reality. It might take thirty minutes or it might take hours to build up a satisfactory force.

Individuals are different, and each must work out his individual technique. Dianism is not to be regarded as an end in itself, but as a great means to further very great ends. In time one will learn through practice to *concentrate* on a chosen point, while at the same time suffering the sexual ecstasy. The fire of concentration will replace the preoccupation with sexual sensation.

What seems difficult at first will become greater pleasure with accompanying spiritual awareness with experience.

Dimensions: Each Plane or level of reality has certain distinctive characteristics of Space, Substance, Energy, Consciousness, Nature, and "Rules of Engagement" that must be recognized as determinate for phenomena at that particular level and for efficient and effective functioning of consciousness at the chosen level. According to the esoteric teachings of Henry Laurency the increase from three dimensions at the physical plane to four at the astral, five at the mental, etc. seven at the manifestal.

Dispensation: A special empowerment to dispense and manage religious or spiritual instruction and practice. Within Christianity, it is the official granting of a license to organize a church. It is also a special time period designated by God for certain things to happen. For Esotericism, it is believed to be both a time period and a *licensing* to a particular group or groups to establish themselves and their message seemingly granted by spiritual *higher-ups.*

There are those of us who believe that we live in a special time when dispensation is universal for all who will open their mind and spirit to the influx of higher consciousness happening now. We are approaching a turning point when the "world as we know it" will end and a new world order will begin to replace the old. Few things happen overnight, but time is critical and changes will be rapid as global conditions require new world organizations and new worldwide solutions to problems arising from the past.

Divination: It is important to understand that "real" Divination is not only an amusing game of "Fortune Telling" but has all the potential to become forms of Clairvoyance (the *psychic* skill of "clear seeing" behind superficial appearances), Distant Viewing (a form of "astral travel"), of Prediction ("Tomorrow's News Today"), and Prophesy (the *shaping* of "tomorrow's news" to personal goals).

Through the ages, an enormous variety of divinatory methods have been developed, including Dream Interpretation and Prophetic Causal Dreaming as developed in this book. Some methods, like Astrology, Handwriting Analysis, and Palmistry, are most appropriate as means to Self-Analysis and Self-Understanding, and can be used as guidance to Self-Improvement.

Many of the methods listed here are archaic and are included to give a broad understanding of human ingenuity when "facing the Unknown."

Prophesy and information by 'occult' methodologies:

By reading naturally produced signs ranging from the shape of clouds to the positions of planets (astrology).

By reading artificially produced signs ranging from tea leaves to the throwing of dice or dominoes.

By reading symbols such as the Tarot cards or the I Ching hexagrams.

By reading visions as seen in Dreams or in Trance.

In each situation, something experienced is interpreted usually by means of long-established rules justified by many years of observation across many cultures. In most cases, these interpretations are supplemented by psychic factors of impressions or intuition naturally arising in either conscious or Sub-Conscious (trance) states.

Divination is not a game undertaken for amusement. You should only undertake a divination because of true need for an answer. We ask the question when it becomes *imperative* to the questioner, so imperative that it will reverberate in your mind and cause an equal reverberation in the cosmos leading to the answer given in the form of a traditional set of rules or "code" yet to be interpreted.

It is likewise important to make the question concise and clearly worded. There should be no ambiguity, and the question should confine itself to earthy, practical matters, unconcerned with issues of morality or judgment. The best question is one that can be simply answered with either a "yes" or a "no." The simpler the question, the more precise the answer. The more serious the question, the more accurate the answer.

How Divination Works. In some sense, avoiding technical details, the future already exists; but it is also important to know that your future is *not* fixed. Changes in your current situation can make changes in your future situation. At the same time, in terms of the bigger universe of which each of is a minute part, small changes rarely have much impact on the future.

Nevertheless, it is *your* future we are talking about without a lot of concern about the world around us. Always there are points of leverage that, if discovered and manipulated with willed intention, can make a difference. *But, that's magic, another subject altogether.*

However, most readings are not concerned with changing the future but with answering questions about the present and near future. Please read the following few paragraphs carefully with your full attention.

Each person is surrounded by a field of energy called the "aura." Your own aura permeates your entire body and represents your feeling, your mind, and your spirit. It's all about you.

Every cell in your body contains of all the information about you—not only the present but the past and the probable future. Not only that, but every cell also contains a hologram of the universe; that is, all knowledge is resident within each one of us, and it is ours to retrieve if we know how.

Your aura further permeates your immediate surroundings—out to about three feet—and especially things you touch. Some substances more easily absorb the auric influence than others, and wet tea leaves are especially sensitive to this influence, serving as an ideal medium for our reading. The minute particles, actually right down to the sub-atomic level, of the tea leaves or other materials being used are responsive to your energy field—including the questions and concerns you have at the moment of the reading. The more often you practice this psychic talent, the more able will your aura project the image-forming energy to the sensitive media.

It is important to realize that all divinatory systems have to connect the Conscious Mind to the Sub-Conscious and thence to the Universal Consciousness. Successful divination and, hence, our personal "psychic empowerment" depends on our abilities to consciously *channel* our questions to these *lower* realms and to take the answers into our *awakened consciousness* for their analysis and application.

Divination, in contrast to "fortune telling" is not a *passive* mere acceptance of answers from the "cards" or the "stones" or the "stars" or other objects that are converted into "tools," but uses those tools in *inter-active* communication between the Unconscious and the Conscious Mind. The "language" of that communication—ultimately—is symbolism but the symbols themselves are not static but instead constantly evolve in response to "the times."

The challenge for the diviner is to use symbols as a frame or vehicle in asking questions, and then to newly interpret those symbols conveying the answers.

Suggested Reading:

Cunningham, Scott. *Divination for Beginners: Reading the Past, Present, and Future.* St. Paul: Llewellyn, 2003.

Slate, Joe H., and Carl L. Weschcke. *Psychic Empowerment: Tools and Technologies.* Woodbury: Llewellyn, 2011.

Divinatory Practices: There are hundreds, perhaps thousands, of different forms of divination and clairvoyant practice. The following tables organize some of the more familiar by the major styles. It is a preliminary effort.

Analytical Table of Clairvoyant and Divinatory Practices
Direct Psychic Perception of an event, object, or person
(mostly contemporary) external to and hidden
from the observer, including:

<u>Clairalience</u>—*the smelling of odors without a physical source that provides some kind of insight*

<u>Clairaudience</u>—*the hearing of sounds and voices without a present physical source that either provides information or messages*

<u>Claircognizance</u>—*knowing without reference to a physical source, sometimes experienced as a "hunch."*

<u>Clairgustance</u>—*tasting without a physical source that provides a stimulus leading to some kind of insight*

<u>Clairsentience</u>—*the acquisition of knowledge through the feeling and touching of an object or contact with an organic substance or part of a person or other creature*

<u>Clairvoyance</u>—*"clear seeing," i.e., the perception of information without the use of physical senses and sometimes knowledge not limited to the physical dimension*

<u>ESP</u>—*"ExtraSensory Perception"*—*basically an alternate expression for clairvoyance clearly indicating something "extra" to ordinary physical senses*

<u>Futurology</u>—*predicting the future based on present conditions through ExtraSensory means*

<u>Precognition</u>—*ExtraSensory perception of events that will occur in the future*

<u>Premonition</u>—*warning of a future disaster through ExtraSensory means*

<u>Psychometry</u>—*reading the history of an object, in particular its association with humans*

Remote Viewing—*direct ExtraSensory perception of events at locations remote from the viewer.*

Retrocognition—*perceiving events that occurred in the past, often leading to a better understanding of present circumstances.*

By Direct Psychic Perception by means of Altered States of Consciousness:

Dream Interpretation—*while often associated with the use of a "dream diction-ary," it really involves methods of allowing the dream "to speak" to the dreamer*

Oracles—*making contact with spirits or gods usually at a special location of-ten associated with unusual environment conditions and a dedicated person in trance*

Ouija—*while commonly used as entertainment, the proper use would be to enter into a trance and let the planchette spell out messages on the board printed with the alphabet and numbers*

Prophecy—*revelation about the future, often ostensibly from a spiritual pres-ence or deity*

Shamanic techniques—*deliberate repression or excessive stimulation of the physical senses through various techniques of Ecstatic or Exhaustive Dancing, Fasting, Sleep Deprivation, Bondage, Isolation, Flagellation, Psychoactive Drugs, Drumming, Sexual or Physical Exhaustion, etc.*

Theomancy—*receiving messages or answers to questions through an oracle or direct contact with Deity*

Direct Psychic Perception by means of Extended Consciousness:

Astral Projection—*intentional acquisition of information while Out-of-Body using the astral vehicle*

Aura Reading—*perception and interpretation of the auric field usually involv-ing some degree of etheric or even auric vision*

Etheric Projection—*projection, or more communally, extension of part of the etheric vehicle (sometimes perceived as ectoplasm) to obtain information by touch or to move objects*

Intuition—*a somewhat vague term for a non-verbal "feeling" message from the Higher Self*

Mental Projection—*projection of the mental vehicle. (It should be clarified that all projections involve more than just the etheric, or just the astral, or just the mental vehicle but rather are inclusive with each having one substance and level of consciousness that is predominant.)*

Indirect Psychic Perception through another person or entity:

Animal Communication—*most often a form of Mental Telepathy by which information is transmitted between the animal and a human generally by uncharacteristic behavior*

Automatic Writing (aka **Autography** and **Psychography**)—*unconscious written communication involving a spirit while the writer is in a trance*

Mental Telepathy—*contact and exchange of information with another person*

Projection of a Familiar—*this is a variation of etheric projection in which a Thought Form of an animal or person is created from etheric and astral substance under direction of the projector—either with a single duty "charge," or a longer term duty charge. It is sometimes called "indirect psychic spying" in contrast to Remote Viewing*

Sciomancy—*communication through a spirit guide who, generally, appears spontaneously*

Spirit Communication—*contact with "spirits" of the deceased or other entities most often through a person acting as a "Medium" or "Channel" under the direction or "Control" of a Spirit Guide*

Telesthesia—*indirect psychic awareness of a distant condition or happening involving a person related to the receiver*

Augmented Psychic Perception by means of Divinatory Tools:

Dowsing (see also **Radiesthesia**)—*the use of a forked stick or bent steel clothes hanger or other metallic imitation of the forked stick in order to sense the presence of water or other resource or lost object. The instrument moves in the dowser's hands when he walks over the searched for substance believed to radiate a perceptive energy*

Handwriting Analysis—aka **Graphology** and **Graphoanalysis**—*measurement and interpretation of size, shape, spacing, impression, and other factors of handwriting, including most particularly signatures, the personal pronoun "I," and also doodles*

Pendulum Work (Radiesthesia) aka **Divining**, **Dowsing**, **Water Witching**—*using a pendulum instead of a rod to determine the location of water or other resource, and also to respond to questions.*

Related techniques include:

    Cleidomancy or Clidomancy: *using a key attached to a cord or string*

    Coscinomancy or Cosquinomancy: *using a sieve suspended from shears or tongs*

    Dactylomancy or Dactlomancy: *using a suspended ring*

Rhabdomancy: *by using a stick or rod.*

Scrying—*seeing a vision while gazing into a transparent, translucent, or reflective object, inducing a mild trance.* Such objects include:

Crystal ball gazing

Crystal gazing

Fires Scrying

Ink Scrying

Mirror Scrying

Smoke Scrying

Water Scrying

Wine Scrying

Tea Leaf Reading:—*interpreting the shapes, size, and patterns of wet tea leaves either by inspiration or a special dictionary of symbols.* Similar practices include:

Coffee Ground Reading

Egg Yolk Reading

Strewn Rice Reading

Wine Sediment Reading

Augmented Psychic Perception by means of manually manipulated complex Symbolic Divination Systems with established rules and meanings:

Cartomancy—*using a deck or ordinary bridge or poker playing cards*

Geomancy—*interpreting dots, lines, and figures traced in sand, dirt or pebbles, or naturally occurring formations either intuitively or by standard meanings. It is a divinatory system prominently used by Golden Dawn magicians and with variants employed throughout Africa and parts of the Arabian Peninsula*

I Ching aka **Yi King**—*the casting of sticks or coins to establish 64 Hexagrams each consisting of six solid or broken lines. The I Ching is the oldest and most universal system of Chinese divination originating at the very foundation of Taoism*

Oghams, aka the **Celtic Tree Alphabet**—*a series of sticks marked with cuts to represent each letter of the Tree Alphabet, and then thrown and selected randomly for divinatory interpretation*

Runes—*similar to, but older and more complex than Oghams and based on a very rich mythic system of Nordic/Teutonic mythology giving definition to each image. Runes are used both in divination and in magic (as charms and spells). Runes should be ranked with Tarot Cards for their symbolic interpretation and magical use*

Tarot Cards—*a complex deck of 78 cards illustrated with symbols and images associated with the Hebrew and Greek Kabbalah. The Tarot is the most popular and important divinatory system in the Western world*

Augmented Psychic Perception associated with Scientific Measurable Physical Phenomena:

Astrology—*the most scientific system for determining the value and meaning of "the moment" by measuring the celestial positions of the Sun, Moon, Planets, and sometimes of the fixed stars and asteroids and the appearance of comets in relation to exact "birth locations" on Earth. The resultant pattern is cast as a wheel, the horoscope, and interpreted through long established meaning based on thousands of years of observation and logical associations. The time and place of birth sets the "plan" and meaning for the life of a person, event, corporate or other legal entity, while changes to the celestial positions (transits) in relation to the birth horoscope will forecast coming events*

Cheiromancy—see **Palmistry** (aka **Palm Reading**)

Gematria—*Each letter of the Hebrew alphabet has a numeric value representing a different creative force. When the numeric values of the letters in particular words, names, and phrases are calculated it is assumed that words, names, and phrases with the same numeric value have associated or equivalent meanings. Those values and meanings may be found in Kabalistic dictionaries and are employed in divination, prayer, and magic*

Numerology (aka **Arithmancy**)—*a system of somewhat arbitrary assignment of numbers to the letters of the alphabet by which names and birthdates are given meaningful interpretation*

Palmistry—*Like Astrology, Palmistry is more a scientific system of divination than it is psychic—nevertheless the psychic faculties always supplement the scientific reading. Palmistry is the science of the reading and interpretation of lines and shapes in the hand, often using detailed measurements of proportionate length, width, depth, and angles of the lines and apparent symbols. The system has been extended to include the proportionate length and width of the thumb and fingers, their flexibility, lines on the knuckles, and the shapes and lines in the fingernails (also called Onychomancy when treated separately from the palm)*

Pegomancy—see Palmistry

Common types of Divination involving extended psychic awareness

The following is just a selection of many divinatory systems, basically demonstrating the point that anything can be manipulated and "read" because the real meaning is found not in the object but in intentional human consciousness. In most cases, the "reading" is accompanied by a light state of trance. In some, but not all systems, there are established "dictionary" meanings. Further information may be found in the on-line *Llewellyn's Paranormal, Magical, and Occult Encyclopedia*.

Types of Divination involving extended psychic awareness

Aeromancy—interpreting atmospheric and related phenomena, such as perceived images in clouds, and also:

> **Austromancy**—*interpretation of winds*
>
> **Ceraunoscopy** and **Keraunomancy**—*interpretation of thunder and lightning*
>
> **Chaomancy**—*Sky Visions*
>
> **Meteromancy**—*Shooting Stars*

Alectormancy, Alectromancy, Alectryomancy—*observing birds, usually a rooster, pick through scattered grains, and noting sequentially when the bird crows signifying a letter of the alphabet. If the rooster pecks at three grains and then crows it denotes the third letter: "c"*

Aleuromancy—*messages are written on paper and then inserted into units of dough that are then baked, such Fortune Cookies that will be selected at random*

Alomancy or **Halomancy**—*interpreting images drawn in spilled salt or dry sand*

Alphitomancy, also called "**Cursed Bread**"—*if a person has indigestion after eating a loaf of barley bread, he or she will be judged guilty of a crime. A similar irrational tradition involved tying a Witch (always a woman in that historic period) and throwing her in water. If she drowned, she was presumed guilty; if she survived, it was sometimes said it was by supernatural force, so again it proved guilt.*

Amniomancy—*interpreting the caul (the part of the placenta remaining on the head) at a baby's birth*

Anthropomancy, Antinpomancy, Splanchomancy—*interpreting the entrails of a human sacrifice*

Apantomancy—*interpreting the chance encounter with an object, animal or person, such as a black cat crossing your path*

Arithmancy: Divination using numbers, including:

Gematria—*interpreting Hebrew bible passages by assigned numeric values to letters of the Hebrew Alphabet*

Numerology—*dates and words (often birthdates and names) are converted into numbers sequentially identified with the alphabet, and interpreted by a number dictionary.*

Aruspicy, Extispicy, Haruspicy—*interpreting the entrails of a sacrificed animal.*

Astragalamancy, Astragalomancy, Astragyromancy, Cleromancy—*interpreting dice casts by number associations*

Axinomancy—*throwing an axe and observing the direction of the handle*

Belomancy, Bolomancy—*shooting, tossing, or balancing an arrow, and interpreting what is observed*

Bibliomancy or **Stichomancy**—*reading or interpreting randomly chosen passages in books, most often religious books. Also:*

  Rhapsodomancy—*Using a book of poetry*

Botanomancy—*interpreting burning or burned leaves or branches*

Brontoscopy—*interpreting the sound of thunder*

Capnomancy—*interpreting rising smoke*

Causimomancy—*observing changes in objects placed in a fire*

Ceromancy and **Ceroscopy**—*interpreting shapes taken by melted wax poured into water*

Cledomancy—*interpreting random events and statements*

Crithomancy and **Critomancy**—*interpreting sacrificial cakes and breads*

Cromniomancy—*interpreting the sprouting behavior of onions*

Cybermancy—*divination through a computer*

Cyclomancy—*interpreting the revolutions of a spinning bottle*

Daphnomancy—*interpreting a burning laurel branch*

Dendromancy—*divination by oak or mistletoe*

Fractomancy—*interpreting the structure of fractal patterns*

Geloscopy—*interpreting the sound or manner of laughter*

Gyromancy—*walking or twirling around in a circle marked with letters until one is dizzy and stumbles or falls, thus spelling a prophetic message*

Hepatoscopy, Hepatomancy—*interpreting the liver of a sacrificial animal*

Hieromancy and **Hieroscopy**—*interpreting burnt offerings or ritually slaughtered animals*

Hydromancy—*interpreting of water by color, ripples, and its ebb and flow, including:*

  Hydatoscopy—*interpreting rainwater*

Lecanomancy—*interpreting the sounds or the ripples as stones are dropped into water*

Pegomancy—*interpretation of waters of sacred springs, wells, pools, or fountains*

Ichthyomancy—*interpreting the behavior, or the entrails, or fish*

Lampadomancy—*interpreting the flame of a candle, torch, or lamp*

Libranomancy or **Livanomancy**—*by interpreting the smoke made by burning incense*

Lithomancy—*divination with crystal or gems by their reflected light or their placement when cast*

Lychnomancy—*interpreting the flames of three candles*

Metoposcopy—*interpreting the lines and wrinkles of the forehead*

Moleoscophy—*interpreting the moles of the body*

Molybdomancy—*interpreting the hissing sounds as molten lead, or tin, when dropped into water*

Oculomancy—*interpreting the eye,* also

Iridology—*interpreting the iris of the eye*

Oenomancy or **Oinomancy**—*interpreting wine*

Omphalomancy—*Interpreting the shape of the first born's navel, or the knots in the umbilical cord to determine the number of children that mother will have in her lifetime*

Onomancy—*the interpretation of names*

Oomancy, **Ooscopy**, **Ovomancy**—*divination with eggs*

Phyllorhodomancy—*Interpreting the sound made by slapping a rose petal against the hand*

Physiognomy—*Reading a person's character by interpreting the facial features*

Podomancy—*by interpreting the lines and details of feet*

Pedomancy—*by interpreting the impression made by a footprint*

Phyllordomancy—*interpreting the sound made when slapping a rose petal between the hands*

Premonition—*A warning of a future event, typically an accident or disaster*

Prophecy—*A vision or revelation of the future, typically provided by a deity*

Psychomancy—*Soul Reading, perceiving a person's values and beliefs*

Pyromancy—*by watching fire*

Pyroscopy—*by burning paper*

Schematomancy—*observing and interpreting the face*

Selenomancy—*interpreting the appearance and phase of the moon*

Sideromancy—*by placing straws on a hot iron and observing the resulting shapes*

Spasmatomancy—*interpreting convulsions*

Spatalamancy—*interpreting skin, bone, or excrement, including:*

>   **Scapulimancy, Scapulomancy, Patulamancy**—*interpreting the cracks in the burned shoulder bones of an animal*

>   **Scatamancy**—*interpreting excrement*

>   **Spatilomancy**—*interpreting animal excrement*

Spodomancy—*by interpreting ashes, cinders, or soot*

Stareomancy—*interpreting the classical elements of wind, water, earth, or fire.*

Sternomancy—*interpreting the marks or bumps on the solar plexus (breast to belly).*

Stolisomancy—*interpreting a person's style of dress*

Sycomancy—*by writing a question on a leaf and observing how quickly the leaf dries*

Tephramancy—*by interpreting the ashes of burnt tree bark*

Tiromancy—*by interpreting the holes in cheese*

Transataumancy—*by accidentally seeing or hearing*

Trochomancy—*by interpreting wheel ruts or tracks*

Uromancy or **Urimancy**—*by interpreting the appearance of urine*

Urticariaomancy—*by the location of an itch (e.g. your palms itch, you'll get money or your nose itches, someone is thinking about you)*

Water Witching—see Dowsing

Xenomancy—*by interpreting meetings with strangers*

Xylomancy—*by interpreting burning wood*

Zoomancy—*interpreting the appearance and behavior of animals*, including:

>   **Entomancy**—*interpreting the behavior of insects*

>   **Ailuromancy**—*interpreting the behavior of cats*

>   **Arachnomancy**—*interpreting the behavior of spiders*

>   **Myrmomancy**—*interpreting the behavior of ants*

>   **Skatharomancy**—*interpreting a beetle's tracks*

>   **Hippomancy**—*interpreting the behavior of horses*

>   **Myomancy**—*interpreting the behavior of mice and rats*

>   **Ophiomancy**—*interpreting the behavior of serpents*

>   **Ornithomancy**—*interpreting the behavior, flight, and song of birds*

>   **Theriomancy**—*interpreting the movements of groups of animals*

Zygomancy—*Divination by using weights*

Suggested Reading:

Slate, Joe H., and Carl L. Weschcke. *Clairvoyance for Psychic Empowerment: The Art and Science of "Clear Seeing" Past the Illusions of Space & Time & Self-Deception.* Woodbury: Llewellyn, 2013. PDF e-book.

Slate, Joe H., and Carl L. Weschcke. *The Llewellyn Complete Book of Psychic Empowerment: A Compendium of Tools & Techniques for Growth & Transformation.* Woodbury: Llewellyn, 2011. PDF e-book.

Divinatory Response: (Divination) The answer to the question asked.

Divine Self (aka Divine Body and Divinity Within): Name of the vehicle for functioning consciously at the 6th level or plane up from the physical. Alternate names include Submanifestal, Monadic, and Anupadaka.

Esoterics believe that each of us has some form of Divinity Within—called a Divine Spark, the Power, the Goddess Within, even—as in Quantum Physics—a God Particle. For some this is the same as *Spirit,* for others the Soul. Whatever name be it in Sanskrit, Hebrew, Greek, Tibetan, etc., there is this distinct core point that connects the physical body with some similar point in each of the higher bodies, and which can be activated to cleanse and transform the physical body and initiate a progression through the higher bodies. When we undertake a conscious program of self-development it is another form of *Spiritual Communication.* In yoga, it is the "awakened" Kundalini that transforms consciousness as it spirals upward through the body's centers to bring union with the Divinity within each of us and unity with Spirit and Universal Consciousness. Some variation of this is present in all spiritual development systems including Christianity and the image of Christ's Heart center.

Dramatic Ritual: Although Aleister Crowley is given much credit for modern *Magickal* Dramatic Ritual, the origins are not only ancient but continuous into modern times supporting Crowley's definition of Magick as "the Science and Art of causing Change in conformity with Will."

In other words, a *Dramatic Ritual is constructed to bring about Change in accordance with Purpose.* This poses two important questions: *(1) Progressive Change in the Inner World of the person or persons at the center of the ritual?* Or *(2) Change in the Outer World of composed of <u>masses</u> of people or in the physical structure of "things themselves?*

Progressive Change in the Inner World is the highest goal of Ceremonial Magick and involves the invocation of a specific Deity into the "targeted" person in such a manner that the Ritualist directs a corresponding deific force to bring about such action as Healing, "Correction" of Character (undesired addictions and habits), Awakening of Psychic Power, even the Recovers of Past Life Memories, etc. It is often constructed as an Initiatory Rite; and to ask the invoked deity for "Messages" or "Prophecies."

Crowley himself states: "The object of all magical ritual" is "the uniting of the Microcosm with the Macrocosm" as in The Supreme and Complete Ritual of the Invocation of the Holy Guardian Angel."

The most powerful dramatic rituals not only invoke specific deific powers but incorporate myths associated with the particular deity. Examples can be found through careful examination of Greek, Egyptian, and Tantric "performance" rituals" which often combined both Inner and Outer World change. Other examples can be found in various shamanic rituals involving techniques to alter conscious of the participants. Gerald Gardner adapted these techniques in his reconstructions of British Witchcraft into modern Wicca.

Change in the Outer World of the Masses was the object and accomplishment of the public rituals (theatrical pageants) of Hitler's Nazi Party and of Stalin's Communist Party. Nevertheless, these were mostly inspired by the dramatic rituals of the Catholic and Orthodox Churches likewise intended for a kind of "Crowd Control."

Change in the Outer World of Things is the object of various demonstrations of Psychokinesis, forms of "Low Magic" intended to attract Luck, Success, Money, Love, etc. While not generally practiced within the context of Dramatic Ritual, such "Spell Work" can be enhanced by the deliberate invocation of a deific force corresponding in nature to the object of the working.

Suggested Reading:

Slate, Joe H., and Carl L. Weschcke. *Communicating with Spirit.* Woodbury: Llewellyn, 2015.

Slate, Joe H., and Carl L. Weschcke. *Moving Objects with Your Mind: The Power of Psychokinesis.* Woodbury: Llewellyn, 2011. PDF e-book.

Ecstasy: "Ecstasy" is defined variously under categories of Emotion, Religion, Mysticism, Psychology, and even in Philosophy. Most such efforts fail because their focus is external; it's like defining Orgasm—as it was until later in the twentieth century—as "ejaculation of spermatic fluid" without any mention of the feminine experience or accompanying emotion or changes in consciousness.

"Ecstasy" results from an *exhilaration* of consciousness arising from:

A series of repetitive physical and sensory actions leading towards sensory overload, such as extended dance, running, or whirling, prostrations, bowing, gesturing with arms and hands, rotating through prayer beads, etc.

An extended experience of sensory deprivation, as in total isolation, the use of a sleep or meditation mask, the combination of restrained movement with a meditation mask, or the use of "sleep sack" in imitation of the traditional *Witches Cradle* (see the chapter on techno-shamanism in our *Clairvoyance for Psychic Empowerment* (Llewellyn, 2013). Also the unique form of artistic Japanese Rope Bondage and swinging suspension known as *Shibari*—originally shamanic but now a "Performance Art" in night clubs.

An extended experience of sensory reception, such as flashing strobe lights, drumming (often with a very slowly accelerating beat but with an overall rhythm of 200-220 beats per moment), the sound of repetitive chanting or ocean waves;

An extended focus of attention on a particular image, as in mediation*—best if combined with Tratak and the chanting of a related mantra (see our *Astral Projection for Psychic Empowerment* (Llewellyn, 2012) and the earlier mentioned *Clairvoyance for Psychic Empowerment.* Also see recommended titles at the end of this chapter.).

*As a mental and emotional exercise. "Meditation" is either a *passive* kind of "listening"—waiting for a message, vision, or revelation—or an *active* "reaching upward" as in prayer, or "projecting inward" as in a "Tattvic Conditioning" of body and psyche or a "Chakra Awakening" to progressively expand spiritual consciousness. See our *Clairvoyance for Psychic Empowerment*, 2013, Llewellyn.

A controlled experience of pain, particularly when applied repetitively as in "scourging" (light, ritual flagellation) often applied in ritual dance, or carefully controlled light electro-shocks known as Transcutaneous Electrical Nerve Stimulator (more commonly referred to as a TENS unit) and sometimes known as erotic electro-stimulation. (Frankly, we entirely recommend against this as too easily misapplied or abused, leading to injury and even death. *Stay away from electricity, from fire, from ice, and other applied force.*)

A continuous singing or chanting of one or a series of words, names, or mantras, most often associated with a particular spiritual or deific entity or with a particular part of the subtle body to excite its activity.

Through prolonged intercourse and visualization of woman as the Goddess Incarnate, sexual ecstasy can be made to become psychic ecstasy, the fire that excites and powers the magickal imagination. Body, Mind, and Spirit are united with a transfusion of energy to transform subjective reality into objective reality.

Tantric sex involving extended arousal through stimulation of many of the physical "trigger points" to the edge of orgasm, and then "holding back" until starting again (and perhaps again and again) to finally "explode" in a long and sometime multiple orgasm.

The infusion of Kundalini energy through particular physical actions extended to the automatic induction of a trance state.

Any of these may be combined either sequentially or coincidentally. The point is to arrive beyond a climatic state, entering into a trance of focused attention and inner awareness, with a self-conceived goal or as guided by an external source. Ecstasy is that point beyond climax, beyond orgasm, beyond external and objective awareness to the point of "union" with something "Deific" and beyond personal limits. It may be a "going out-of-the-body" but it's not ordinary astral projection but a merger of "human" spirit with limitless "Divine" Spirit.

That "Divine Spirit" cannot be defined nor named as it comes from outside reality and giving it any name is to humanize it within all the limits of human experience and emotion, to encumber it with human desires, hates, prejudices, and selfish goals. Somewhere it says "No man can see the face of God and live!" The God is outside of all creation but the Spirit is everywhere and in everything.

Enoch: "He who walked with God," Hebrew prophet said to be the seventh master of the world following Adam.

Enochian Language: (Also known as the Language of the Angels, and the Secret Angelic Language) The words transcribed by Dr. John Dee (1527–1608) and Edward Kelley in their spiritual contacts, starting in 1582, were eventually seen to form a genuine language as well as a system of magic.

Enochian is pronounced Eh-no-kee-an, is supposedly the same language spoken by the angel Ave to the prophet Enoch whose name in Hebrew is spelled *Heh Nun Vav Kaph.*

Enochian Words: In the magickal workings of Dr. John Dee (1527–1608), astrologer to Queen Elizabeth I (and some also claim him to have been her spymaster), he made contact with certain angelic beings who used a language distinct from any other. Dee believed these beings to be the same angels that transported the Hebrew prophet, Enoch, to heaven, and hence the name for the language. Enochian words are sometimes called "barbarous" because their pronunciation is so evocative.

Esoteric Knowledge, Esotericism: In many ways, Esotericism and Occultism are just alternative words for the same teachings, yet Esotericism is commonly perceived as more Spiritual and Eastern, and Occultism as more Magickal and Western. Both teach that the human person is more than what we believe we perceive as only the physical body, and that the physical universe is the smallest aspect of the entire Cosmos.

Neither are "religions," yet they both share common themes with religion of Spirituality, Ethical Guidance, belief in a Creator Source and many Spiritual Intermediaries and Guides, some of which can be various evoked in service to the person, to humanity as a whole, and to all life.

What's the difference between them and religion? Esotericism and Occultism perceive the human as an evolving being intrinsic to the purpose of the Cosmos, while religions perceive the human as serving God under the dictates of priests proclaiming for themselves spiritual authority.

Exemplar: *An ideal example, worthy of being copied.* Lou Culling liked *words* and liked to get his listeners and readers to take note of his sometimes unusual terminology. I think I more than once caught him making up words to fit what he wanted to say. I believe "example" would have been a better choice than "exemplar" because he was not pointing to something worthy of being copied; but by using it he was saying, "Pay attention to this example."

Frater Genesthai: The Magickal name of C. F. Russell, founder of the G.˙.B.˙.G.˙..

Fu His: Fu Hsi (about 4,000 BC) is the father of the Chinese Tai Chi Philosophy, of yin and yang and thus the **I Ching**. He is the first in recorded history to have invented a theory of everything—that everything is a combination of just 8 trigrams which are also phases in a universal cycle. For the first time, he symbolized yin as a broken line, yang as an unbroken line. These were observed to appear as vacated turtle shells cooked in a fire. Their appearance (it usually took three shells to get a reading) indicated the phase in the focus of attention. By the law of synchronicity, appearing symbols relate to the appearing world.

Suggested Reading:

Wu, Wei. *A Tale of the I Ching: How the Book of Changes Began.* Malibu, CA: Power Press, 2005.

G.˙.B.˙.G.˙.: The 'G.˙.B.˙.G.˙.' stands for *The Great Brotherhood of God.*

The promise of the Order was "A Shortcut to Initiation." That was the headline of a 1931 announcement appearing over a Chicago box office number. The founder of the G.˙.B.˙.G.˙. was C. F. Russell whose magical name was Frater Genesthai. Lou Culling described Russell ". . . as a teacher in Practicing Magick, was, without question, the greatest genius of this century, or of several past centuries that I have been able to trace." This was the man who had a tiff with Aleister Crowley about giving up his room at the Abbey in Cefalu, Italy and spent the next sixty hours in magical retirement sitting on 'The Rock' without food or water.

Unless you are both interested and a good historian in regard to the world of Crowley, this information won't mean much to you, and perhaps it really doesn't mean anything other than to tell you that Russell was a magician who studied with Crowley and was intimate enough to be part of Crowley's inner circle.

Following this event, Crowley gave Russell his blessing to found his own Order to be based on these three points:

Liber Legis. Crowley's "Book of the Law."

Thelema

The Aeon of Horus

Reading that 1931 announcement, Louis T. Culling wrote of his interest, and was the first to have responded. He was required to pay a fee of $5.00 and to secure at least eight "loyal and active" members to form a "Neighborhood Lodge." We have only limited information about the full size of the Order. In San Diego, there were 25 members, in Los Angeles 75, in San Francisco 50, and in Denver 125. Culling writes that there were other local lodges in all the large cities.

The G∴B∴G∴ was not an exclusively male organization and had both men and women in equal status. A "Brotherhood of God" becomes an association of men and women *with God*. Perhaps this is not a claim to equality with God, but when we look to Biblical texts we see that *God created man in His own image, in the image of God created He him, male and female created He them.* (Genesis 1:27). Elsewhere we read that Jesus—equated with God—promises that men will be able to perform miracles just as He does. *Does this make us equal to God?* Perhaps, for we are all part of one creation, and quantum theory demonstrates that the process of creation is continuous and that with will and intention we can bring about change.

The G∴B∴G∴ closed its doors to new members in 1936, and then ceased entirely in 1938. In 1936 Russell, as Head of the Order, wrote to Lou Culling: *The closing of the doors of the* G∴B∴G∴ *does not mean that the Great Work must be lost to the ken of man. I appoint you to reveal the entire curriculum of our Magick Order. This is not to be before the year 1956, and furthermore, only when you are ready to assume the responsibility.*

Why was the Order closed? Apparently the closing was planned at the time of its beginning. Culling writes, "As early as 1932, I received official notice that the doors would be closed to new members after 1936, after which the existing members would continue operations until the final closing period of 1938." He also noted in an interview transcribed in 1971 that "Russell's prediction was that after the G∴B∴G∴ closed its doors, that all occult orders were losing their dispensation (amount to nothing) and there would not be another legitimate order of any kind with any real dispensation until the year 1972."

What the G∴B∴G∴ claimed to have accomplished was to reduce all the extensive magickal material derived through the Golden Dawn and Aleister Crowley to an efficient and essential curriculum of personal or group study and practice as a true "Short Cut to Initiation."

The purpose of all magickal study is this Initiation, which culminates in the attainment of the Knowledge and Conversation of one's Holy Guardian Angel—one's true Inner, or Higher, Self. While Culling claimed that the practice of this curriculum would also lead to the attainment of magickal powers, these are considered here only as aids in the Great Work, described in psychological terms as "the integration of the subconscious with the conscious personality," and ultimately *union with the Highest Self.*

German Spirit, The: The great Goethe thought that the dominant characteristic of the German is the ideal of individualism as exemplified through such men of genius as Goethe himself, Wagner, Nietzsche, Luther, Bismarck, and others.

However, comparing the individualism of the German Spirit with the American, we see the American demanding a state that assures that each individual has the opportunity to achieve the perfect life and the greatest liberty, while the German sees the individual as subordination to the state in order that it will perfect all society to thus perfect the individual. Art, Music, Education, Literature, Industry, Science, Religion—indeed all "culture"—are all directed to that end so that unity of perfected individuals serves the Greatness of the German State—which then is the same as "the German Spirit."

The American, however, demands that the state prevent any inhibition of individual freedom of choice and maximum opportunity free of any inhibition whether by religion, government, corporations, natural disaster, or other individuals. He further sees government as obligated to provide the individual with the fundamentals of secular educational, civil society, and maximum resources for personal growth and development.

Golden Dawn, Hermetic Order: Founded in England in 1888, this magical order provided the impetus and source for magical study and practice within the Western Esoteric Tradition.

Israel Regardie's *The Golden Dawn* is an encyclopedic resource for the rituals and knowledge lectures of the GD, while his *The Tree of Life, The Middle Pillar,* and *A Garden of Pomegranates* provide in-depth exposition of the GD's magical system.

Suggested Reading:

Christopher, Lyam Thomas. *Kabbaalah, Magic & the Great Work of Self-Transformation: A Complete Course.* Woodbury: Llewellyn, 2006.

Cicero, Chic, and Sandra Tabatha Cicero. *The Essential Golden Dawn: An I*troduction to High Magic. St. Paul: Llewellyn, 2003.

Cicero, Chic, and Sandra Tabatha Cicero. *Self-initiation into the Golden Dawn Tradition: A Complete Curriculum of Study for Both the Solitary Magician and the Working Magical Group.* St. Paul: Llewellyn, 1995.

Denning, Melita, and Osborne Phillips. *The Sword and the Serpent: The Twofold Qabalistic Universe.* St. Paul: Llewellyn, 2005.

Regardie, Israel, and Carl Llewellyn Weschcke, ed. *The Golden Dawn.* With revision, expansion, and additional notes by Israel Regardie, Cris Monnastre, David Godwin, Sam Webster, Mia Dhyan Anupassana, Hal Sundt, and George Wilson. St. Paul: Llewellyn, 2002.

Great One: (Yi King/I Ching) To see or consult the Great One means to invoke the wisdom or aid of the supraconscious.

Great Stream: (Yi King/I Ching) Expanded advancement beyond the normal sphere (see Line Positions).

Great Work: The path of self-directed spiritual growth and development. This is the object of your incarnation and the meaning of your life. The Great Work is the program of growth to become all that you can be—which is the realization that you are a 'god in the making.' Within your being there is the seed of Divinity, and your job is to grow that into the Whole Person that is a 'Son of God.' It is a process that has continued from 'the Beginning' and may have no ending but it is your purpose in life. It is that which gives meaning to your being.

In this new age, you are both teacher and student and you must accept responsibility for your own destiny. *Time is of the essence!* Older methods give way to new ones because the entire process of growth and self-development has to be accelerated. Humanity has created a *time bomb* that's ticking away, and only our own higher consciousness can save us from self-destruction. But—have faith and do the Great Work for it is all part of a Great Plan.

The Great Work is not denial and restriction but fulfillment. There's not just one narrow Path, but many paths—one for each of us.

Suggested Reading:

Denning, Melita, and Osborne Phillips. *The Foundations of High Magick.* St. Paul: Llewellyn, 1991.

Heaven and Earth: (Yi King/I Ching) Another term for Yang and Yin.

Hexagram: 1) (Yi King/I Ching) A figure consisting of two Trigrams. The lower Trigram conditions the ruling force and nature of the upper Trigram (see Trigrams). A hexagram is one of sixty-four combinations of long and broken lines used in

Yi King) system of Chinese divination that are traditionally de-
rowing Yarrow Sticks, or by means of coins (heads, tails), dice,
other means. 2) (Magick) A six-pointed star consisting of two su-
iangles, one whose apex is up and the other apex down. The upward
sculine, the downward is feminine—together they symbolize union
sexual congress. In ritual magic they are used to invoke or to banish
planetary forces. 3) (Judaism) As a symbol, it is the Hebrew "Star of David."

Suggested Reading:

Culling, Louis T. *The Pristine Yi King: The Pure Wisdom of Ancient China*. St.
Paul: Llewellyn, 1989.

Kraig, Donald Michael. *Modern Magick: Twelve Lessons in the High Magickal
Arts*. Woodbury: Llewellyn, 2010.

McElroy, Mark. *I Ching for Beginners: A Modern Interpretation of the Ancient
Oracle*. St. Paul: Llewellyn, 2005.

Nishavdo, Ma. *I Ching of Love*. St. Paul: Llewellyn, 2002.

Regardie, Israel, Chic Cicero, and Sandra Tabatha Cicero. *The Tree of Life: An
Illustrated Study in Magic*. St. Paul: Llewellyn, 2001.

HGA: The Holy Guardian Angel.

High Magick: Contrary to the practice of "Spell Work," High Magick is less focused
on bringing about direct physical change such as altering the weather or attracting
love or money than in identifying the individual with the Divine within and without through "Love under Will."

It is this ability to grow and exercise all our capabilities under Will to alter the
World and ourselves that is the direct expression of our Divinity within. However it is our task to learn the purpose of our power in order to align our work
with that of the Divine throughout all manifestation, and—in truth—we can only
learn that through direct experience and extended observation.

We learn, not from others, but by applying the methods taught by others to
our own experiment and verification. The goal of High Magick is *to become more
than we are, and all that we can be!*

Higher Self: The third aspect of personal consciousness, also known as the Super-
Conscious Mind. As the Middle Self, or Conscious Mind, takes conscious control
of the Lower Self, or Sub-Conscious Mind, the Higher Self becomes more directly
involved in functioning of the Personal Consciousness.

Even though the Higher Self is also known here as the Holy Guardian Angel,
there is value in using a more easily comprehended psychological term. Words are
words and there are often many names for the same thing. But each gives a par-

ticular shape or color or tone to the thing named to expand our understanding comprehension when we are relating to larger concepts.

Qabalistically, it is the Super-Conscious Mind in Tiphareth that mediates between the Divine Self and the Lower Personality.

Holy Guardian Angel: (Also the HGA) The transcendent spiritual self that mediates between the Divine Self and the Lower Personality and serves as guardian and guide. The term was used by Abramelin the Mage as the focus of the magical operation known as "the Knowledge and Conversation of the Holy Guardian Angel." The HGA is also called the Higher Self, the Augoeides, the All-Knower, the Divine Genius, the True Ruler, Adonai, the Indwelling Spirit, etc. Carl Jung calls it his Daemon (not demon!).

Contact between the Higher, Divine Self, and the Lower Self/Personality, has to be initiated by the Personality, and that contact is the first step in the Great Work that leads to integration, and thus to Initiation.

Homer: The greatest of the Greek epic poets and author the Iliad and the Odyssey. He is believed to have lived around 850 BCE. Much of the content of his writings were speeches and these provided models for persuasive speaking and writing that was emulated throughout the ancient Greek culture.

Icarus: In Greek myth, Icarus and his father Daedalus escaped from prison flying on homemade wings of wax and feathers. Against his father's advice, Icarus flew too high, and the sun melted his waxen wings so he plunged to his death for overreaching.

I Ching: (Also Yi King) A Chinese divinatory system of 64 'hexagrams' that express the dynamic flow of energies into their physical manifestation. Like most divination, it is a manipulative system calling forth the practitioner's psychic abilities. The 64 hexagrams are all the possible combinations of pairs of eight trigrams—which are blocks of three parallel lines either broken in the center or unbroken.

In the ancient form, 50 yarrow stalks charged with 'magical' powers were used in a complicated system of spontaneous division and division again until a final number indicated either a broken or unbroken line. After six lines were obtained, a book was consulted for the meanings.

In contemporary practice, the system has been simplified to twelve sticks, half marked with a yang line and half with a yin line, all held in one hand as a prayer is made, and then six are drawn to reveal the hexagram of the moment in time. Some even use coins to determine the hexagram. By placing yourself in touch with the flow of universal energies through the random draw you will find your place in the scheme of things—at this moment. The I Ching is not so much predictive as revealing of your circumstance if you continue to follow the path you are on. The interpretation will suggest ways to realign yourself with the deeper harmony.

Suggested Reading:

McElroy, Mark. *I Ching for Beginners: A Modern Interpretation of the Ancient Oracle*. St. Paul: Llewellyn, 2005.

Brennan, J. H. *The Magical I Ching*. St. Paul: Llewellyn, 2000.

Imagination: The ability to form and visualize images and ideas in the mind, especially of things never seen or experienced directly. The imagination is an amazing and powerful part of our consciousness because it empowers our creativity—the actual ability to create. On the Tree of Life, imagination is found in Tiphareth as part of Ruach, the Conscious Self. It can be told that the Magickal Imagination may well be over 50% of the total of Magick itself. Naturally, it is meant that kind of Imagination that is brought to a point of *Subjective Reality* and most certainly never the non-willed and uncontrolled ramblings of what can hardly be called "mind" in the undisciplined person.

The imagination is one of the most powerful tools that a human has. Through the imagination we can see what is not yet existent, and can change one thing into another. We can fly without wings, see with our eyes closed, hear sounds beyond sounds or silence in place of sound. We can test things in our imagination and work out any problems. Tesla, the great electrical genius, is said to have been able to design a motor in his imagination, set it running, and then come back to it at a later time and check for wear on the bearings and other parts so he could make improvements in the design.

Imagination is the making of images, and magick is accomplished by making images and their movement real. Some of that reality comes in the process of charging those images with energy, but more comes by the acceptance of their reality on the astral plane. As images are charged in the astral world, they can be drawn into the physical world, or to have an effect on the physical plane.

The Magickal Imagination is a major factor in Magick itself—to the point where "Subjective Reality" is equal to "Normal Reality." At some point, *Inner* can be substituted for *Outer*, and *that which is imaged happens!* With new understanding of Quantum Theory, "Subjective Reality" finds new expression in Magickal practice.

The Magickal Imagination is that process at work—an *Imago* of perfection imposed to change ordinary reality into the ideal.

This is demonstrated well in Sex Magick where it is the careful role-playing of the imagination that allows the partners to exchange one reality with another. In your ritual, you submerge the personality of your partner into the imagined identity of a god or goddess. It isn't illusion, for the more often this is done, the more attributes of the god or goddess will manifest into the old personality.

The skill of the magician is enhanced by the skilled use of correspondences so that the imagined identity is supported by the established attributes associated with the god or goddess. This is why it is important to memorize and know the various appropriate correspondences.

Imago: Botanically, the last stage an insect attains during its metamorphosis. It is the name of a form of marriage therapy that addresses the relation itself rather than focus on the individual partners.

Magically, Imago is an idealized mental picture that can be recalled in its perfection at any time. While still in the realm of the Imagination, it is a manifestation of the *Force of Spirit*, taking it beyond ordinary imaginary images. To illustrate, the *Imago* was the name of the death mask worn in a special ritual on behalf of the deceased in Ancient Rome to establish his immortality. Similarly, I once had a dream about a "Life Mask" to be molded when a person was at their peak, and then worn ritually to enforce that image of youth, strength, and beauty.

Incarnating personally: After death, the familiar personality that was the person we knew in life slowly moves "upward" through the Astral and Mental into the Causal levels while "letting go" of the previously accumulated non-essential memories and addictions (chemical and otherwise) to become its "essential" self. It is at the causal level that all the lessons of the past life are extracted and the remaining a new personality is shaped with a plan for the next life. The new personality, with only a few "unfinished" memories of its previous lives, incarnates in a new body.

In a recent Boston University study published online January 2014 in the *Journal of Child Development* shows that up to age seven children often have a strong sense of their own existence extending back long before their birth into this life. Some children at this early age have memories of previous lives and others recognize persons known in a previous life.

Suggested Reading:

Newton, Michael. *Destiny of Souls: New Case Studies of Life Between Lives.* St. Paul: Llewellyn, 2000.

Newton, Michael. *Journey of Souls: Case Studies of Life Between Lives.* St. Paul: Llewellyn, 1994.

Newton, Michael. *Life Between Lives: Hypnotherapy for Spiritual Regression.* St. Paul: Llewellyn, 2004.

Newton, Michael. *Memories of the Afterlife: Life-Between Lives Stories of Personal Transformation.* Woodbury: Llewellyn, 2009.

Slate, Joe H., and Carl L. Weschcke.*Doors to Past Lives.* Woodbury: Llewellyn, 2011.

Indwelling Spirit: A largely Christian term with dual meaning. Spirit is always present in the Incarnating Personality but at the same time is rarely active. It is one of life's goals to more fully manifest that Spirit in the Personality as the Holy Guardian Angel.

Inferior/Superior: (Yi King/I Ching) The lower Trigram represents the inferior. The upper Trigram represents the superior. These descriptions may apply to one's own inferior and superior qualities or to another person.

Initiates: Culling is using this word to mean that these people were "masters" of this particular manner of esoteric working rather than being formal initiates of any occult or masonic order, although Dr. Randolph was indeed an initiate of the Rosicrucian Fraternity. Culling was also an advocate of "self-initiation" as described in his as yet unpublished book, *A Shortcut to Initiation.*

Initiation: The word has been given a variety of definitions over the years—everything from the pledging and hazing of college (and even high-school) students into fraternities and sororities to the admissions trials of secret societies, entry into occult and Masonic lodges and their grade or degrees, and to the more serious dramatic and transformative rituals of Wiccan and other esoteric groups. In some cases, the initiation rituals are truly effective in raising the consciousness of the "candidate," whereas in other cases the initiation is more a certification of the levels of study and practice the student has mastered.

In the true Occult (and psychological) sense, *Initiation* is more an inner experience than an outer one—even though a dramatic ritual may induce an inner transformation and flowering of the psychic potentials and powers of the person. Despite the promises of various teachers, gurus, priests and adepts, it is less something done to the person and more something that happens "when the student is ready."

It has been called a "tearing away of the veil" so that the new initiate now sees with new eyes, and perceives a world of greater complexity—one of added dimensions, forces, and living beings. Progressive initiations mark further growth and development as the person becomes more of the Whole Person each is intended to be. The potential is there from birth and before, and can be realized through knowledge, experience, and growth practices.

In the Theosophical concept, Initiation refers to a non-magical and more eastern process of expanding consciousness of which there are ten in number usually administered by an enlightened teacher. *And maybe there are not enough of them to go 'round'*. Self-Initiation bypasses that shortage along with the high costs of travel and the possible dangers of international travel in troubled times.

Initiator: (Yi King/I Ching) Starting energy and force. Represents Yang, to which its partner Yin responds and nourishes, develops and sustains.

Inner Relationship with the Holy Guardian Angel: This is the goal for the Retirement Ritual, and of the Great Work. Think what it is saying—that you can and will establish an actual relationship with your Higher Self. Through this relationship—the knowledge and conversation with your Holy Guardian Angel—you have the opportunity to bring together all the "parts" that are your Sub-Conscious Mind, your personal consciousness (the personality that you think of as yourself) with the super-Conscious Mind, or Higher Self—into a unified, integrated, Whole Person.

Thus you become a fully conscious, fully awake, whole person in whom lost memories are restored, lost knowledge is regained, your psychic powers developed into usable skills, your magickal abilities energized, and your Divinity awakened.

Integration: Integration is more than a bringing together: it the uniting of parts into a new whole. It is used to describe the goal of psychological development in Jungian Psychology culminating in the person actually becoming the Higher Self rather than the personality.

It is a difficult concept because it is a change of identity from the "I" of the personality into a new "I" that incorporated the transformed elements of the old personality into a new Whole Person centered on the Higher Self. "Who am I?" requires a new answer.

Intuition: A blinding flash of insight answering a question or solving a problem originating at the Soul level of consciousness. Instinctive knowing without actual knowledge and sensory validation. "Our central nervous system automatically responds to events that have not yet happened and of which we are unaware in the present." (Research by Dean Radin of the Institute of Noetic Sciences quoted in Larry Dossey's *The Power of Premonitions*.) However, there are programs that teach "intuitive thinking" in relation to specific professions, such as Nursing, and in practices such as "Creative Thinking." It is considered a faculty of the High Mental or Causal Body.

Invocation: Invocation and Evocation are often, mistakenly, used interchangeably and with little appreciation of their vast difference. Invocation precisely means to actually bring a spirit or divine presence (or <u>concept</u>) *into* the psyche and even the body of the magician. Evocation, in contrast, calls a spirit or other entity (or concept) into the presence, not the being, of the magician and usually into a magical triangle placed outside the magic circle of the magician. Invocation requires psychological and spiritual strength as well as proper preparation. It's not just that there are dangers but that the opportunities are so great.

Jesus: Whether there was a historical Jesus or only a mythical one assembled from nearly a dozen mythical processors with a nearly identical story, we may never know. The "real" Jesus we have today is an empowered "Thought Form" living for the 2.1 billion Christian Believers. As such a continually empowered thought form it has taken on archetypal quality.

It is written that Jesus said "ye are Gods . . . these things I do ye shall do and even greater." To me, that reads as both prophecy and promise; He doesn't say we will become gods but that we *are* gods who will do miracles. As we grow in Wholeness, our latent powers become skills we can perform at will. We refer to this as "Self-Empowerment" because it is not given to us by others, nor do we have to be Christian for this to happen. On the other hand, merely having psychic powers does not make us a *spiritually powerful* person who has become Whole.

Jungian Psychology: Also called Analytic Psychology—the system developed by C. G. Jung. After studying with Freud he advanced a more spiritual approach to psychotherapy evolving out of his studies of occult traditions and practices including, in particular, alchemy, astrology, dream interpretation, the I Ching, the Tarot, and spiritualism.

For Jung, the whole range of occult and religious phenomena have evolved out of the relationship between the individual consciousness and the collective unconscious. While the personal unconscious or Sub-Conscious Mind is the 'lower' part of the individual consciousness, it is through it that we also experience and have experience of the elements of the collective unconscious—most importantly the role of the archetypes.

The archetypes are 'collectives' of images and energies relating to 1) role specific functional, formative and universal experiences such as Mother, Father, Lover, Judge, Hero, etc., 2) those that are more personal with karmic content including the Shadow (repressions), the Anima (expressions of the Feminine in men), the Animus (expressions of the Masculine in women), and 3) the Self (the evolving Whole Person that overshadows the Personality).

Kabbalah: Kabbalah is a complete system of knowledge about all the dimensions of the universe and of the human psyche organized into 'the Tree of Life' diagram showing the inner construction and the connections between levels and forms of consciousness, energy and matter.

The Kabbalah—spellings of "Kabbalah" and "Kabala" generally refer to the original Jewish version, "Cabala" refers the Christian version, and "Qabala" and

Qabalah" for the magical or Hermetic (and Greek) version—is probably the most complete purview of the world as perceived and experienced through spiritual vision that we have. It is a systematic organization of spiritual reality into a manageable formula for human study along with a methodology of "correspondences" to organize all of human knowledge.

It is a treasure trove for practicing magicians and the most expert self-study program of progressive mediation the world has ever seen.

It provides a resource for understanding and applying the principles of Magick, for understanding the dynamics of the psyche, and for interpreting human history and action.

The present day Tarot specifically relates to the Tree of Life.

Suggested Reading:

Andrews, Ted. *Simplified Qabala Magic.* St. Paul: Llewellyn, 2003.

Christopher, Lyam Thomas. *Kabbalah, Magic & the Great Work of Self-Transformation: A Complete Course.* Woodbury: Llewellyn, 2006.

Dennis, Geoffrey W. *Encyclopedia of Jewish Myth, Magic & Mysticism.* Woodbury: Llewellyn, 2015.

Godwin, David. *Godwin's Cabalistic Encyclopedia: A Complete Guide to Cabalistic Magick.* St. Paul: Llewellyn, 1994.

Gonzalez-Wippler, Migene. *Kabbalah for the Modern World.* St. Paul: Llewellyn, 1993.

Gonzalez-Wippler, Migene. *Keys to the Kingdom: Jesus and the Mystic Kabbalah.* St. Paul: Llewellyn, 2004.

Malachi, Tau. *Gnosis of the Cosmic Christ: A Gnostic Christian Kabbalah.* St. Paul: Llewellyn, 2005.

Regardie, Israel, Chic Cicero, and Sandra Tabatha Cicero. *A Garden of Pomegranates: Skrying on the Tree of Life.* St. Paul: Llewellyn, 1999.

Regardie, Israel, Chic Cicero, and Sandra Tabatha Cicero. *The Middle Pillar: The Balance Between Mind and Magic*St. Paul: Llewellyn, 1998.

Stavish, Mark. *Kabbalah for Health and Wellness.* Woodbury: Llewellyn, 2007.

Trobe, Kala. *Magic of Qabalah: Visions of the Tree of Life.* St. Paul: Llewellyn, 2001.

Karma: In general, the force generated by a person's actions, many of which are created in life by thoughtless action in response to such emotional drives as lust, greed, blind hate, and particular ideologies and theologies—themselves an excuse for "not thinking about it." *Following orders* is no excuse for the killing, mutilation, rape, theft, and other crimes executed under direction of power driven leaders.

Kelley, Edward (1555–1595): Dr. Dee's assistant. As a clairvoyant he could see the angels and what they were doing.

Kerner, Ian: A nationally recognized sex and relationship counselor and *New York Times* best-selling author of numerous books, including the very important *She Comes First.*

Khien: (Yi King/I Ching) The Trigram with three Yang lines. Also referred to as Lingam. Khien is the Great Initiating Force.

Khwan: (Yi King/I Ching) The Trigram of three Yin lines. Also referred to as Yoni. Khwan is the Great Womb, the nourisher and developer. Invokes and receives.

Life Goals and Purpose: Every life has purpose: We are here to grow, to become more than we are. Each of us has the ability to apply our inherent powers and our emerging skills to the challenge of accelerating personal growth.

Individually, we have instinctive, and consciously determined goals—some inspired by outside events, such as reactions to observed poverty, gender discrimination, hate-actions, etc., others in response to observed opportunities. Some are distinctly personal—as in the drive to overcome a physical handicap—others are individual as career goals, the writing of books, and other accomplishments. Other than those that are criminal and injurious to others, the setting of life goals are both simply and expressly that which amplifies the evolutionary process. It is not enough to just express the biological force of reproduction, the fight to be king of the herd, to "feather your own nest," or even to climb the next hill. Those are givens; you must add to the givens with personal and social goals, ambitions to accomplish, to improve. It's the *management* of your life, and it comes from the spiritual level. Seek guidance from within.

Line Position: This is an important key in the Yi King. Marc Edmund Jones, an eminent authority on reformulated concepts in astrology, wrote about the three Fire Signs—Aries, Leo and Sagittarius—in relation to their natural houses, the first, fifth, and ninth, as follows: "The First House corresponds to starting a sphere. The Fifth House, to attaining autocracy in one's sphere. The Ninth House, to going beyond one's sphere or expanding it."

This concept has a remarkable correspondence with the three line positions. Line number one (the lowest) is symbolized as Earth and as being the human body per se, including the desires and emotional drives. Line number two—the central line—is the thinking man—the Conscious Mind. Line number three—the top line—is symbolized as "heaven"—superior-inspired wisdom.

Although in a Hexagram the upper three lines constitute the upper Trigram, the customary way of counting is to continue with four, five, and six lines. The upper Trigram is superior and the lower Trigram is inferior.

Love under will: It's the second part of the phrase that begins with 'Love is the Law.' "Love magickally directed, and used as a spiritual formula," says Crowley. This is an important clarification for what otherwise has commonly been interpreted as justification for a kind of 'free love' movement. As a 'spiritual formula' it is a concise instruction for Sex Magick as practiced by the G∴B∴G∴. This "Will," is the True Will of the Higher Self, while sexual love arouses the energy directed by the True Will in fulfillment of our magickal goals.

Low Magic: Generally, it is the intentional ritual action supported by various physical correspondences with particular herbs, astrological factors, symbols, etc. lending strength to the visualized accomplishment through psychic powers to make things happen as a materialization of desire. It is the practical magic of Spell Craft—simple rituals for Success, Money, Love, Health, etc. It is found in most books on Wicca and Witchcraft, the Power of Attraction, and Success Power.

Lower personality: Generally conceived as the Sub-Conscious Mind, also called the Personal Unconscious.

Lower Self: The Conscious Mind and the Sub-Conscious Mind, together, are the Lower Self.

Ma'at: The ancient Egyptian concept of truth, balance, order, law, morality, and justice. Ma'at was also personified as the goddess who regulated the stars, seasons, and the actions of both humans and the deities, who established order out of chaos at the moment of creation.

Magic Mirror: A device, similar to the crystal ball, to focus attention in a process of self-hypnosis to open a channel to the astral world, i.e., the Sub-Conscious Mind.

Magical Oaths: The two oaths taken by the G∴B∴G∴ members can be seen and used to describe the importance of understanding the true nature of a magical oath—which is to establish a new relationship with your Higher Self that puts meaning into life.

I swear to tell myself the truth.

I swear to regard every event (or condition) as a particular dealing between myself and the Holy Guardian Angel.

Truth is generally a *relative* term for the simple reason that we can never know all the facts around any situation. At the same time, in a legal sense an oath is binding to honestly answer every question and perform every duty to the best of your ability.

A magickal oath is different. It requires that you continuously tell yourself the truth, which may mean thinking over what you previously thought to be true and then telling yourself a new truth. It isn't honesty before the Law, but honesty before your own Higher Self.

An "event" isn't really *every* event, but those which take on a special kind of "halo effect" of calling itself to your attention. It must arise within your own personal sphere of awareness. It may be a completely ordinary event, but suddenly it stands out as if speaking to you. Yet to regard, or rather to believe, that everything which a person sees, feels or hears is an omen or message, is a psychopathic condition.

The main point is that one must maintain a sense of keen awareness. When this is done, the way is open for one's intuition or inspiration to inform one on any possible oracular import. As part of a devoted program of relating to your Higher Self, then one can get much symbology and "conversation" concerning his Great Work in the many things that touch your life. As you progress, both the events and their messages are greatly increased—those that are of value.

Under this Oath, the budding magician stands between two extremes. On the one side is the near-psychopath who regards everything that touches the eye and ear as a particular secret personal message. On the other side is the impervious one who sees no soul message in anything. Here, the neophyte stands in the middle ground, with open eye and ear to heed anything that may be relevant to his Great Work.

Magickal Curriculum: Simply a concisely developed program of study and practice.

Meditation: Over the years there's been a lot of nonsense written and spoken about this subject than perhaps anything other than dieting for weight reduction. Simply put, meditation is: 1) An emptying of the mind of all thoughts and 'chatter' often by concentration only on the slow inhalation and exhalation of breath and is characterized by slow alpha and theta waves. It induces relaxation and a 'clean slate' preparatory for receiving psychic impressions. 2) A careful thinking about a particular subject in a manner that brings access to physical memories as well as astral and mental level associations of knowledge about that subject. 3) A state of consciousness characterized by relaxed alertness reducing sensory impressions with increased receptivity to inner plane communications.

Meditation, hypnosis, and self-hypnosis are all associated with special mental states which facilitate positive personality changes and connect with higher dimensions of the psyche. In addition, those particular mind disciplines being used to achieve particular therapeutic results are receiving increasing professional and scientific attention.

Hypnosis is increasingly used with healing applications in all fields of medicine: to modulate pain, reduce certain side effects of medications, and to accelerate healing during and after convalescence. It is also used to prepare patients for surgery and hospital procedures, and childbirth by reducing anxiety and instilling affirmative healing imagery. It should be understood that any discussion of hypnosis is inclusive of self-hypnosis, and it should also be understood that anything that can be accomplished through hypnosis can be accomplished through meditation, but we have to go beyond the common perceptions about meditation as just a state of soulful self-oblivion to understand the worldly practical applications.

Hypnosis has been called the most powerful non-drug physical relaxant available. In addition it has the potential to reach beyond the neuromuscular system to involve the autonomic nervous system to positively influence the mechanisms of disease while integrating the healing process with the emotional system and the higher realms of the psyche.

Meditation, hypnosis, and self-hypnosis are all associated with special mental states which facilitate positive personality changes and connect with higher dimensions of the psyche. In addition, those particular mind disciplines being used to achieve particular therapeutic results, are receiving increasing professional and scientific attention.

Meditation, hypnosis, and self-hypnosis, all progress from the relaxation of the physical body to remove or by-pass emotional blockage and open the mind to possibilities beyond past restrictive conditioning. Meditation has a particular value in reduction of stress—considered by most health professionals as a genuine "killer" of older people because it is cumulative in physical damage and tends to become a habitual mental pattern.

Like Self-Hypnosis, meditation is mostly self-administered and can be applied entirely for physical, emotional, and mental benefits. From a Mind/Body perspective, meditation is a non-drug way to lower stress levels, relax any area of the body, reduce blood pressure levels, calm the emotions, and clear the mind.

Before going too deeply into the "overlay" of various traditional yogic and religious practices and teachings, we need to discuss the single most important key: deep, regular, and relatively slow breathing. Study yourself: when you focus on many activities, physical and mental, *you tend to tense up, breathe shallowly and often hold your breath.* Don't! Practice your full and regular breathing at all times and you will improve your health, reduce stress and tension, think more clearly, and control emotional reactions to external stimuli.

This controlled breathing should become habitual, but conscious observation will enable you to restore any interruption of that fundamental pattern. Physical relaxation results, correcting many health "disturbances" that result from physical stress. Control breathing and you control stress. But, for a body already habitually stressed, additional programs of relation of both mind and body will deliver more results, and will facilitate psychic development and spiritual growth. You will find benefit in silently speaking the phrase "breathing deeply and evenly" in a relaxed rhythm coordinated with your breath. "Breathing deeply" as you inhale, "and evenly" on the exhale. Let it become a constant reminder.

Body-Mind Relaxation. To get started with Body/Mind meditation requires no training, just common sense. The keys to success are found in:

1) A comfortable posture, preferably seated in either a modest reclining or a spine upright position;

2) Deep but not exaggerated breathing at a comfortably slow pace;

3) An intentional stilling of the mind. While not a requirement, in most meditative traditions, the eyes are closed. In some traditions, different eye focus points have different effects, and points such as the "third eye", or gazing over the nose, help to lock the brain into a point of stillness. Different meditations may call for staring into at a candle flame, or other object of focus (Tratak meditation).

Often, especially when first beginning a regular practice of meditation, there is noticeable tension in the body. You can easily add a Tension and Release procedure to aid Body-Mind Relaxation.

Start by pointing the toes of both feet like a ballet dancer, and hold them pointed for 60 seconds, and then relax. Next, spread the toes of both feet apart as hard as you can and hold them that way for 60 seconds, and release. You will feel mild warmth and relief. Repeat tensing, holding, and releasing with both ankles and calves. Then move upward, repeating for each muscle group: thighs, buttocks and groin, chest, upper arms, forearm and wrists, hands and fingers, neck and shoulders, mouth and facial muscles, brow and scalp.

Alternatively, you might prefer first with working up the left leg, then the right, and similarly with the arms. Either way, *feel* the whole body as relaxed while restoring the breathing rhythm, slowly and deeply. Silently or quietly tell yourself "breathing deeply and evenly, I am more and more relaxed." Repeat to yourself, "breathing deeply and evenly" in a relaxed rhythm several times as you note that your mind is only involved with that one thought.

"Mantra Meditation" is by far the best known form of meditation, and you've already engaged in mantra meditation as you slowly repeated the phrase "breathing deeply and evenly" in a relaxed rhythm coordinated with your breath. Instead, in mantra meditation you can repeat other words, phrases, and short prayers in a similar fashion. Every tradition includes such mantras that may be used in the same way but with effects that do reach into the spiritual dimension.

Each mantra, while having similar physical and mental effects, will also produce different emotional feelings and induce unique spiritual effects identified with the particular tradition and the words or names used. Phrases containing "God Names" are especially powerful, as you would expect.

Words aside, meditation can be classified into three types according to their orientation which in turn can be distinguished from each other by brainwave patterns.

Concentration is focused attention on a selected object, thought, image, sound, repetitive prayer, chant, mantra etc., while minimizing distractions and constantly bringing the mind back to concentrate on the chosen object.

Mindfulness requires a non-reactive monitoring of present experience: perception, thought, feelings, etc. The meditator centers focuses awareness on an object *or* process—such as breath, sound, visualized image a mantra, koan, or on a physical or mental exercise—while maintaining an "open" focus that may lead to insight or enlightenment. The meditator must passively observe without reaction.

Transcendent Mindfulness requires that the meditator is open to experiencing a *shift* in consciousness and even changes in the physical/etheric body, all the while focusing on a thought, image, or object to the point of identifying with it.

Meditation can be practiced while seated or standing in particular positions (called *asanas* in yoga), but once you have broken habitual mental patterns that produce stress, you can be meditating while walking or doing simple repetitive tasks.

In a form of meditation using visualization, such as Chinese Qi Gong, the practitioner concentrates on flows of energy (Qi) in the body, starting in the abdomen and then circulating through the body, until dispersed (http://en.wikipedia.org/wiki/Meditation-cite_note-Perez-8).

Mantra meditation is also the most familiar form of concentration, particularly when you expand the definition of "mantra" to include chants and prayers. Mantras are usually associated with Hinduism and Buddhism, but the method is generic and can apply to any tradition. Chants are commonly associated with Judaism and many neo-Pagan religions. Sometimes magical "spells" are chanted. Repetitive Prayers are found in most religions, but are particularly associated with

Christianity, Judaism, and Islam. In Hinduism, one of the oldest sacred texts, the Brihadaranyaka Upanishad says the goal of meditation is: "having becoming calm and concentrated, one perceives the self (the *tman*) within oneself."

Yogic science teaches that man-tra ("man" meaning mind, "tra" to cut) helps "yoke" the mind to a more conscious and harmonious vibration. The repetitive use of mantras can aid meditation, clear the Sub-Conscious of unhealthy attachments, and break accumulated mental patterns.

While I list some of the best known Hindu mantras transliterated into English, we still need to provide phonetic pronunciation guide.

Sanskrit Pronunciation Guide

a = *a* as in *sonata*	ai = *ai* as in *aisle*
ah = *a* as in *alms*	I = *I* as in *big*
ey = *ey* as in *they*	oh = *o* as in *no*
ee = *ee* as in *reed*	u = *oo* as in *fool*
s (at the beginning of a word = *ss* as in *Ssiva*)	
s or sh (in the middle of a word = *sh* as in *she*)	

From *Words of Power* by Brian and Esther Crowley, Llewellyn.

OM, or AUM

Pronounced: *Aum,* or *Ah, Oo, Mm.* Note: The Ah can start at the solar plexus, moving up to the heart, and then to the throat. Repeat several times, and then the Ah should commence at the throat; then move up to the brow with the Oo; and up to the crown with the Mm. The full mantra should be extended out in vibratory fashion to *Ahuu-oooo-muummm,* feeling the vibrations as indicated.

Meaning? There is no meaning as this is said to be the primal sound that initiated the universe. Still, it can be considered in three parts: the "A" as in "the beginning," the "U" as the maintenance and preservation of what was created, and the "M" as transformational power. Another perspective views the "A" and the Physical Plane, the "U" as the Astral and Mental Planes, and the "M" as Spirit.

OM MANI PADME HUM

Pronounced: *Aa-oo-mm Mah-nee-Pad-may Hoom.* Note: In extended meditative work, colors may be visualized with each syllable as follows:

Om—White, the world of the devas.

Ma—Green, the realms of spirits.

Ni—Yellow, the realm of human.

Pad—Blu, the realm of animals.

Me—Red, the realm of nature.

Hum—Gray, the realm of the underworld.

Meaning: "Hail to Him who is the Jewel in the Lotus." It is the Infinite bound within the Finite. It is used as a protective mantra, and as an attunement of the person with the Divine.

OM HRIM KRIM HUM SHRIM

This mantra is actually four mantras general pronounced as one, but also separately. The "Four Great Goddess Mantras" bring about development and integration of the mind, body, and soul. Each governs primal forms of energy.

HRIM: (pronounced *Hreem*) rules over the cosmic magnetic energy and the power of the soul and causal body. It is the prime mantra of the Great Goddess, ruler of the worlds, and holds all her creative and healing powers. HRIM awakens us at a soul or heart level, connecting us to Divine forces of love and attraction, opening the lotus of the heart to the inner Sun of consciousness (*The Mantric Approach of the Vedas* by David Frawley).

KRIM: (pronounced *Kreem*) rules over prana as lightning or electrical energy. KRIM grants all spiritual faculties and powers—from the arousing of kundalini to opening the third eye. It has a special power relative to the lower chakras, which it can both stimulate and transform. It helps awaken and purify the subtle body. It is the great mantra of Kali, the Goddess of energy and transformation. KRIM carries the supreme life force (*The Mantric Approach of the Vedas* by David Frawley).

HUM: (pronounced *Hoom)* is a mantra of the inner fire. It represents the soul hidden in the body, the Divine immanent in the world. It both calls the divine down into us and offers our soul upward to the Divine for transformation in the sacred fire of awareness. It is used to destroy negativity and creates great passion and vitality (*The Mantric Approach of the Vedas* by David Frawley).

SHRIM: (pronounced *Shreem*) is a mantra of love, devotion and beauty. SHRIM is a mantra directed to Lakshmi, the Goddess of Beauty and divine grace. Yet SHRIM works at a deeper level than merely to give us the good things of life, including health. It takes us to the heart and brings faith and steadiness to our emotional nature (*The Mantric Approach of the Vedas* by David Frawley).

Another group of mantras are used individually to stimulate the psychic centers, or *chakras as follows:*

LANG (pronounced *LAM*)—Muladhara: Root Center

VANG (pronounced *VAM*)—Swadhistana: Sex Center

RANG (pronounced *RAM*)—Manipura: Navel Center
YANG (pronounced *YAM*)—Anahata: Heart Center
HANG (pronounced *HAM*)—Vishuddhi: Throat Center
ONG (pronounced *OM*)—Ajna: Third Eye Center
Silence—Sahasrara: Crown Center

There are many, many more traditional Hindu and Buddhist mantras with various applications. As indicated above, some have specific transformational effects, while others are chanted or sung to produce feelings of peace, unity, and communion.

Judaism: The core of Jewish meditation disciplines are found in the Kabbalah in which the ultimate purpose is to understand and cleave to the Divine. Classic methods include mental visualization of the higher realms through which the soul navigates to achieve certain ends.

The basic belief is that through meditation one can separate his soul from his body and transcend to the upper universes. The Kabbalah serves as a map telling one how to prepare and where to go.

Meditation involves controlling ones thought process, blocking out the five senses, and entering expanded consciousness. Without meditation a person uses only three to five percent of his brain. Part of the brain receives signals of spirituality, but these signals are very sublime and are blocked out by the other five senses. When one clears his head of all thought he can feel spirituality and eventually can transcend to the upper worlds.

Jewish meditations are, of course, in the native language of Hebrew, and the mantric words will be presented in transliterated English. Here is a phonetic pronunciation guide:

The Hebrew letter *chet* is pronounced "ch" as in the Scottish word *loch.*

The letter *zayin* = "dz" as in *adze.*

Kaph = "kh" as in *Khmer.*

Tzaddi = "tz" as the *ts* in *cats.*

Quf = the guttural "q" as in *Qoran.*

The proclaimed goal of Kabbalah meditation is able to answer three of life's most critical questions: *who we really are, where we came from, and why we are here.* The answers provide the means to achieve true joy and a deep sense of accomplishment. You are able to experience life under the light of the Higher Being of your own realization.

The central focus of Kabbalah is on the Tree of Life, a unique diagram representing the Macrocosm and the Microcosm—the whole of that which is without and the whole of that which is within, the Universe and the Whole Person.

This Tree of Life and the wisdom of the Kabbalah are the foundation of most Western metaphysics and *invisibly* of the whole of Western science and philosophy. With it, we have the means to understand and relate to the body of the Universe and of Man, and the Soul of Man and of the Universe.

While there are individual Hebrew mantras, the premier form of meditation is found in the practices of "Path-Working" often in combination with individual cards from the Tarot. These are imaginative journeys or *guided meditations* following the twenty-two paths between the ten Sephiroth which should be understood as the "God Forces" behind the universe.

From a psychic perspective, Path-Working has been described as *the art of clairvoyantly investigating the Paths of the Tree of Life.* The technique was largely developed by adepts of the Golden Dawn and Aurum Solis but has become a comprehensive meditative system outside the magical orders. Once the meditator has passively followed the guided meditation, he should then attempt to re-tread the Paths while out-of-body following certain ritual techniques involving visualized symbols, performing certain gestures and vibrating Divine Names.

Path-working can be classified as a *Transcendent Mindfulness* form of meditation in which shifts in consciousness are the intended result. These are *astral* learning experiences that can be understood as "initiations."

Generally included in the visualized symbols used with each path are the related Tarot cards (major arcana) and/or the related Hebrew letter. Just as the individual Tarot Arcanum communicates particular information and *energies,* so do the individual Hebrew letters. That is a deep subject unto itself.

Because Path-Working is a visual exercise, it needs some sort of visual focus and the images of the Tarot Trumps are the most convenient for this purpose, and often serve to frame the type of vision that ensues.

We can't go into even an overview of path-working in this short space, so we refer the reader to *A Garden of Pomegranates: Skrying on the Tree of Life,* by Israel Regardie with Chic and Sandra Tabatha Cicero for a full exposition.

To the kabalistic student, speech is the medium of revelation and hence language itself is sacred and an object of contemplation. The 22 letters of the Hebrew alphabet are profound realities embodying those primal spiritual forces that are, in effect, the "building blocks of Creation." Hebrew is called a "flame language" and each letter appears to be shaped out of *flames* that can channel forces connecting Heaven with Earth is special ways.

Because of the belief that these letters (the forces embodied therein) predated Creation the letters themselves and the order and manner in which they are utilized are of crucial significance, and their properly pronounced sounds transformative.

Hebrew chants (mantras) were designed as special formulas able to arouse spiritual forces.

As with Hindu mantras, the purification of the divine power within is attained through the correct and persistent vibration of the sacred sounds and can result in powerful effects of a physical and paranormal nature.

Active Imagination: The pre-eminent psychologist, C. G. Jung developed a technique of meditation called "Active Imagination," which is similar to Path-Working.

The meditator is instructed to choose a dream or fantasy image, and then concentrate on the image to fix it in the mind. Contemplating it serves to animate it, and the alterations that occur must be noted as they reflect the psychic processes occurring in the unconscious which appear in the form of images of "conscious memory material," thus uniting conscious and unconscious.

Instead of merely observing events, the meditator participates as a real character in drama that is taking place within his psyche. The goal is to assimilate lessons from the Unconscious into Consciousness in "Individuation"—the conscious process of psychic healing and integration of all parts of the psyche. The importance of being involved in the vision rather than just being an observer is to integrate the statements of the unconscious and to assimilate their compensatory content—thereby producing a whole new meaning.

Jung observed in his own active imagination sessions two types of fantasies: one was related to images from his own past, but the others were mythological, archetypal, spiritual, and religious". He recognized these as symbols of basic drives common to every man throughout history—leading him to form the theory of the Collective Unconscious, perhaps his greatest achievement.

In Path-Working, the meditator likewise must experience himself as a character fully participating in the vision he is experiencing. In addition, the symbolism of the Paths of the Tree of Life is likewise "mythological, archetypal, spiritual, and religious," and the Tarot Arcana are direct representations of the Archetypes. The Path-Worker has a set framework within which to explore the archetypes himself.

Likewise, we can compare the self-initiatory process of path-working with the individuation process of Jung's Analytical Psychology.

The Middle Pillar Exercise: Perhaps one of the most important magickal exercises based on the Kabbalah and given here in Hebrew was developed by the Golden Dawn, and described in *The Middle Pillar* by Israel Regardie (edited with new material by Chic and Sandra Tabatha Cicero). The following version is a variation practiced by Carl Llewellyn Weschcke in his personal discipline.

Essentially, it is a meditational exercise intended to open and balance the five specific psychic centers (chakras) that correspond with the Sephiroth on the central pillar of the Tree of Life as visualized within the physical body.

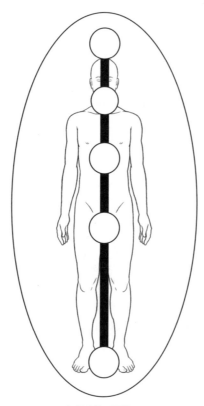

Middle Pillar

While visualizing the Sephirothic Centers within the body as shown in the illustration, reach up to center above the head (Kether) with both hands, see the center fill with white light from the Cosmos above, then vibrate the holy name AHIH (Eh-he-yeh) three times, pausing in between each to take a deep breath. After the third vibration, inhale and bring your hands down to the throat center (Daath) while visualizing the light descending from the crown to the throat, and vibrate the holy name YHVH ALHIM (Ye-hoh-voh E-loh-heem) three times as previously.

Continue on down the Middle Pillar in the same manner, vibrating YHVH ALOAH ve-DAATH (Ye-hoh-voh El-oah ve-Da-ath) at the heart, SHADDAI AL CHAI (Shah-dai El Chai) at the genital center, and then ADNI HARTZ (Ad-doh-nai ha-Ah-retz) at the earth center.

In review, you have brought light from above down the central column of the Tree and your spine, filling each center with that white light. Each center is pulsing with the light.

Continue experiencing the light continuing down the central column, but now slowly bring your hands from their down position (just like in the illustration) up on each side while seeing and feeling Earth energy rising upward through the spinal column in your inhalation, and when you reach the crown see and feel it fountain out and down outside your body to sweep back in at the feet. Now comes the more challenging part: With each inhalation pull energy up the center column, and with each exhalation let energy flow down the center column as well as outside the body in a complete and continuous full circulation of light and energy. It sounds more complex than it is. Continue this for several minutes, and then let it dissipate as you feel calmly energized in your body and aura.

The Open Dialogue: There is one particular form of meditation dear to writers and researchers alike—that of tapping into the Unconscious to secure answers to specific questions.

In the *Mindfulness Meditation* there is focus on a single object or idea combined with openness to insight. In the "Open Dialogue" our focus is on a specific question while we are open to a variety of answers that might be specific to the question but more often will be "clues" that can be noted and then become the object of further continued meditation, or taken up again at a later meditation.

In essence, we are entrusting the Unconscious to come up with generally nonspecific answers to our specific question that may lead to further questions and further answers that are more clue-like than specific. It's a kind of inner brainstorming that can be continued over a period of time. And even though it is presented here in this presentation on meditation, the same process can be continued with the use of Tarot cards, Tea Leaf Reading, Pendulum Divination, Dreaming, Crystal Gazing, Spirit Communication, etc.

The "Open Dialogue" is for Big Questions that may even be your Life Work, but more often are chapters in your "book of life."

And, in closing . . . And for our final mantra we remind the readers that the primary purpose of all meditation and all psychic work is to bring each person to union with the Divine Spirit that is everywhere but most easily found within:

SOHAM, HAMSA

(So-ham, Hahm-sa)

He Am I; I am He.

Suggested Reading:

Chadwick, Gloria. *Inner Journeys: Meditations and Visualizations.* Woodbury: Llewellyn, 2006.

Clement, Stephanie. *Meditation for Beginners: Techniques for Awareness, Mindfulness, and Relaxation.* St. Paul: Llewellyn, 2002.

Crowley, Brian, and Esther Crowley. *Words of Power: Sacred Sounds of East and West.* St. Paul: Llewellyn, 1991.

De Biasi, Jean-Louis. *The Magick of the Upper Paths*, Forthcoming, Llewellyn.

Denning, Melita, and Osborne Phillips. *Magical States of Consciousness.* St. Paul: Llewellyn, 1985.

Denning, Melita, and Osborne Phillips. *The Sword and the Serpent.* St. Paul: Llewellyn, 1988.

Paulson, Genevieve L. *Meditation as Spiritual Practice.* St. Paul: Llewellyn, 2005.

Regardie, Israel, Chic Cicero, and Sandra Tabatha Cicero. *A Garden of Pomegranates: Skrying on the Tree of Life.* St. Paul: Llewellyn, 1999.

Regardie, Israel, Chic Cicero, and Sandra Tabatha Cicero. *The Middle Pillar: The Balance Between Mind and Magic.* St. Paul: Llewellyn, 1998.

Regardie, Israel, Chic Cicero, and Sandra Tabatha Cicero. *The Tree of Life: An Illustrated Study in Magic.* St. Paul: Llewellyn, 2001.

Slate, Joe H., and Carl L. Weschcke. *Psychic Empowerment: Tools and Techniques.* Woodbury: Llewellyn, 2011.

Tyson, Donald. *The Power of the Word: The Secret Code of Creation.* St. Paul: Llewellyn, 1995.

Middle Consciousness: An alternate name for the Conscious Mind.

Mother Earth: All life on this planet is born of Mother Earth, living on Her Home and within her Aura. She is our Mother and is known by many names.

Nature Religion: All ancient religions were Nature Religions. Today, modern Wicca is referred to as a Nature Religion as its adherents attune themselves to the natural cycles perceived in the movements of Sun and Moon and reflected in the growth of plants and the movement of animals. A practical to these natural rhythms is Llewellyn's annual *Moon Sign Book.*

Netzach: The seventh Sephirah on the Tree of Life, Victory. It is located at the bottom of the Pillar of Mercy.

> God Name: Tetragrammton Tzabaoth (Lord of Armies)
> Archangels: Hanial
> Angelic Host: Tarshishim
> Astrological Correspondence: Venus
> Body: the left hip

Colors: in Atziluth: amber, in Briah: emerald, in Yetzirah: bright yellow green, in Assiah: olive flecked with gold.

Consciousness: the Emotions, as part of Ruach, (the Conscious Self)

Element: Fire

Magical Image: a beautiful naked woman

Symbol: the rose

Tarot: The four Sevens

New Aeon: Also known as *The New Age.*

New Aeon of Horus: *Is this the same as "the New Age" or "the Age of Aquarius?"* Perhaps yes, perhaps no. Crowley predicted the coming of *the "New Aeon of Horus" when Every Person is a Star moving by his own inner light and will.* Sincere followers of Crowley would likely say there's no connection. Astrologers are just as likely to say that the zodiacal entry into Aquarius has little connection to either, while maintaining that Aquarius does embody much that is claimed for the New Age and for the New Aeon.

My own inclination is to believe they are all manifestations of the same thing—that we are indeed in a New Age opening up opportunities for growth and development of the Whole Person. Maybe the astronomical/astrological precession triggers a more *Aquarian perception* in all of us, leaving behind what has been claimed as repressive in the Age of Pisces. And maybe this is the same as the New Aeon of Horus. *Why not?*

I believe we are in a new *era* (to substitute those three loaded concepts with a neutral word for purposes of discussion) in which there has been a shift of energies allowing more people to open up to new ideas and to respond to new ideas. And, yes, it is likely that the transition from Piscean to Aquarian energies facilitates this. Again: *Why not?*

Regardless, any study of history will demonstrate that we have more intellectual freedom and opportunity today than in any previous era we know anything about. Myth may claim that in some ancient past, perhaps in some Atlantean civilization, we had a similar situation that led to abuse of knowledge by the few to the detriment of all.

Crowley tells us that this new age brings us the freedom and the *impetus*—a "call" urging to step ahead of the external regimentation. Individually, we have to make the effort while the energies of the age make it possible to succeed. Magick is no longer for the few, the elite priesthood of the secret lodge, but for everybody who makes the effort. Magick is the technology for self-transformation and self-empowerment. Every Man and every Woman can become a Star by employing the esoteric technology now available to everyone.

Myth always contains some kind of truth, and perhaps this warns us of needs for awareness of potential hazards as more people are enabled to develop their psychic powers and to more easily gain deeper understanding of the human psyche and of quantum theory.

New Age: A phrase adapted by certain occult writers to describe 1) A belief in a new level of consciousness coincident with the Aquarian Age. 2) A social movement of diverse spiritual and political elements directed toward the transformation of individuals and society through heightened spiritual awareness obtained through practices of meditation, yoga, ritual, and channeling. 3) A cultural phenomenon often associated with the psychedelic and mind-altering substances widely available in the 1960s.

It is an ideal of harmony and progress that includes feminist, ecological, holistic, and organic principles expressed through an alternative lifestyle that developed its own music, fashions, communal living, open sexuality, and political activism.

It became a commercial category, particularly in the book trade, which brought together subjects related to self-understanding, self-transformation, and self-development including acupuncture, alchemy, ancient civilizations, angels, anthroposophy, aromatherapy, astral projection, astrology, Atlantis, auras, biofeedback, Buddhism, channeling, chanting, chakras, Chinese medicine, complementary healing, creative visualization, crystals, divination, dream interpretation, Egyptology, energy healing, ESP, extra-terrestrial life, ghosts, Gnosticism, handwriting analysis, herbalism, hypnosis, Kabbalah, magick, martial arts, meditation, natural foods, numerology, occultism, organic gardening, Paganism, palmistry, paranormal phenomena, past lives, psychic healing, psychic powers, reiki, reincarnation, runes, self-hypnosis, sex magick, shamanism, spiritual healing, Spiritualism, Tantra, Tarot, Theosophy, UFOs, Wicca, witchcraft, yoga, Zen, etc.

The New Age movement is inclusive of a resurgent paganism and rejection of formalistic religion in favor of Nature Mysticism and personal spirituality. While it generally includes roles for ministers and spiritual counselors along with those for priest and priestess as in Wicca, the religious aspect is participatory rather than hierarchical, ecstatic rather than puritanical, initiatory rather than theological, and inner-directed rather than outer. Divinity is found both within the person and in Nature, directly experienced rather than requiring an intermediary, and self-responsible rather than authoritarian.

While there are numerous organizations and groups, they are mostly informal, usually centered around lectures and workshops, and non-restrictive.

Odysseus: Hero of Homer's epic poem, the *Odyssey*.

OTO: O∴T∴O∴ - O∴T∴O∴ (Ordo Templi Orientis—The "Order of the Temple of the East") The OTO was or is (depending on how you look at it) a magickal order founded by Karl Kellner (1851–1905) in 1890. Upon Kellner's passing in 1905, the leadership passed to Theodore Reuss (1885–1923) and then to Aleister Crowley in 1922.

Currently there are (or were) two O∴T∴O∴ organizations: One in England headed by Kenneth Grant and the other headed by successors to Grady McMurtry.

The distinguishing characteristic of O∴T∴O∴ rituals is their overt intention to arouse and direct sexual energy. Kellner claimed to have been given secrets of a sexual yoga during travels in the Middle East and India, and he believed that the Knights Templar had this same knowledge.

Per their website, the "O∴T∴O∴ is dedicated to the high purpose of securing the Liberty of the Individual and his or her advancement in Light, Wisdom, Understanding, Knowledge, and Power through Beauty, Courage, and Wit, on the Foundation of Universal Brotherhood. U.S. Grand Lodge is the governing body of O∴T∴O∴ in the United States. It is the most populous and active branch of O∴T∴O∴, with 44 local bodies in 26 states as of March 2009. If you are interested in becoming a member of Ordo Templi Orientis, see the membership page for more information. To find an O∴T∴O∴ body near you, consult our list of local bodies. Our FAQ answers many common questions about O∴T∴O∴ and Thelema." www.oto-usa.org/

Pa Kua: Eight trigrams, the eight signs which form the basis of I Ching, and from which the sixty-four hexagrams are constructed.

The Pa Kua is also used in various decorative and religious motifs incorporating the eight trigrams of *I Ching; specifically* in a circle around the yin-yang symbol.

Though the origin of the Pa Kua, and hence of the I Ching, is often attributed to Fu Hsi, the legendary Chinese emperor thought to have ruled at the beginning of the millennium BC, the eight trigrams used for divination were not invented until about 1000 BC. Fundamental to their divinatory usage, these three-lined figures, in their sixty-four combinations, form the basis of Chinese cosmological speculation.

© Bob Sadler

Parrott, Wanda Sue: Wanda Sue Parrott is only one of this veteran writer's by-lines. She is a retired journalist and co-founder of the National Annual Senior Poets Laureate Poetry Competition for American poets age 50 and older, which she administered from 1993 through 2013.

Wanda was born in Kansas City, Missouri in 1935. She made her debut as a stand-up-comedy poet as Professor Parrott in Springfield, Missouri poetry slams in 2007. "I love to experiment, and to invent," she says.

As Diogenes Rosenberg, in 1997 she invented the world's shortest—and only purely horizontal—sonnet, the Pissonnet (pronounced Pee-so-nay if intoned for delicacy with a French accent). It is a popular poetic form in contemporary literary contests.

As Edgar Allan Philpott, in 2009 she won the Louisiana Senior Poet Laureate Award by masqueraging as an itinerant musician from New Orleans. As Philpott, she also self-published *The Boondogller's Bible*, which was reissued in 2014 under her own name.

As Prairie Flower, a name that evolved decades ago, she has produced poetry inspired by the Native American influence.

During the 1970s she wrote Swamiwanda's Metaphysical Mailbag column for the old *Hollywood Citizen News*, and for nearly forty years, survived an on-and-off career as journalist under her legal name, Wanda Sue Parrott. Under this name, while living in Springfield, Missouri from 1988 through 2009, where she was syndicated columnist with *Senior Living Newspapers* and teacher of writing at Ozarks Technical College, she invented the 100-word Story Stanza.

Wanda has been a Rosicrucian since 1963. She now lives in Monterey, California, where as an active Unitarian Universalist, she is an advocate for the homeless. She is a member of the Tap Bananas, a troupe of senior performers.

Founder of the Amy Kitchener's Angels Without Wings Foundation, she was born in 1935 in Kansas City, Missouri but was raised and educated in Southern California. She returned to Missouri in 1988 where she has been president of Springfield Writers' Guild, honorary life member of Missouri State Poetry Society, and founder of Springfield Writers Workshop which has been meeting in Springfield-Greene County Library since 1992. More recently she has returned to California.

She was an investigative reporter with the *Los Angeles Herald-Examiner*, syndicated feature writer with Ozarks Senior Living newspapers, and holds many awards for poetry and short fiction, as well as newspaper columns and features. She won several "Best Feature" awards in the Hearst Corporation's chain of newspapers. In 2002 she was the honored recipient of the Alumnus of the Year Award from her alma mater, Citrus College in Glendora, California, where she served as president of the Associated Women Students in 1953-1954. In 2004 her sci-fi story "Power Lunches" won 1st Place in the Writer's Challenge Literary Association's transcendental tales contest. She won the 2007 Mistress of Mayhem Award from Sleuth's Ink Mystery Writers for her short story "Elfinetta's ETs."

She has published under 18 pen names, including Prairie Flower and Edgar Allan Philpott. As Diogenes Rosenberg, she invented the Pissonnet in 1997; the world's shortest sonnet form is now in public domain and she has admitted being its inventor. She is co-founder and sponsor of the National Annual Senior Poets Laureate Poetry Competition for American poets age 50 and older, now in its 17th year. Visit her website: http://www.amykitchenerfdn.org

Pentagram: Five-pointed star, single point upward to represent Spirit as dominant over the four lesser elements of Earth, Fire, Water, and Air.

Piscean Age: The passing old zodiacal age being replaced by the incoming Aquarian Age.

Proteus: The Greek god of rivers and bodies of water large enough to have waves—thus indicating "ever-changing characteristics." The derived word, "Protean" conveys the positive meaning of flexibility, versatility, and adaptability.

Psychological and Esoteric Models of the Whole Self: Words such as Soul, Higher Self, Spirit, Psyche, Inner Self, the *Atman,* the Whole Personality, Causal Self, *Chiah, Neshamah,* Higher Manas, Higher Ego, Holy Guardian Angel, Spiritual Soul, Intuitional Self, *Buddhi,* Higher Causal Self, Super-Conscious Mind, and many more in all languages and cultures have been used variously with little definition other than a presumed meaning of "other than physical consciousness," "that which survives physical death," and "that which is immortal."

In modern psychological and esoteric terminology these same words and related concepts have been associated with the Personal Unconscious, the Collective Unconscious, the Archetypal Mind, the Subtle Bodies making up the complex structure of the whole person, and more.

For our purposes here, we see a basic psychological model that parallels a similar esoteric model as follows:

The Psychological Model and the Esoteric Model of the Whole Person

PSYHOLOGICAL MODEL	ESOTERIC MODEL
Lower Self, aka Sub-Conscious Mind	Astral Body and Consciousness (Self)
Middle Self, aka Conscious Mind	Mental Body and Consciousness (Self)
Higher Self, aka Super-Conscious Mind	Causal Body and Consciousness (Self)

In both models, at each level, there is more complexity than shown. Generally, and in relation to their multiple functions, each level in both models is further divided into seven sub-levels. Our focus is on the highest sub-level of Level 3, simply called the Higher Self and the Causal Self. Essentially, they are the same, but because our focus in this book is magickal and esoteric, we will target the Causal Self.

The Causal Self is not the Soul, nor is it the Spirit, but it is magickally called the "Holy Guardian Angel" and is the highest aspect of <u>personal</u> consciousness in *the incarnating personality*. Understand that *the Soul, itself, does not incarnate,* but abstracts the life lessons from the incarnated personality through the Causal Self, which then "dies" along with that personality. The Soul then creates a new "Causal Seed" with the abstracted memories of many life times and a new life plan which generates a new incarnating personality, step-by-step, following the Esoteric Model into physical incarnation from which new levels of psychological consciousness develop as the physical body grows and matures to work side-by-side with the esoteric selves through a new life time.

It is the Higher Self communicating with the Causal Self that is our aspiration in what we call the "Knowledge and Conversation with the Holy Guardian Angel" which is the goal of all High Magick, the purpose of all Self-Development, the ultimate accomplishment of all Meditation. It is the fulfillment of this process that fully transfers "command & control" of the entire personality from the reactive emotional-centered Lower Self and the more-or-less brain-centered mental Middle Self to the Spirit-centered Causal Higher Self. That the state of self-mastery we call "adepthood." (The chances of you encountering such an adept—whether in this world or the next—is very slight. No real adept will ask for your obedience, devotion, or your money—so don't give it!)

Qodosh: In the Third Degree of Sex Magick in the G∴B∴G∴.. Physical ecstasy must become psychic ecstasy that in turn 'fires' the Magickal Imagination. In the now empowered imagination we aim for realization of the objective of the operation. All the while, the chosen objective is the central focus of the concentration and imagining from beginning to end of the sexual union.

If the objective of the operation is a quality, such as the vision of Beauty, then the experience, the trance, may continue on for a week or even more. And if the operation is repeated, the experience extends more and more, and becomes Reality.

Even though the objective may seem "external," the effect on the two partners is internally transforming. It bears a lot of thought.

Recurring Dream: The repetition of a specific dream without significant change or variation in content.

Retirement Ritual: A "retirement ritual" or "retreat," is common to many magical, shamanic, and spiritual systems. As a time of isolation and self-deprivation, it involves a challenge to one's self-identity and an opening to the Higher Self whether conceived as the Holy Guardian Angel or God.

A familiar task of the retirement ritual is to record one's visions and realizations in a diary, and/or to discuss the experiences with the shaman or teacher, and to return to that record in future times to review those insights from an evolving perspective.

Retirement rituals, retreats, vision quests, wilderness journeys, periods of silence, etc., are all common to Initiatory Practices. Each tradition has its own unique practices, many symbolic and dramatic, and intended to "shake the foundations" and "stir the pot." The intention is to mark the ending of one part of your life and to mark the beginning of another. All involve a "change of pace" during which things can happen.

Some may demand a life-changing accomplishment at their culmination—a "Big Dream," the finding of an amulet, the making of a talisman, a substantial fasting and purging, the killing of an animal that then becomes one's totem, and other ways to establish a transition from one phase of life to another.

Aside from the Retirement Retreat, there is proven value to periodic retreats, even annually, to encourage review and communication with the Higher Self, the Holy Guardian Angel. Various businesses and organizations, churches, and other groups provide for such retreats for their own purposes—*shouldn't you do the same for the most important personal purpose of all?*

It doesn't demand much on your time and resources, and can be combined—as long as you are honest and disciplined about it—with a family vacation. But, you don't really have to go somewhere beyond your own home for a weekend retreat or personal vacation. The advantage of a change of place is the same as for a change of pace—you plan the time and environment to get the most out of your reflection time.

The only equipment you need is your journal and a pen, or your laptop computer provided you use it only for your journaling purpose. No e-mails, no online searches, just your journal. Your *ideal* program should call for three periods of meditation, 30 to 60 minutes each, followed by one to two hours of writing. That's it, a maximum of nine hours over two days once a year for the most important endeavor of your life. But, even as an ideal it may be too much. Adjust it if necessary.

If you have BIG questions about your spiritual progress, write them down and start your morning meditation with them. If you have no questions, just ask your Higher Self to communicate with you, and patiently *listen*. Make no demands; just be open to your Holy Guardian Angel.

Expect nothing specifically. You do not know your own self-created necessity in relation to the Angel or Daemon. You can in no way command your Daemon! You may have an energized feeling of freedom or of being rejuvenated, and it may last for many weeks. You may have a completely empty feeling that absolutely nothing has taken place—and this is a sure sign that something of no value has been taken from you, which you will later realize. On the other hand, something outstanding may manifest almost immediately. Above all things, as an aspiring magician you must learn in your aspiration to "Lust not for result." To lust for result is anathema in Magick.

Of course, you can do lesser meditations for this sort anytime, but there is value to this larger, weekend, retreat that will pay unlimited dividends.

Rite of Diana: A sex magick ritual bringing one or both partners into the Borderland State and the imagination subjectively real, during one Dianism congrex lasting for hours without break.

Rosicrucianism: According to legend, a German doctor and mystic philosopher called Christian Rosenkreuz studied in the Middle East under various Moorish masters, possibly including Sufis, then returned to Germany and gathered a small circle of friends-become-disciples and founded the Rosicrucian Order around 1407.

During the Founder's lifetime, the Order consisted of just eight members, each a doctor and a sworn bachelor. Each swore an oath to heal the sick without payment, to maintain a secret fellowship, and to find a replacement for himself before he died. By 1600, scientific, philosophical and religious freedom had grown such that the Order determined that the public might benefit from the Rosicrucian's knowledge, so they started seeking good men.

It is believed that the first Rosicrucian manifesto was influenced by the work of the hermetic philosopher Heinrich Khunrath, author of the *Amphitheatrum Sapientiae Aeternae* (1609), who was in turn influenced by Dr. John Dee, author of the *Monas Hieroglyphica* (1564).

Rosicrucianism was first associated with Luther's Protestant movement in opposition to Roman Catholicism and its preference for dogma over empiricism. Early seventeenth-century occult philosophers such as Michael Maier, Robert Fludd, and Thomas Vaughan became interested in the Rosicrucian world view. It also influenced the development of Freemasonry then emerging in Scotland and later such magickal orders as the Golden Dawn and Aurum Solis. Today, many modern societies exist for the study of Rosicrucianism and allied subjects.

Rosicrucian (AMORC) Order: AMORC has been operating since 1915, and has affiliated lodges and chapters all over the world. The Rosicrucian system is unique—it provides a foundation that ties together all of the different aspects of metaphysical study, and demonstrates their interconnectedness. Contact them at www.rosicrucian.org/ for more information.

Rosicrucian Fellowship: Founded by Max Heindel with its main teaching presented his book *The Rosicrucian Cosmo-Conception*. This Christian Mystic Philosophy presents deep insights into the Christian Mysteries and establishes a meeting ground for Art, Religion, and Science. Max Heindel was selected by the Elder Brothers of the Rose Cross to publicly give out the Western Wisdom Teachings in order to help prepare mankind for the coming age of Universal Brotherhood, the Age of Aquarius. Although the Rosicrucian Fellowship books are sold, the services of our Healing Department, the Correspondence Courses, and the various School activities continue to be offered on a free-will love-offering basis. Visit www.rosicrucian.com/ for more information.

Rosicrucian Fraternity: Formed in Germany in 1614 bringing together groups identified as Hermetists, Pythagoreans, Magi, Platonists, Gnostics, Alchemists, and Paracelsians. The Fraternity came to America in 1774 under the governorship of

Benjamin Franklin, George Clymer, and Thomas Paine who was succeeded by La-fayette, like Franklin, a member of the Paris Rosicrucian lodge. In 1842, the nov-elist, George Lippard, rewrote the exoteric ritual, giving it a patriotic-Christian basis. During the Civil War this Great Council was composed of Paschel Beverly Randolph, General Ethan Allen Hitchcock and Abraham Lincoln.

The Fraternitas Rosae Crucis has two missions: (1) To offer spiritual teachings to individual members who desire to develop their soul from a "slumbering em-ber" to a fully conscious spiritual being; (2) To disseminate spiritual and scientific truths for the betterment of the physical, moral, and intellectual condition of all humanity.

The Fraternity teaches that there is one God, the Creator and source of all. That within each of us is buried a Divine Spark, of and from God that is our soul. In our essence we have free will and the opportunity to either diminish or grow this tiny spark by our mode of life, our thoughts, desires, and actions. To develop this celestial soul spark, we must transmute our lower nature and increase the feeling of love within our being, and thus become a conscious Soul with a direct link to God. This state of spiritual development is termed Soul Illumination sym-bolized by the fully bloomed rose in the centre of the cross of transmutation, the Rosy Cross. Soul Consciousness is followed by God Consciousness.

Russell, C. F. Cecil Frederick Russell (1897–1987): Russell wrote in 1922: "Magick is aptly defined as the science and art of doing one's Will, and achieving one's purpose, fulfilling the Law of THELEMA. Thus theoretical magick is the art of perfecting mental processes, and practical magick the art of perfecting volitional processes. These definitions are hardly conclusive, but they are scholarly enough for practical purposes, I think. I think that every member should be drilled in cer-emonial magick until he subconsciously acquires the attitude of doing the right thing at the right moment with omnipotence at his command and eternity at his disposal. The ideas that dissolve the sin complex, viz that nothing really matters, that it is impossible to make a mistake, etc, cannot be rooted in the organism by any other method."

Russell was a member of the A∴A∴ and O∴T∴O∴ (known as Fr. Genesthai) and was secretary to Aleister Crowley during the (in) famous 1920s Cefalu period. Some speculation suggests that Russell's experiences on "the Rock" during this period at Thelema Abbey subsequently led to his establishment of the Gnostic Body of God (G∴B∴G∴) and his personal magickal explorations into the fields of mathematics and logic. More can be found at the website: www.cfrussell.home-stead.com/

(Note that there is some dispute as to the meaning of the acronym G∴B∴G∴. Culling says it means the "Great Brotherhood of God," but the above description says it means the "Gnostic Body of God." Both Russell and Culling are no longer with us, so let's just stick with "G∴B∴G∴.")

Seven-pointed Star: "Seven" is itself an important number. The geometrical shapes and the manner of their drawing and use utilize the power of the number.

Astrologically, the ancients saw only seven visible heavenly *moving* bodies composing our solar system: the Moon (not a planet), Mercury, Venus, the Sun (not a planet), Mars, Jupiter, and Saturn. The remaining planets Uranus, Neptune, and Pluto are not visible to the naked eye. Everything upon Earth was thought to be under the astrological rulership, of these seven "planetary" influences. Each of the four lunar periods lasts seven days. The summer solstice takes place when the sun passes in the seventh zodiacal sign; the winter solstice when it traversed seven signs starting from this last. There are seven signs from one equinox to the other. There are seven types of characters in the traditional astrology. A Hindu tradition attributes to the sun seven rays.

The number seven regulates the life of the man: after seven months of gestation the fetus is viable. Seven marks the periods of the life: the first childhood until 7 years which is the age of reason; to 7 x 2 years, end of the childhood; to 7 x 3 years, majority, end of the adolescence; to 7 x 4 years, youth; to 7 x 5 years, adult age; to 7 x 6 years, maturity followed by the decline of the forces. It is also the duration of the human cycle: every seven years, the body is regenerated entirely.

Commonly, seven is a Lucky Number and is seen throughout Man, Nature, and the esoteric dimensions: the seven magickal directions with their own magickal energies and correspondences that "bend" those energies to human pujrpose: North, East, West, South, Above, Below, and Within; the seven major Chakras that factor the subtle energies of both the physical and subtle bodies: Muladhara, Swadhistana, Manipura, Anahata, Vishuddha, Ajna, and Sahasrara.

Seven is the Egyptian symbol of eternal life, symbolizing a complete cycle of dynamic perfection; seven is the number of the Perfect Man and the Symbol of the totality of the created Universe; seven is the number of the initiation.

In the Roman Church, seven are the virtues of faith, hope, love force, justice, prudence, and temperance; seven the sacraments: Baptism, Confirmation, Eucharist, Penitence, Unction of the patients, Order, Marriage; seven are the feasts of the Virgin Mary: the Purification, the Annunciation, the Visitation, the Assumption, the Nativity, the Presentation of the Virgin, and the Immaculate Conception; Seven the number of Archangels: Gabriel, Michael, Uriel, Raphael, Chamuel or Samael or Sealtiel, Japhiel or Orifiel or Jehudiel, Zadkiel or Zachariel or Barachiel;

Seven are the seven capital sins, corresponding to the seven material desires: pride, avarice, impurity, envy, greed, anger, and laziness.

The apocryphal Book of Enoch speaks of the seven watchmen, the seven great mountains, the seven great rivers, the seven great islands, and the seven paths to the paradise. Plato says that man is composed of seven souls, as also does Hinduism. There are seven emblems of the Buddha.

Sufism names seven cosmic plans: Zat, the not-expressed; Ahadiat, the conscience; Vahdat, the interior self; Vahdamiat, the internal light; Arwah, the spiritual plan; Ajsam, the astral plan; Insaam, the physical plan. It recognizes also seven aspects of the manifestation: the stars, the moon, the sun, the reign mineral, vegetable, animal, and human. To the image of the man, the Earth is composed of seven "chakras" and it is located in the seventh super-universe.

The human person is composed of seven bodies: physical, etheric or vital, emotional or astral, causal, mental, body of divine vitality or Buddhic, and the body of divine spirit or Atmic. The etheric body of the man is completely developed and installed only around the age of seven. The number seven regulates the rhythm of development of the woman: at 7 months, appearance of the baby teeth which will be lost at 7 years old; at 7 x 2 years, appearance of the menstruation and to 7 x 7 years it is the menopause.

There are seven symbolic colors of the Tarot, seven pillars of the Wisdom; seven Greek vowels used by the gnostic: alpha, epsilon, eta, iota, omicron, upsilon, omega; seven fundamental notes, or modulations, of the musical scale; seven colors of the rainbow.

In the legend of the Grail there are seven virgins defended by seven knights confronting the hero Galahad. The seven skies of Zarathustra. The seven oxen pulling the chariot of the sun in the Scandinavian legends.

Among all prime numbers, seven is the first number that does not enter in the Euclidean circle—the heptagon cannot be built in a circle of 360 degrees like the triangle or the pentagon. The number 7 has some curious particularities. For example 1 divided by 7 gives a simple recurring decimal of six digits:

0.142857142857142857...

and this one multiplied successively by 2, 3, 4, 5, 6, gives products where we find the same numbers in the same order:

142857 x 2 = 285714
142857 x 3 = 428571
142857 x 4 = 571428
142857 x 5 = 714285
142857 x 6 = 857142

The seven-pointed heptagram is the symbol of perfection in many Christian religions. The heptagram is also known among <u>neo-Pagans</u> as the *Elven Star* or *Fairy Star*. It is treated as a sacred symbol in various modern Pagan and witchcraft traditions. <u>Blue Star Wicca</u> also uses the symbol, where it is referred to as a *septagram*. The heptagram is also a symbol of <u>magical power</u> in some <u>Pagan</u> religions. The seven-pointed Faerie Star is the symbol of the Tuath De Dannan (Children of Danu).

In <u>alchemy</u>, a seven-sided star can refer to the seven planets which were known to ancient alchemists.

The seven pointed **septagram** is a continuously drawn figure having seven points. It is a less common religious symbol than the pentagram, but it is a sacred symbol to many Wiccans.

The septagram is important in Western kabbalah, where it symbolizes the sphere of Netzach, the seven planets, the seven alchemical metals, and the seven days of the week. It is an important part of the seal of the A∴A∴, the inner order of the O∴T∴O∴, the secret society made famous by Aleister Crowley.

The seven-pointed star is the distinctive symbol of the New Age as seen in the Star Tarot card.

Sex Magick: Sex Magick is the whole thing—the persisted application of all that has been learned and gained as skills in the training of Alphaism, Dianism, Qodosh, the exercise of the Magickal Imagination, the memorization of correspondences, the learning of concentration and visualization, and the glory of union.

For I am divided for love's sake, for the chance of union.

What is "Sex Magick?"

Hey Baby, want to get together and do some Sex Magick?

NO!

At least, I hope she says "no" to that proposition because what he's after is not what we call "Sex Magick." Nor are we proposing "the magic of sex." And to clarify, romance and relationship are not fundamental to Sex Magick. You will find out why as we progress in this discussion.

Every man thinks he's an expert on sex, and most women know that he's not. He does know how to make babies, but he doesn't necessarily know how to make love, or to make magic. Women instinctively know how to make magic but both men and women need to learn Sex Magick.

The simple truth is that men simply get an *itch* in their penis, and want it scratched—preferably by a woman. Women yearn for something more complex: they want to be attractive and desirable; gathering men like honey gathers flies. They want to feel adored and they want to know that they cause a man to have an erection and desire sex. And they want romance and intimacy, to feel that they are the only one in his life. They want to be held and kissed, and to have lots of slow foreplay.

Women's pleasure is the key, and orgasm is not the biggest part of it. Prolonged intercourse, with or without her orgasm, is vital to create the energy field needed for the transformation of consciousness fundamental to Sex Magick. Women are the *engines* that power-up the field whereas men are just the mechanics and the best of them learn how to carefully manage the process while she just swoons in enjoyment.

Every woman should feel herself as a goddess incarnate in the lead-up to sex, during sex, and after sex. His role as a god is a secret—else his ego inflates and robs the mission. She should become filled with energy, but her energy is 'magnetic' while his is 'electric.' They should both enter into the "Borderland" state of consciousness where there is only pleasure but no climax, and hold that state for two or more hours. When the "moment is right," her magnetism should simply draw his electricity into her person, body and soul, with or without his sperm which is of no particular interest to the Sex Magick operation.

And when the "moment" comes, he projects his special intention, the magickal goal of the operation, right along with his electricity and semen. His role is primarily that of the Magician who projects the imaged goal with the release of his power into her. She receives, transmutes, and makes it happen in dimensions beyond the physical and mostly beyond her awareness. Some women claim to know when they're impregnated, but it's not likely and not necessary. Instead of a physical child, here there is a "magickal childe."

In Giving and Receiving there is Magick, and Love

Yes, all this does require preparation, discipline, and restraint. And the importance of preparation precedes foreplay and should include the planning and execution of drama to elevate the feeling of importance of the ritual and the roles of the players. Sex Magick evolves from Dramatic Ritual with the staging of place, costuming, incense or aromatic oils, soft lighting, music possibly romantic or with a stimulating base beat, and possibly a non-intrusive script leading to awareness of the intended result.

In this case of a Magickal Curriculum, it is the Knowledge and Conversation with the Holy Guardian Angel. It can be the objective for either partner, or both.

It calls upon the Magickal Imagination to see the partner as god or goddess, or as Holy Guardian Angel. *What does the god or goddess or Holy Guardian Angel look like? Do they move? Do they speak?* Some answers can be found in reference works in religion and mythology, while others will arise from your subconsciousness.

Do what thou Wilt. Love is the Law; Love under Will

In your planning, let awareness of pleasure and arousal be your guide. Don't neglect the possible role of fantasy roll playing and fetishes in costuming. Goddesses wear anything they want, and what they want includes knowing and witnessing the arousal and lust of their partner. The challenge remains the required discipline and restraint, especially on the part of the man so that you can remain engaged for two or more hours. Even though the emphasis in a Sex Magick operation does not call for the partners to be an established couple, knowledge and understanding of each other's needs and 'turn-ons' is helpful in holding the man back from orgasm and leading the woman to the edge, and then pushing that edge beyond previous limits. The edge should not be a cliff to fall down but the start of a spiral upward to heaven. An important side note: fantasies and fetishes should be her choices, not his. We have been conditioned to think that only men have fetishes and sexual fantasies, but that's not accurate. Hers are more subjective and his more objective but in Sex Magick it is "She who must be obeyed." An important book is *She Comes First,* by Ian Kerner.

See yourselves enjoying the extended bliss of the Borderland state rather than the immediacy of satisfaction. Make Love for an Eternity! You will find that extended bliss is healthful, will rejuvenate you, and will lower blood pressure, bathing your inner bodies with health-giving energies and secretions.

Love is the Law

Suggested Reading:

Kerner, Ian. *She Comes First: The Thinking Man's Guide to Pleasuring a Woman.* NY: Regan Books, 2004.

Kraig, Donald Michael. *Modern Sex Magick: Secrets of Erotic Spirituality*. St. Paul: Llewellyn, 1998.

Shortcut to Initiation: A shortcut obviously contrasts with the longer route. Often a shortcut is a rougher road; one with particular hazards and without some common comforts and resources, and sometimes it doesn't even show up on the official map. But there are reasons to take the shortcut: it is more efficient, often both shorter and faster, and sometimes more adventurous.

A shortcut may go through dangerous territory, and sometimes it may leave the paved road completely and take you cross country through which you have to make your own trail. There may be no rest areas or food stops or gas stations—so you have to plan ahead and be able to take some risks. There's no guide to lead you. *You are on your own!*

But, ultimately, you are always 'on your own.' The work can't be done for you—so whether you take the 'high road' or the 'low road,' the better mapped route or the shortcut across country—you are the one! You will learn more because you are your own guide, your own resource. Instead of a teacher watching over you, you have only your own Higher Self *who will respond to your need!*

Initiation is one of those ambiguous words that are used variously. In esoteric practice, it sometimes seems to mark one's "graduation" for the completion of *under-graduate studies*. But 'to initiate' also means to start a process.

In our magickal curriculum it means both. The goal is to make you a Whole Person so that you can become a Greater Being. Like the good Scout, the Initiate is prepared because of the work he has completed. The Initiate is ready for the Great Adventure leading to God.

The only mysteries are the Inner Mysteries

Sincerity: Implies self-honesty—knowing one's self to be ethical and honest in motive and action, firm and correct in both attitudes and methods.

Soul: *"You" are not your Soul.* The "You" you know is best understood as a partial and temporary manifestation of "Soul" that we call "personality." This personality is not the *whole* soul but one of many aspects of it incarnating life after life and occupying a series of temporary vehicles each composed of the substance of one dimension after the other. Then the essence of each life's lessons is abstracted and eventually "absorbed" and further refined into the soul until the soul itself is ready to move on into still higher spiritual dimensions. The soul continues on its journey through the Cosmos, learning and/or "working" on behalf of the *Great Plan* set in motion by the "Creator Source" of all that is—which is better realized as *Unity* when not given a defining and hence *limiting* name.

The soul is the absolute ultimate and immortal essence of who you are. The eternal part of the human being, attributed Kabbalistically to Chesed, Geburah, Tiphareth, Netzach, Hod, and Yesod.

Soul's Vehicles :		
Causal Body (Higher Mental)— Thought.	To evolve with—	Ideals and Abstract
Mental Body (Lower Mental)— Thoughts	To think with —	Ideas and Concrete
Astral Body (Upper and Lower)—	To feel with—	Emotions and Desires
Physical Body (incl. Etheric Body)—	to act with—	Sensorial Reactions and Actions
Personality, the Lower Self—	Lower Manas	Mental
	Concrete Mind	Body
	Astral, Desire	Astral
	Nature	Body
	Physical, Functioning	Body
	Physical/Etheric	Body
Body Consciousness—	Autonomic nervous system	
Source: Jinarajadasa. *First Principles of Theosophy*, 1861.		

Spirit: See also "Ether" and "Akasha." This word has multiple meanings.

   a. The Spiritual Body, or Soul.

   b. The entity surviving physical death—believed to temporarily function on the Astral Plane.

   c. The fifth element from which the lower four—Fire, Air, Water, and Earth are derived.

   d. Entities from other dimensions or planets channeling to humans.

   e. A non-physical entity functioning on the Astral or other planes.

   f. The 'collective' of etheric, astral, mental, and spirit bodies other than the physical.

   g. God, or an aspect of Deity.

   h. A collective term for non-individual spiritual power and intelligence, probably an aspect of the Collective Unconscious or Universal Consciousness.

   i. Non-human inhabitants of the astral plane.

   j. The inner reality of something—as in "the spirit of the times."

k. The Alchemical element symbolized by an eight-spoked Wheel is the higher level of reality of Eight Dimensions from which other elements and levels flow.

l. Symbolized by the "Egg," it is the Great Mother Goddess, the source of all physical manifestation.

m. The "Interdimensional" function through which all things and entities seem to appear and disappear with a change in their nature.

n. Spirit is also the "Space" between things and around things. In a broad sense, it is the old, pre-Einstein *Ether* of empty space which being non-physical could not be observed.

o. The 'Holy Spirit' which may be the Primal Consciousness or Matrix that can be activated by prayer or other affirmative thoughts.

p. That part of the Human Being attributed to Kether, Chokmah, and Binah.

There is another way to look at Spirit, and that is that some Spirits may be projections of human consciousness. "Nature abhors a vacuum" is an old adage. A modification would be that "Empty Space invites <u>active</u> Consciousness." *Thought and Feeling, guided by Will, create Forms and Energizes them.* Whether these forms are created consciously or unconsciously, they exist, and the more attention, and <u>intention,</u> is focused on them, the more Life and Power they have.

There are, then, perhaps, three kinds of *Spirits:*

1. Bodies of consciousness created by the Soul to progressively incarnate into a series of vehicles, such as now occupied by you and me, and all living people. And then at death, these include the traditional spirits of the surviving personalities of people and—in a different fashion—animals.

2. Units of consciousness created as functioning parts of the Cosmos out of the substance and energies of each cosmic plane, such as the Sun, Moon, and Planets for the physical plane; such as Elementals and Nature Spirits and others for the astral plane; such as Thought Forms and Magickal Constructs for the mental plane; and Angels and Archangels for the Causal Plane. But, notice—contrary to materialist beliefs—we are stating the stars, their satellites, and the planets all are active forms of consciousness, and are all spiritual entities.

3. Forms of consciousness created through the human imagination, drawing substance and energies from all four of the lower planes, in varying degrees dependent on unconscious to conscious to intentional responses to initial stimulus and opportunity.

   a. In this third category we include unconscious projections via the imagination of thought forms created in response to natural stimulus—such as the energies surrounding a natural spring inhabited by water sprites and other elementals. The human response might picture a feminine deity (water being a feminine element) who then acts to further draw energies to herself to protect the spring from harm, and to create an atmosphere of love and nurture beneficial to all who come to the spring.

b. A second form as humans respond to natural forces and earth currents (ley lines) that instinctively trigger thoughts and images of snakes and dragons. With repetition, and recognition of their importance as guides to planting and other activities, the images take on life and consciousness, and become objects of worship or magickal interaction.

c. A third form of unconscious projection comes in response to strong and repeated emotions such as love, lust, hate, fear which take on person-like images of goddesses and gods. Here we have not only the opportunity for worship but for magick—defense again objects and causes of hate and fear, invocation for the goddesses of love and lust. With more conscious attention focused on these deities, they become multiple and specific, and are presented in detailed symbolism to represent all the variations of their manifestation.

d. A fourth form comes with conscious projection developed from knowledge of magickal principles where abstract symbols become charged with energies of attraction and repulsion. Gods and Goddesses of the household, of the city and the nation, sometimes projected on to the memories of heroes and great leaders. Many of the Christian and Buddhist saints are so charged with energies that they too function as spirits. Sometimes, animals are the matrix for projection of consciousness and psychic energies—in particular the horse, the cow, the goat, the dolphin, the cat, and the dog—because of their special role between Man and Nature.

Star, The: The seven-pointed star is the sigil of the Goddess Babalon. In the Tarot, the Star is the 17th Major Arcanum—image: a bright star overhead and most commonly a naked woman kneeling at the edge of a body of water pouring water from two vessels, sometimes one onto the ground but other times both into the water; Hebrew letter: Tzaddi; Divinatory meaning: spiritual guidance, hope, help; the 28th path on the Tree of Life connecting Yesod to Netzach.

Sub-Conscious, AKA the Sub-Conscious Mind and the Personal Unconscious: The vast inner region of experiences not ordinarily available to the conscious awareness. It is believed to be the repository of all past-life experiences. The term **sub-**

conscious is used in many different contexts and has no single or precise definition. This greatly limits its significance as a definition-bearing concept, and in consequence the word tends to be avoided in academic and scientific settings.

In everyday speech and popular writing, however, the term is very commonly encountered as a layperson's replacement for the Unconscious Mind, which in Freud's opinion is a repository for socially unacceptable ideas, wishes or desires, traumatic memories, and painful emotions put out of mind by the mechanism of psychological repression. However, the contents do not necessarily have to be solely negative. In the psychoanalytic view, the unconscious is a force that can only be recognized by its effects—it expresses itself in the symptom. Unconscious thoughts are not directly accessible to ordinary introspection, but are supposed to be capable of being "tapped" and "interpreted" by special methods and techniques such as meditation, random association, dream analysis, and verbal slips (commonly known as a Freudian slip), examined and conducted during psychoanalysis.

Carl Jung developed the concept further. He divided the unconscious into two parts: the personal unconscious and the collective unconscious. The personal unconscious is a reservoir of material that was once conscious but has been forgotten or suppressed.

The idea of the "subconscious" as a powerful or potent agency has allowed the term to become prominent in the New Age and self-help literature, in which investigating or controlling its supposed knowledge or power is seen as advantageous. In the New Age community, techniques such as autosuggestion and affirmations are believed to harness the power of the Sub-Conscious to influence a person's life and real-world outcomes, even curing sickness.

Though laypersons commonly assume "subconscious" to be a psychoanalytic term, this is not in fact the case. Freud had explicitly condemned the word as long ago as 1915: "We shall also be right in rejecting the term 'subconsciousness' as incorrect and misleading." In later publications his objections were made clear:

"If someone talks of subconsciousness, I cannot tell whether he means the term topographically—to indicate something lying in the mind beneath consciousness— or qualitatively—to indicate another consciousness, a subterranean one, as it were. He is probably not clear about any of it. The only trustworthy antithesis is between conscious and unconscious." As outlined above, psychologists and psychiatrists exclusively use the term "unconscious" in situations where many lay-writers, particularly such as those in metaphysical and New Age literature, usually use the term "subconscious." It should not, however, be inferred from this that the orthodox concept of the unconscious and the New Age concept of the Sub-Conscious are precisely equivalent.

Psychologists and psychiatrists, unsurprisingly, take a much more limited view of the capabilities of the unconscious than are represented by the common New Age depiction of a transcendentally all-powerful "subconscious."

The Sub-Conscious retains memories of everything through the feelings associated with that memory. In general, however, we are mostly concerned with childhood memories, fears, and misunderstandings that have been—often—repressed. As childish memories, they live on and may still influence our adult understanding and feelings erroneously and painfully. By recalling those memories, an adult perspective can replace the childish one and at the same time release energies tied up in those childish fears and misunderstandings.

The Sub-Conscious Mind is never asleep, always aware. It is the *Nephesh* on the Kabbalistic Tree of Life. That part of the mind below the threshold of consciousness. Normally, unavailable to the Conscious Mind, it can be accessed through hypnosis and self-hypnosis, meditation, automatic writing, etc.

More importantly, in the studies of Joe H. Slate and Carl Llewellyn Weschcke, it is the *lower* part of the Personality which while containing forgotten and repressed feelings and memories and our emotional nature, it is also the fundamental Belief or Operating System that filters Reality, that collection of guilt feelings called the 'Shadow,' the 'Anima' or 'Animus' collection of feelings representing our idealization or fear and hatred of the opposite gender, the various Archetypes and Mythic images formed though the history of human experience, all of which can operate as doorways or gates to the astral world and connect to the higher or super consciousness. The Sub-Conscious is also home to our instincts and the autonomic system that cares for the body and its operation.

"The Sub-Conscious is not only a content domain but a dynamic constellation of processes and powers. It recognizes that the wealth of our Sub-Conscious resources is complementary to consciousness rather than counteractive. It's a powerful component of who we are and how we function" (from Slate and Weschcke: *Psychic Self-Empowerment for Everyone*).

According to the self-empowerment perspective, the Sub-Conscious never sleeps—it's in continuous interaction with consciousness. It embraces the physical, spiritual, and psychical nature of our existence. Awareness of future events, telepathic communications, and clairvoyant insight are all among its powers. The subconscious, with communication to the Collective Unconscious and the Super-Consciousness has very nearly unlimited resources available to you through your Guide. Almost like a forgotten best friend or favorite mentor, the Sub-Conscious welcomes our probes and challenges us to use its powers.

The Sub-Conscious Mind has no ethics or morals; it is your Conscious Mind that must make choices and impose order on chaos, develop distinct channels to reliable resources, and otherwise understand and learn that your Sub-Conscious Mind is your key to the infinite resources of the Universe. Helping you to build the relationship between the Sub-Conscious Mind and the Conscious Mind is the purpose of Self-Empowering procedures (see Slate and Weschcke: *Self-Empowerment and the Sub-Conscious Mind*).

But the major message we want to give you is that the Sub-Conscious Mind is an unlimited resource, not only of memories and information but also of powers and skills. It is the foundation and matrix to all we are and all that we will become. Our personal unit of consciousness is part of the Universal Consciousness so we have unlimited potential and have yet to discover any limits to our capacity or ability to use that potential. Our goal is to become <u>adept</u> at upon calling these powers and resources to match our needs and interests, and to keep "pushing the envelope" towards yet greater capacity and ability.

Aside from the integrative process, there's evidence suggesting that the Sub-Conscious can literally generate new potentials and growth energies independent of our conscious interactions through processes not yet fully understood, possibly through the synergistic or holistic results of the integrative process alone. What we need to understand is that the Sub-Conscious Mind is <u>not </u>a passive by-stander but always aware and always active. As you grow in consciousness and integrate more of your psychic and other powers into your Whole Person, the Sub-Conscious Mind grows and contributes more to the Whole Person you are becoming.

Understanding these creative processes of the Sub-Conscious Mind is among our greatest challenges with potentials for enormous benefit. The point here, as elsewhere, is always that the greater our understanding, the greater the benefit, *but even as we face the continual challenges, the very attempt at understanding stimulates positive developments.*

Contrary to some views, the Sub-Conscious is "the essential you," the essence of your being as an evolving soul. Without the subconscious, you would not exist at all. It's the vast totality of your existence: the 'old you' of the past, the 'dynamic you' of the present, and the 'infinite you' of the future.

There are a number of methods in use in the contemporary New Age and paranormal communities to try to directly affect the latter, such as Affirmations, Autosuggestion, Hypnosis and Self-Hypnosis, Meditation, Prayer, Pre-Sleep suggestions followed by Dream Analysis, Ritual, and various Shamanic techniques.

Suggested Reading:

Slate, Joe H., and Carl L. Weschcke. *Psychic Empowerment for Everyone.* St. Paul: Llewellyn, 2009.

Slate, Joe H., and Carl L. Weschcke: *Self Empowerment and Your Sub-Conscious Mind.* St. Paul: Llewellyn, 2010.

Subjectively Real: While Subjective is the obverse of Objective, the result is two kinds of "reality:" the Inner World of feeling and thinking vs. the Outer World of observation and measurement. The Outer World as we perceive it is not simply the actual Physical World but how our "Mental World" interprets it. Thus Objective Reality cannot be true Physical Reality since all perception including that of observation and measurement results in a mental interpretation, a mere "picture." Subjective Reality is more than Feeling and Thinking and includes all forms of subtle perception through clairvoyance and astral travel. Difficulties arise when the perceiver doesn't distinguish between these different realities in the same manner as the person who can say, "my interpretation is."

Super-Conscious Mind: The higher level of consciousness of the triune personal consciousness of Sub-Conscious, conscrious, and Super-Conscious "minds." It is the apparent source of intuition and inspiration and the act of pure will-power (uninfluenced by biological drives and emotion). It is the "target" of self-hypnosis and constructive meditation.

Your Sub-Conscious Mind is mostly conditioned by the past, and your Conscious Mind by the present. But you were born with a basic purpose, with some specific learning goals for this life time. The Super-Conscious Mind is your doorway to and from the future. The Super-Conscious Mind is the higher self and the source of your inspiration, ideals, ethical behavior and heroic action, and the very essence that is "the Light of Men" as it was in the beginning and as it is now and as it will always be . . . .

The Super-Conscious Mind is the *higher* level of personal consciousness with access to the universal of Collective Unconscious. It is where the 'gods' or powerful archetypes and spirit guides can be found, and where the Akashic Records are accessed.

Thelema: (Will, in Greek) This is one's True Will, which can be discovered through the sincere practice of Magick. Crowley constructed this into his axiom: "Do what thou wilt shall be the whole of the law, Love is the law—Love under Will." The word of the Law is Thelema.

In the original writing of the *Book of the Law*, the word Thelema is in Greek letters; and by Greek gematria, the letters total the number 93. Thelema and 93 are synonymous with PURE WILL.

Thelema implies drawing closer and closer to the consciousness of one's real Individuality (the Khabs), in contradistinction to the active conscious Personality (the Khu). It then becomes the aim of the aspirant to be and to express one's True Individuality as much as possible, instead of being submerged in the Personality.

The key to the cryptic word "Thelema"—Will—is to recognize and DO THE TRUE WILL in conformity with the Conversation of the H G A, the Daemon.

Third Degree of Sex Magick: This is fully developed in the previously referenced book, Culling, L.T. and Weschcke, C.L.: *The Complete Magick Curriculum of the Secret Order G.·.B.·.G.·.—Being the Entire Study Curriculum, Magick Rituals, and Initiatory Practices of the G.·.B.·.G.·. (The Great Brotherhood of God)*, 2010, Llewellyn print book: XLI + 310 = 351 pages, 6 x 9; Llewellyn e-book: 4210 KB, 360 pages, Text to Speech.

Tree of Life: (Qabalah) A diagram with ten spheres and twenty-two connecting paths that functions as a kind of 'Interdimensional' 'cross-indexing filing cabinet' for you to relate corresponding facts and experiences with others of the same nature along with the information similarly experienced and related by millions of other students over hundreds of years.

Trigrams: A trigram is a block of three parallel straight lines, each line being either complete (unbroken) or broken. See Pa Kua and I Ching for more details.

Tzaddi: In the <u>Qabalah</u>, the <u>22 Paths</u> (named after the letters of the Hebrew alphabet) connect the ten <u>Sephiroth</u> on the "<u>Tree of Life</u>." The eighteenth is the **Path of Tzaddi**, which connects <u>Netzach</u> with <u>Yesod</u>. It expresses as the number 90, the Element of Air, the **Sign of Aquarius, ruled by Saturn, with Neptune exalted.**

"Tzaddi is not the Star." Aleister Crowley transposes the Tarot Trump of the Star and the Emperor, so that the Emperor then corresponds to the Hebrew letter tzaddi, and the Star to heh.

Unconscious: 1) A lack of consciousness. 2) An alternate word for the Sub-Conscious Mind. 3) A particular reference to the *personal* Unconscious region of the mind where suppressed desires, memories, and feelings reside. In common usage, the personal unconscious is somewhat lesser than the Sub-Conscious Mind. Some theoreticians believe that at least some psychic phenomena rise from these areas of the personality as *quanta* of energy/matter packets manifesting in poltergeist-like phenomena.

Unconscious Mind: The Unconscious Mind is a term coined by the 18th century German philosopher Christopher Riegel and later introduced into English by Samuel Taylor Coleridge. The Unconscious Mind is generally defined as that part of the mind which gives rise to mental phenomena that manifest in a person's mind but which the person is not aware of at the time of their occurrence. These phenomena include unconscious feelings, unconscious or automatic skills, unnoticed perceptions, unconscious thoughts, unconscious habits and automatic reactions, complexes, hidden phobias and concealed desires.

The Unconscious Mind can be seen as the source of night dreams and automatic thoughts that appear without apparent cause; the repository of memories that have been forgotten but that may nevertheless be accessible to consciousness at some later time; and the locus of implicit knowledge, i.e., all the things that we have learned so well that we do them without thinking. One familiar example of the operation of the Unconscious is the phenomenon where one fails to immediately solve a given problem and then suddenly has a flash of insight that provides a solution maybe days later at some odd moment during the day.

Observers throughout history have argued that there are influences on consciousness from other parts of the mind. These observers differ in the use of related terms, including: Unconsciousness as a personal habit; being unaware and intuition. Terms related to semi-consciousness include: awakening, implicit memory, subliminal messages, trances, hypnagogia, and hypnosis. Although sleep, sleep walking, dreaming, delirium, and coma may signal the presence of unconscious processes, these processes are not the Unconscious Mind. Science is in its infancy in exploring the limits of consciousness.

Universal Consciousness: "In the Beginning is the Word." But before the manifestation of the physical cosmos there was the emanation of Consciousness and the Great Plan that first guided the formation of Spirit and then of Space/Time and Energy/Matter leading into the Big Bang of physical creation. With physical creation we have Universal Consciousness (or the Unconscious, or the Great Unconscious) functioning in the background of all there is, and permeating every life, visible and invisible, and everything, visible and invisible.

Universal Field of Possibilities: The Universal Field of Possibilities manifests first as Energy/Matter under the guidance of packets of information/instruction. Thus we can see an analogy with a computer with its Operating Program and its Application Programs.

See Field.

Universal Force: The Force, the Tao, the Energy behind all existence, physical and otherwise.

Universal Mind: *Everything is connected.* Universal Mind, including our individual minds, is the energetic connection that enables you, with your mind, to access and work with these fundamental energies and forces behind all material manifestation.

Wagner, Richard: (1813–1883) Regarded himself as "the most German of men" who projected "the German spirit" in his 13 operas and other compositions. He is best known for 'the Bridal Chorus' familiar to most married couples. He was also a vociferous writer of about 230 books and articles. He was a vegetarian and a socialist, and has been called an anarchist, a nationalist, and even a fascist and anti-Semite. Hitler adored Wagner, and was often heard humming his operas.

Wedding March, The: A moving composition written in 1842 by Felix Mendelssohn and now the frequently used recessional played on a pipe organ regardless that the Catholic Church strongly discourages its use. It is frequently teamed with the "Bridal Chorus" from Richard Wagner's opera *Lohengrin*, played for the entry of the bride.

Western Magick: *In this now global civilization, is there a distinction between eastern and western magick?* Yes, but it is less a distinction than so sincerely proclaimed when it was assumed that the eastern mind was different than the western. We can understand that various esoteric methods have a cultural history without saying that yoga is only for people born in India just as we've learned that computer science is not the sole province of Americans.

Western Magick has a distinctive system of knowledge and application, just as does Indian Tantra and Chinese Alchemy, but anyone can learn and apply these techniques without limitation.

Western Magick is largely founded on the Kabbalah and today includes Tarot and Ritual Magick. At the same time, there are differences in different traditions as to the understanding of various correspondences and symbols. At the practical levels, one system is not necessarily enriched by another. Learn the basic correspondences and symbols of the system you practice.

Suggested Reading:

Hulse, David Allan: *The Western Mysteries.* St. Paul: Llewellyn, 2002.

Regardie, Israel, Chic Cicero, and Sandra Tabatha Cicero. *The Tree of Life: An Illustrated Study in Magic.* St. Paul: Llewellyn, 2000.

Skinner, Stephen. *The Complete Magician's Tables.* Singapore: Golden Hoard Press, 2007.

Skinner, Stephen, and David Rankine. *The Veritable Key of Solomon*. Singapore: Golden Hoard Press, 2008.

Tyson, Donald. *Ritual Magic: What It Is and How to Do It*. St. Paul: Llewellyn, 1992.

Whitcomb, Bill. *The Magician's Companion: A Practical and Encyclopedic Guide to Magical and Religious Symbolism*. St. Paul: Llewellyn, 2002.

Wiccan: A practitioner of Wicca also known variously as the *Old Religion,* as *Modern Witchcraft,* and as *The Nature Religion.* Wicca is an *experiential* religion in contrast to a primarily ceremonial religion performed by priests for their "flock." As a result, a Wiccan is commonly known as a "solitary" practitioner, joining with others mainly for the major celebrations of Sabbats (Solstices and Equinoxes) and Esbats (Full Moon). These celebrations usually involve invocations of the God (Drawing Down the Sun) and of the Goddess (Drawing Down the Moon).

World of the Mind, The: The modern world is the World of Mind that man has imposed upon the pure physical world. Every bit of creation first exists in the World of Mine, and the manifests into the physical world. This is true for every individual's personal world, and even more so for the composit world we all share. We are the creators of the world we now know, and are responsible for that it is. To the extent that it is a man-made "mess," we can fix it and build a better tomorrow. That's what we are for—to grow towards perfection in ourselves and to grow a more perfect world for all.

Yang/Yin: The cosmic principles of non-dualism, one of the keys to the "language" of the Yi King. Yang represents the male energy in all nature, and Yin is its complement, the female energy. They are co-equal and cooperating.

Yesod: The ninth sephirah on the Tree of Life, Foundation, located on the Middle Pillar between Tiphareth and Malkuth.

God Name: Shaddai El Chai (Almighty Living God)

Archangel: Gabriel

Angelic Host: Kerubim

Astrological Correspondence: Moon

Body: the genitals

Colors: in Atziluth: indigo, in Briah: violet, in Yetzirah: very dark purple, in Assiah: citrine flecked with azure.

Consciousness: the Sub-Conscious Mind, instincts, animal intelligence, the Nephesh

Element: Air

Magical Image: a handsome and strong naked man

Symbol: the truncated pyramid

Tarot: The four Nines

Yi King—See I Ching

Yi King System of Divination: This very ancient Chinese system of divination is comparable to Western geomancy, a fact often overlooked among scholars and others who still want to divide the world into East and West. In addition, during "Warring States Period," the old text was re-interpreted as a system of cosmology and philosophy that became the foundation for many aspects of Chinese culture. Basic to all is recognition of "constant change" and the evolving nature of any situation.

INDEX

A PERSONAL EMPOWERMENT BOOK

COMMUNICATING
WITH
SPIRIT

LONG SUPPRESSED IN
WESTERN CULTURE AND RELIGIONS

HERE'S HOW YOU CAN COMMUNICATE WITH *(and Benefit from)*
Spirits of the Departed, Spirit Guides & Helpers, Gods & Goddesses,
Your Higher Self and Your Holy Guardian Angel

Includes
VERIFIABLE TECHNIQUES DRAWN FROM
World Religions, East & West – New Age Spirituality: Yoga, Tantric Sexuality,
Taoist Martial Arts, the Pagan Revival, Theosophy and Empowering Meditations
– Quantum Science & Paranormal Research – Esoteric & Psychological Studies
– New Psychic Developmental Practices - Ageless Shamanism, Ecstatic
Consciousness & Out-of-Body Journeys - Modern Intuitive Shamanism, Power
Animals, Sensual Magic & Sub-Space – Pre-Hindu Shamanic Tantra & Deific
Possession – Spiritualist Mediums & Channelers – Magic, Evocation & Invocation
– Spiritual Communication between Mind & Psyche – The Ways of Attainment:
the Astral Room, Magick Circle, Qabalistic Cross, Evocation of Guardian Powers,
American Middle Pillar & Auric Energizer, Invoking Your Holy Guardian Angel,
Opening the Third Eye, and Meditation to Raise Consciousness
to the Highest Human Potential

CARL LLEWELLYN WESCHCKE
JOE H. SLATE, PHD

Communicating with Spirit

Here's How You Can Communicate (and Benefit from)
Spirits of the Departed, Spirit Guides & Helpers,
Gods & Goddesses, Your Higher Self and Your Holy Guardian Angel
CARL LLEWELLYN WESCHCKE

Spiritual communication is no longer a passive state of waiting to hear the spirits speak through a medium or channel. Discover how to manifest an active state of conscious and create direct communication with specific spirits and spiritual entities. This is a "do it yourself" book, personal and individual, so you know longer have to depend on groups and institutions for power or authority.

Communicating with Spirit shows you—with clear and precise instructions—how to return Spirit to your inner self, open the doors to communication at the spiritual levels, and extend perception from the material limitations toward the inclusiveness of higher-dimensional awareness. Explore yourself and the world of spirit—the answers come from within.

978-0-7387-4468-1, 792 pp., 7 x 10 $34.99

CLAIRVOYANCE
FOR
PSYCHIC
EMPOWERMENT

THE ART & SCIENCE OF "CLEAR SEEING"
PAST THE ILLUSIONS OF SPACE & TIME
& SELF-DECEPTION

Includes

DEVELOPING PSYCHIC CLARITY & TRUE VISION

The Tattva Connection Meditation & Visualization Program
Microcosm to Macrocosm & Macrocosm to Microcosm

Based on the Ancient Tantra Tradition
An Eastern Gift to Western Psychic & Paranormal Science

25 Developmental Practices for Accurate Clairvoyance
Divination · Dream Interpretation · Invocation · Magick

CARL LLEWELLYN WESCHCKE
JOE H. SLATE, PH.D.

Clairvoyance for Psychic Empowerment
The Art & Science of "Clear Seeing" Past the Illusions
of Space & Time & Self-Deception
CARL LLEWELLYN WESCHCKE

This magnificently comprehensive resource combines little-known spiritual techniques of the East with Western scientific practices and research, providing readers with the best methods to develop clairvoyant abilities. More than just an interesting phenomenon, the insightful writing and clarifying illustrations reveal how the skills the book teaches can be applied to every level of your spiritual and daily life. Its breadth makes this an instant classic. All other books on this subject will compare themselves to this, but only the wideranging knowledge of Weschcke combined with the scientific rigor of Slate could produce this book.

978-0-7387-3347-0, 864 pp., 7 x 10   **$29.99**

A PERSONAL EMPOWERMENT BOOK

ASTRAL
PROJECTION
FOR
PSYCHIC
EMPOWERMENT

The Out-of-Body Experience,
Astral Powers, and their
Practical Application

CARL LLEWELLYN WESCHCKE
JOE H. SLATE, PH.D.

Astral Projection for Psychic Empowerment
The Out-of-Body Experience, Astral Powers, and their Practical Application
Carl Llewellyn Weschcke

Astral projection is far more than an out-of-body experience. It is a doorway to new dimensions— and opportunities to grow spiritually, increase your love potential, develop psychic skills, and change reality. More than in-depth theory, this innovative and comprehensive guide introduces the huge benefits and applications of astral projection. Learn to induce an out-of-body experience, safely visit astral realms, explore past lives, practice astral sex, communicate with astral guides and entities, create powerful thought forms, and much more. Fascinating case studies reveal astral projection's undeniable therapeutic value in overcoming fears and healing. The empowering seven-day developmental program will help you grow in more ways than you can ever imagine.

978-0-7387-3029-5, 528 pp., 7 x 10   **$24.95**